KASHMIR

Praise for the book

Saifuddin Soz, correctly points out in *Kashmir: Glimpses of History and the Story of Struggle* that Pakistan and India have no option but to resolve their outstanding disputes, particularly that of Jammu and Kashmir. Giving figures of deaths and disappearances running into tens of thousands, he correctly highlights the sufferings of the people of Kashmir as a result of hostility between the two countries.

Soz rightly emphasizes that Jammu and Kashmir is a purely political dispute and cannot be handled administratively or through use of force.

During our tenure, Pakistan and India were almost able to resolve the dispute over Jammu and Kashmir which has been the cause of at least five wars and four near war situations. With both countries being nuclear powers, possessing second strike capability, and with huge standing armies, war is just not an option.

A win-win situation for Kashmiris, Pakistanis and Indians is possible as I detail in my book *Neither a Hawk Nor a Dove*. Although I listed eleven or twelve very important features, the plan has become popularly known as the four-point formula including inter alia, demilitarization, self-governance, joint mechanism, defining units of Kashmir, monitoring and review mechanism.

Khurshid Mahmud Kasuri,
former minister of foreign affairs of Pakistan between
November 2002 and November 2007

To most outsiders, Kashmir appears to be an intractable problem that will continue to extract a high price, especially in terms of human lives, well-being, development and neighbourly relations, for the indefinite future. In this accessible study, underpinned by reasonableness, a secular and democratic approach, and uncompromising independence of thought, Professor Saifuddin Soz steps back from his engaged politician's role to argue that especially in this case, understanding the past clear-sightedly and showing the political courage and imagination to act on the hard lessons it offers is the way forward. A must-read for anyone who wishes to understand what needs to be done to make the seemingly intractable challenge of Kashmir tractable in a reachable future.

N. Ram,
chairman of The Hindu Group of Newspapers and
former editor-in-chief of *The Hindu* and *Frontline*

Kashmir is a complicated story. Not many people have the hang of it. Professor Saifuddin Soz, former Union minister, has lived it. He knows how New Delhi has spread itself all over while the Kashmir's popular leader Sheikh Abdullah had acceded only partially. Things came to such a pass that Prime Minister Jawaharlal Nehru had the Sheikh dismissed and arrested, though grudgingly, as he was outvoted on this issue by his own Cabinet.

Soz tells us how Srinagar made efforts to have autonomy within India and how New Delhi mistook it as a bid to become sovereign. He has a point when he says that the institution of J&K Constituent Assembly should be the ground on which the structure of a future agreement can come up. His formula is akin to Musharraf-Vajpayee-Manmohan proposals for 'an abiding cordiality' between India and Pakistan. He can't be faulted on his recommendation that India and Pakistan cannot and should not live in perpetual animosity.

Again, it is not easy to disagree with Soz when he says that the Kashmir dispute can be resolved through a purposeful dialogue with all the stakeholders, including the Hurriyat.

Soz's proposals should be discussed both by New Delhi and Islamabad and see if this is the base on which a structure of cordiality can be built.

The book should be read by all serious thinkers because Soz does leave the beaten track and paves a new path which can be taken by all the parties. Whether they would agree to the proposal of Soz remains to be seen, but a wide debate on them is necessary in the country because Kashmir has plagued India since its independence in 1947.

Kuldip Nayar,
author, senior journalist and
former high commissioner of India to the UK

KASHMIR
Glimpses of History
and the
Story of Struggle

Saifuddin Soz

RUPA

Published by
Rupa Publications India Pvt. Ltd 2018
7/16, Ansari Road, Daryaganj
New Delhi 110002

Sales centres:
Allahabad Bengaluru Chennai
Hyderabad Jaipur Kathmandu
Kolkata Mumbai

ISBN: 978-81-291-5192-6

Third impression 2018

10 9 8 7 6 5 4 3

The moral right of the author has been asserted.

CONTENTS

INTRODUCTION

A plethora of historical documents, travelogues and ancient literature has often described Kashmir's historical significance, cultural identity, literary achievements and natural bounty. However, there is hardly any book that provides a comprehensive account of Kashmir and its people with any objectivity.

In the context of the unrest in the Kashmir Valley that has been intensifying of late and the misreading of the unique people of the region, this book tries to cast a dispassionate look at how the Kashmir narrative has unfolded over the centuries.

This book attempts to explore the modern and ancient sources of Kashmir's history, views of numerous travellers—both foreign and Indian who visited the Valley—the diverse cultural landscape of this great land, the distinctive character of Kashmiris and, above all, the contours of Kashmiriyat.

Kashmir has the unique distinction of being a civilization on its own. According to Hungarian-British archaeologist Sir Marc Aurel Stein, who penned the most authentic translation of Kalhana's *Rajatarangini* (written in 1148–49), Kashmir's recorded history is at least more than 3,000 years older than Kalhana's record. Eminent scholar Balraj Puri mentions Kashmir's history to be more than 5,000 years old. No other region in India possesses such an ancient historical record. Even the Burzahom excavations (near Srinagar) establish Kashmir's antiquity to beyond 3000 BC, just as *Rajatarangini* does. *Rajatarangini*'s importance is not confined to the history of Kashmir alone; it is a priceless document of ancient history relevant to the entire Indian subcontinent.

Herodotus, who lived in the fifth century BC considered to be the 'Father of History', had made a reference to Kashmir. Claudius Ptolemy (AD 100–170), a Greco–Egyptian writer, gives a detailed account of Kashmir's geography and its people, although he never visited it. Chinese traveller Hiuen Tsiang, who visited Kashmir in AD 631 and stayed there for two years, gave a detailed account of Kashmir's civilization and its liberal rulers. Kalhana also described how the rulers of Kashmir respected all, irrespective of caste and creed. Al-Beruni (AD 973–1048), who never visited Kashmir, described its geography in lucid detail with wonderful accuracy.

The advent of Islam in Kashmir created a new feeling of equality and harmony among the people and introduced a set of human values that were unknown till then. Kashmiri king Ranchen Shah, who ascended the throne in 1320, became the first Muslim ruler with the title Sadruddin. He accepted Islam and was deeply influenced by the Sufi saint Bulbul Shah. Mass conversions to Islam followed soon and there is no evidence of coercion in the introduction of Islam in Kashmir.

In his book *Kashmir: The Wounded Valley*, Ajit Bhattacharjea writes, 'Islam came to Kashmir initially by peaceful rather than enforced conversion. This was of considerable significance to its future history.'

Thereafter, Muslims and Hindus (Pandits) had a long history of living together in peace and harmony. Even the recent rise of armed militancy couldn't impair the spirit of this harmony. Temples in the Kashmir Valley have always been safe and protected even during the long period of militancy, barring a few stray attempts to damage some during the recent spell of turmoil.

In the immediate aftermath of the spread of Islam in the Valley, a unique situation of cultural synthesis was forged, thanks to the efforts of Lal Ded and Sheikh Nooruddin. Laleshwari (Lal Ded) was born into a Brahmin family in 1335 and she got recognition as the first Kashmiri saint.

Sheikh Nooruddin (Nund Rishi) was born in 1377. He was a devout Muslim saint. Essentially, the message of Lal Ded and Sheikh Nooruddin was the same.

Sheikh Nooruddin, who was the founder of the Rishi cult, accepted Lal Ded as his guide. Together, they produced a blend of culture, which is rightly described as the hallmark of Kashmiriyat. Later when Sultan Zain-ul-Abidin (Budshah) ascended the throne after the demise of his father Sultan Sikandar in 1418, he cemented liberalism, togetherness and harmony among the Kashmiris.

The travelogues included in this book represent a balanced description of the people of Kashmir, their traits, qualities and certain failings. These travelogues have been critically examined for their merit and factual accuracy. This book aims at giving a correct view of the current situation in the Valley. It must be said on record that the Kashmiris have always fought for freedom, just as they did against their subjugation under the Mughals, Afghans, Sikhs and the Dogra autocracy.

This book describes in detail a bleak period in Kashmir's history under the Afghan rule (1752–1819) and the Sikh rule, (1819–46) when Kashmiris felt terrorized in their own land. The Afghans didn't know the art of governance and committed atrocities against the people. The Sikh rule was essentially a parochial and sectarian dispensation, which caused widespread unrest and Kashmir remained suppressed, subdued and terrorized. The last governor deputed to Kashmir by the Lahore durbar was Sheikh Gulam Mohyuddin, who was an exception and became popular for his good deeds.

Kashmiris also fought the Dogra rulers who were autocratic and imposed an exorbitant tax burden. As per S.S. Charak's research, everything under the sun except air was taxed and even sex workers were not spared.

The Treaty of Amritsar signed by the British and Maharaja Gulab Singh in 1846 proved to be the final nail in the coffin of Kashmiris' subjugation. It resulted in the 1931 revolt under the leadership of Sheikh Mohammad Abdullah.

It is really unfortunate that in spite of the Union of India having accepted the necessity of the institution of the Jammu & Kashmir Constituent Assembly, it developed a deep suspicion for its working.

After the undemocratic and unfortunate dismissal and arrest of Sheikh Mohammed Abdullah on 9 August 1953, Kashmiris were wounded and could never get over it. Then started an organized effort by the Union of India to dilute the autonomy granted to the state under the Delhi Agreement of 1952. It is said that while the Sheikh was placing the Delhi Agreement at the Jammu & Kashmir Constituent Assembly, the then central government was having second thoughts about the state's autonomy.

The reinstallation of the Sheikh as the chief minister of Jammu & Kashmir in 1975 also did not go well with the people of Kashmir, who thought circumstances had compelled him to compromise with the central government. Even so, the very clause that required the central government to critically examine the laws that had been extended to Jammu & Kashmir since 1953 was never implemented by the Centre. The undemocratic dismissal of the Farooq Abdullah government on 2 July 1984 further created a divide and alienated Kashmiris from India's heartland.

The pre-poll alliance between the Congress and the National Conference in March 1987 also didn't go well with the people. There was rigging in some assembly segments, which could have favoured the newly formed Muslim United Front (MUF). This created tremendous unrest among young Kashmiris.

Pakistan was waiting to take advantage of this anger and enticed the young, disenchanted Kashmiris through their spy outfit, Inter-Services Intelligence(ISI), to cross the border and train as militants. This led to the era of death and destruction in the Kashmir Valley and some parts of Jammu from 1989 till recent times. Almost 70,000 people have died till date, though the government figure is 45,000. It is unfortunate that a vast majority of people killed are innocent men, women and children.

Another episode connected to the armed militancy was the mass exodus of Kashmiri Pandits. Historically, Kashmiri Muslims and Hindus constitute two central pillars of the cultural synthesis that we call Kashmiriyat.

When militancy in the Valley was visibly on the wane, militant leader Burhan Wani's killing by the security forces on 8 July 2016 again created unmanageable havoc, resulting in the killing of more than 150 youths, besides wounding more than 3,000 youngsters with pellets and other means. The call for a shutdown by the Hurriyat meant the closure of all businesses and enterprises, educational institutions and transport, that is, all commercial activities shut down for more than four months starting in the first week of July 2016. Many have described this as an uprising.

Surely, it is not a law and order problem. It is accepted widely in India as well as in other parts of the world that the Kashmir dispute has to be sorted out through dialogue and discussion with the three main stakeholders—the people of Jammu & Kashmir, India and Pakistan. Since the Hurriyat Conference has represented the anger of Kashmiris in recent times, the Union of India would be well-advised to initiate a dialogue with its leaders and thereafter talk to other segments of the society.

The last chapter of this book explains in detail how to move forward through an effective and purposeful dialogue that can yield a permanent solution to the dispute. The solution has to be acceptable to the main parties without playing favourites. That is possible, and the same has been explained in the concept.

I feel confident that the Kashmir dispute will be resolved through an effective dialogue between the Union of India and the main stakeholder, the people of Kashmir. I must share the unease in my mind on why the two sides should not adopt an extreme posture in the dialogue process so that they can move forward towards a possible solution.

The Union of India must see reason and realize that it had gone wrong in its constitutional relationship with Kashmir. It must also realize the significance of corrective measures that it had undertaken in the mid-1960s and, as a part of the process, the Sheikh had held decisive parleys with the then President of Pakistan, General Ayub Khan.

On the other side of the spectrum, among others, I would like the opinion leaders collectively called the Hurriyat to be reasonable in the dialogue process and make a deliberate attempt to avoid extremes of its political demeanour. They must, among other things, realize that the Union of India is a crucial factor in the dialogue process. The Opposition at the national level, led by the Congress, has already given an indication to be part of the solution, rather than part of the problem, so that the Kashmir dispute is resolved forever.

Kashmir and Kashmiris have suffered enormous tragedies during all these years of hostility between India and Pakistan. So stakeholders have to show utmost sensitivity to Kashmiris, who richly deserve an era of hope and dignified peace ahead.

1
KASHMIR'S PREHISTORIC ROOTS

ashmir's recorded history dates back to at least 3000 BC. In *Rajatarangini,* Kalhana had referred to the dynasties ruling over Kashmir and certain related facts covering more than 2,000 years. The details were, however, woven into the texture of mythology. Well, mythology can hardly be bracketed with discernible facts of history. *Rajatarangini* is, however, the first authentic chronicle providing details of Kalhana's time, but also throwing light on the times gone by.

After *Rajatarangini,* there is hardly any worthy chronicle, although Syed Ali, Hassan Khohihami, Birbal Kachroo, Dedamari and Hyder Malik of Chadura wrote treatises that threw considerable light on various aspects of Kashmir's history. But Kalhana has the unique distinction of writing about, apart from Kashmir's past, the entire period covering his times. Nobody before him had ever tried to give such comprehensive details of Kashmir's history.

Marc Aurel Stein studied Kashmir's history so minutely that all subsequent historians on Kashmir admitted plainly that he had put in strenuous effort to bring the facts recorded by Kalhana in his *Rajatarangini* to light. Stein also determined *Rajatarangini*'s merit as the first historical document on Kashmir's history.

The Burzahom excavations executed by the department of archeology in 1961 have assumed tremendous importance in the subsequent years so that it has become the most important reference point for future researchers.

The fact is universally accepted that Burzahom should be accepted as the most authentic archeological site in Kashmir without any parallel.

Now that the Burzahom excavations have proved the fact that it is the first neolithic site discovered in Kashmir, it may, perhaps, become an imperative for researchers to proceed further from that point of reference. Burzahom is located at a distance of 8 km from the famous Shalimar gardens in Srinagar.

Burzahom is a village known as a place that had lot of birch around it. Burza means birch in Kashmiri language. A lot of birch was found during the excavations and that shows that birch trees must have been common in the area in that age. Interestingly, it was also found that food from the forests and foothills, and a good quantity of water supply was also available to Burzahom people. The excavations found that Burzahom was a raised location and it seems to have remained safe from floods.

In his well-researched book *Prehistoric Kashmir*,[1] Aijaz Ahmad Banday has stated in detail that the earliest neolithic houses at Burzahom were pits dug below the ground level and there is clear evidence that these houses were built by using mud and twigs.

There was mud plaster on the walls. The pits were deep and protected the inhabitants from the cold and heat. There is also evidence that Burzahom people made clay pots and tools made out of animal bones; needles for sewing and narrow spearheads and daggers were used for hunting. A grinding stone was also found in a pit. The archeologists found that Burzahom bone and stone tools were better compared to the ones discovered elsewhere.

Apart from human burials, animals were sometimes buried along with humans or in separate graves. The remains of wild and domesticated animals were also found. The seeds of cultivated types of wheat, barley and lentils of different kinds were also found.

There is also evidence that bone and stone tools were gradually discarded in favour of copper tools. At some places in Burzahom, iron objects had also been found.

The tools made of stones and bones found at Burzahom are not found in neolithic sites in any other part in India.

There is evidence that the people at Burzahom were hunters. Experts feel that further excavations at Burzahom and many other sites that have already been identified at places like Gofkral, Olichi Bagh, Pampore, Panzgam, Sombur and Waztal and other places in Kashmir Valley will yield quite a lot of information on the stone-age life.

Banday has also categorically stated in his book that the only historical evidence regarding first human habitations in Kashmir is available through Burzahom excavations.

He has come out with details regarding the excavations and it is almost a new angle on Burzahom. For instance, he takes the position that Burzahom excavations have established the fact that whereas there is no historical evidence on Pishachas and Nagas having lived around mountainous earlier, the people who lived in Burzahom were men and women comparable to the present race with facilities of food and water, etc. He also takes the position that no name can be given to the human race that lived at Burzahom and that they can simply be referred to as Burzahom people.

In his book *Kashmir: Exposing the Myth Behind the Narrative*,[2] Khalid Bashir Ahmad has rightly brought in the Unesco's reference to Burzahom which recorded, among other things, that, 'the entire site retains its physical integrity and is still set in a landscape that is reminiscent to the natural setting of the neolithic men approximately in the fourth milliennium BC'.

Ahmad, therefore, emphatically asserts, 'In the absence of archaeological evidence attesting to the presence of the Nagas or Pisacas, it is hard to take them as historical entities.'

Afaq Aziz of Kashmir University and many others are also working to identify more sites that can yield credible knowledge on archeological assets still buried in different parts of Kashmir.

Gulshan Majeed, associated with the Centre for Central Asian Studies for several years, has also shown considerable expertise in unearthing facts related to Kashmir's history and archaeology.

The latest findings by the retiring additional director general of the Archaeological Survey of India (ASI), R.S. Fonia, have not only confirmed the earliest findings by scholars such as Banday and others about Burzahom, but also brought to surface certain other things also such as the link between Burzahom site to the contemporary Indus Valley civilization. As per Fonia, the inhabitants at Burzahom had regular trade with the Harappans. Fonia regrets that while blood and unrest smear Kashmir's landscape, an ancient past buried beneath the ground has surfaced to remind us of the glorious times.

The findings submitted by Fonia in the last week of June 2017 on the eve of his retirement reveal that ranging from 3000 to 1000 BC, the culture in Burzahom illustrates the various stages of evolution from food gathering to food producing. Evidence of bone, needles, cotton, wool and other fabric point to a fairly dominant textile industry. The report reveals how Kashmiris were traditionally an artisan community adept at weaving and intricate craftsmanship.

The former director general of the ASI, Gautam Sen Gupta welcomed the move. Meanwhile, Ajmal Shah and Mumtaz Itoo, Kashmir-based archaeologists and researchers, have claimed that Kashmir's history may be older than the Burzahom era (see *Sunday Guardian* report dated 2 September 2017 by Noorul Qamrain). Their claim is based on a detailed analysis of the material collected by them from many prehistoric sites in North Kashmir and elsewhere in April 2017. In fact, the Centre for Central Asian Studies has added a new dimension to the quality of research at the University of Kashmir.

Satish Vimal, a programme executive at Radio Kashmir, Srinagar has, in recent times, taken keen interest in promoting discussions on Kashmir's history, particularly, relating to the prehistoric times and has identified credible researchers in the field.

It will be interesting to mention it here that the Burzahom site was identified first in 1935 by researchers Helmut de Terra a reputed geologist and archaeologist and Thomas Thomson Paterson, a prominent archaeologist, geologist and anthropologist who worked at Cambridge University and became a fellow of Trinity College. They were officially associated with the excavations at Burzahom in 1935.

There is plenty of mythology related to prehistoric Kashmiri life. According to Hindu mythology, the valley of Kashmir was formerly a lake, which was drained by the great sage Kashyap, son of Marichi (son of Brahma) by cutting a gap in the hills at Baramulla (Varaha-mula). When Kashmir had been drained, Kashyap asked Brahmins to settle there. In the existing physical condition of the country, we find some truth in this story. The name of Kashyap is by history and tradition connected to the draining of the lake and the chief town in the Valley was called Kashyap-pura, later identified with Kaspatyros of Herodotus. Kashmir is also believed to be the country mentioned by Ptolemy's Kaspeiria. Cashmere is an archaic spelling of Kashmir, and in some countries, it is still spelled this way.

My understanding is that while the mythological analysis can be interesting, the present-day world can't accept mythology as a substitute for organized research. The draining of Mountain Lake that happened to be the most important event in the prehistoric times can be attributed to Rishi Kashyap, as no other person has ever been acclaimed responsible for this important and prehistoric feat. But it is a situation deeply shrouded in mythology. Common sense and circumstantial evidence can guide us better on Rishi Kashyap as for draining the water of lake through the gorge at Baramulla. It is easily understandable that Rishi Kashyap must have been an engineering genius who cut the gorge near Khadanyar, Baramulla, to make the waters flow downwards and then the valley dried-up for human habitation.

In fact, there is no authentic record available as to who were the original inhabitants of Kashmir. The earliest inhabitants have, however, been described as Nagas and Pisachas, but the facts are deeply shrouded in mythology.

Interestingly, a very knowledgeable scholar of Kashmir's history and culture, late Moti Lal Saqi, gives a very comprehensive detail in his book on how mythological details on Kashmir's history can be used as an aid to modern-day research.

Discussing the Vedas, Mahabharata and Puranas with reference to Kashmir in his book *Agur Naeb*,[3] he cautions that history shrouded in mythology can't be brushed aside altogether and mythology, the literature, the language, the customs and folklore, etc. can help us to solve many puzzles. He cites so many examples in this connection. For instance, he tells us that no historical document states that in Kashmir, Hindu women shaved off their hair on the demise of their husbands, but it is a fact of life of Kashmiri Hindus.

His assessment is that at some point of time, Hindu women discarded sati and adopted the practice of shaving off their hair on the death of their husbands.

He asserts that due to the lack of knowledge on customs of the people, the language and cultural moorings, many scholars have ignored the Vedas altogether. He says that Stein is an exception to this general behaviour because he took pains to know things about Kashmir's history through intensive research.

Saqi says, 'While it is true that the ancient Aryans' book Rig Veda doesn't mention Kashmir but in the same Veda, the names of rivers were mentioned but no historian has mentioned this fact (*Agur Naeb,* page number 76–98).'

Rivers like the Ganges, Yamuna, Saraswati, Saturi (Satluj), Iravati (Ravi), Aiksinas (Chenab) and Vitasta (Jhelum) are mentioned.

Saqi says that this gives us an idea that around that time, many Aryan tribes had crossed the Ganges and the Yamuna to reach other places and knew the topography of those areas. It was a transitional period for the Aryans of whom many were nomads and many settled in human habitations by pushing the original inhabitants to mountains or subduing them. The Aryans were basically nomads, but when they saw settled habitations, they also decided to set up habitations of a permanent nature. It is also a fact that the Aryans visited every nook and corner of Kashmir. Around that time, Kashmir was not known as Kasheer or Kashapmar, as these expressions could have been used along with the names of rivers in the Rig Veda.

Saqi explains further that Nilmatpurana was written in the seventh century AD as compared to the Rig Veda, which was written between 2500 and 1400 BC. Strangely enough, Nilmatpurana refers to events that occurred around 3500 to 4000 BC but these facts are based on mythology. It is also interesting that the Vedas mention Mado Wadwan and the rivulet, which is still known by the same name and after covering 160 km, falls into the Chenab. But, *Rajatarangini* doesn't mention it.

The Vedas also proved that Kashmir has been a part of geographical situation of Sapta-Sindu that is, the area where seven rivers flowed. These rivers are Ganges, Yamuna, Saraswati, Satluj, Ravi, Chenab and Vitasta.

In this connection, Saqi gives credit to Stein who added a small book to his original research and published the same in 1921 titled 'Some River names in Rig Veda'.

It is, therefore, necessary to get along some distance with Saqi who takes the position that the language of the Vedas is the basis of knowing that the Aryans happened to be part of the dynasty that have inhabited Iran, Greece and Europe, till today.

Saqi goes further to say that though the Mahabharata is basically an epic poem of North India, but it throws quite a good light on Central and South India. The Mahabharata also explains that the expression Kashmir or Kasheer was because of Kashapmar and therefore, in the mythology, Kashmir is directly connected with the Mahabharata. The names of Nagrajas mentioned in the epic and many names in Kashmir are still connected with those times. Saqi makes other interesting assertion that the Mahabharata happens to be the only text that explains the past history of India and it is, therefore, a fact that whatever is not mentioned in it is mentioned nowhere.

Bamzai in his book *History of Kashmir*[4] says that apart from giving details of mythology related to Kashmir, there have been periods when the people came in contact with the Roman, Greek and Persian civilizations resulting in a happy blending of cultures, at once tolerant and sympathetic towards the ideas and beliefs of others. The Kashmiris demonstrated it practically.

He also says that Buddhism came into ascendency in the second century BC and in contrast to the religious feuds in the rest of India, we find the Buddhist kings and ministers building temples and viharas dedicated to the Hindu as well as to the Buddhist deities.

It is very interesting to notice that eminent historians have taken a lot of interest in explaining the mythological part of Kashmir. Bamzai is no exception to that process.

Bamzai says further that after Islam came to Kashmir, the synthesis of Hindu and Islamic religious thoughts found its greatest champions in

Lalleshwari and Shaikh Nooruddin who are even to this day venerated by the Hindus and Muslims alike. During the darkest periods of religious persecutions by fanatical outsiders, the people of Kashmir lived amicably.

While Kashmir's ancient history continues to remain shrouded in mythology, the authentic details are available regarding the people of local origin of Kashmir. For example, the Karkotas who ascended the throne of the land sometime between the sixth and seventh centuries ruled Kashmir for more than two centuries.

Archaeologist Iqbal Ahmad,[5] who has numismatic knowledge on this aspect of Kashmir's history, says that it is not exactly known when the Karkotas founded their rule; however, scholars have agreed that they ascended the throne sometime in the beginning of the seventh century and its founder was Durlabavardha. Ahmad is of the opinion that the chronology since the ascension of the Karkota had no doubt assumed an authentic sequence, but the dates of the ascension of its various rajas is concerned, it has been a subject of controversy.

G.M.D Sufi in his book *Kashir: Being a History of Kashmir*[6] also explains in detail the legendary aspects of Kashmir in prehistoric times. He thought that the geological evidence and mythological tradition agreed that the valley of Kashmir was perhaps a hundred million years ago with one vast lake hundreds of feet deep.

He says that the above legend corresponds with the results of early geological observations. In the prehistoric times, the basin of Kashmir contained a lake that was very large and deep. The sandstone rock at the western corner of the basin, according to these earlier observations, seems to have been rent by some cataclysm followed by attrition; and the lake was drained by the deepening of the Baramulla gorge, which was the result of the slow process of erosion by water and which must have taken hundreds of years to accomplish. These earlier observations are, however, now contested.

Balraj Puri in his book *5,000 years of Kashmir*[7] accepts James Ferguson's opinion that Nagas were serpent-worshippers and aboriginal race of Turanian stock inhabiting North India, who were conquered by the Aryans.

Puri thinks that the fourth Buddhist council was held at Harvan near Srinagar in Kashmir in AD 100 where the Mahayana school of Buddhism was founded. He also thinks the transition from Naga cults to Buddhism too was smooth.

Puri's mistake is that he takes Ferguson's evidence for granted on the Nagas and he could not have mentioned decisively that the fourth Buddhist conference was held at Harvan.

However, Puri is right in saying that influenced by Shaivite Tantric thought of Kashmir, Buddhism got transformed into its Kashmiri version. He says further that eventually indigenous religious beliefs, Vedic thoughts and Buddhism were synthesized by great Kashmir philosophers Vasu Gupta and Abhinava Gupta into a Kashmiri version of Shaivism called Trikha philosophy. According to him, the influence of Buddhism is discernible in many rituals and customs of Kashmiri Hindus even today.

Seeking support for his thesis of cultural synthesis, Puri says that Sufi had stressed monastic theism that is, Kashmir Shaivism is very close to Islam. He pertinently compares it with the tenets of celebrated Muslim mystic Mansoor-al-Hajaj (AD 858–922) who had proclaimed 'Anal Haq' (I am the creative truth). Kashmir thus accepted Islam not as a negation but as a culmination of a proud spiritual heritage. Sheikh Nooruddin (Nund Rishi) is perhaps the best product of this cultural synthesis and it is not for nothing that a prominent writer, Farooq Nazki, calls Shaikh Nooruddin a Muslim Shaivite.

Shafi Shauq, a Kashmiri historian is of the opinion that Trika (Trikha) can be explained as a philosophy in which three paths meet. Thus, it is another name of Kashmir Shaivism as it is divisible into three schools, namely, Triambika (inseparability of Shiva, Shakti and the human soul), Spanda (all existing beings are because of human consciousness) and Pratibhijnya (recognition of the self).

Shafi Shauq further explains that the three streams of thoughts are complementary and are best represented by Kashmir poetry of the fourteenth century.

HERODOTUS REFERS TO KASHMIR

Considerable research notwithstanding, Kashmir's ancient history is still shrouded in mystery. Available sources focus on Kashmir's past and many historians agree that such known ancient sources have made the history of this land unique. M.A. Stein's book *Ancient Geography of Kashmir*[8] is considered to be a reliable source in this context. He said Kashmir's reference in the classical literature is more ancient than believed to be and one should go by the accounts of Herodotus.[9] Many scholars say that Herodotus mentioned Kashmir as Kaspatyros. He names the city of Kaspatyros as the place where Scylax of Koryanda[10] embarked on his expedition to explore the course of the Indus. Scylax was sent by King Darius.[11]

The place mentioned by Herodotus is evidently the same as Kashmir because Hecataeus (549–486 BC) makes it clear Kaspatyros or Kashpapyros was situated in the territory where the Indus first became navigable. This is ancient Gandhara region, which is present-day Peshawar. Stein made great efforts to prove that the Kashmir Valley is the same area as Kaspatyros, mentioned by Herodotus.

Wilson[12] was the first to connect Kaspatyros with Kashmir. But the idea seems to have occurred earlier, for D. Anville[13] thought it necessary to refer to it and refute it. Wilson realized the city of Scylax must have been situated close to the Indus and hence far away from Kashmir. Still, he proposed to identify its name with Kashmir. Assuming the borders of the latter kingdom extended as far as the Indus, the mistake must be traced to a fanciful etymology of the latter's name.

Stein says Wilson assumed Kashmir got its name from Kasyapapura, which was supposed to have been colonized by Rishi Kashyap. He supported this strange derivation by referring to the uniform assertion of 'oriental writers', who probably consulted the Persian Tarikhs of Kashmir of the seventeenth and eighteenth centuries. He consulted these in connection with his above quoted essay. The Tarikhs indulged in whimsical etymologies, such as Kashmir, that is, Kashyap (Kasyapa) + mar (matha). But neither the etymologies nor the name Kasyapapura are known to be genuine sources. Strangely, Stein mentions Herodotus' reference to Kashmir, but while analyzing, he doubts if Kaspatyros is indeed Kashmir.

Renowned historian P.N.K. Bamzai has no difficulty in accepting Kaspatyros as a reference to Kashmir. In his book, *Culture and Political History of Kashmir* (Vol. I), he says, 'Herodotus, the Father of History, mentioned the city of Kaspatyros as the place where the expedition of Scylax of Koryanda, sent by Darius to explore the course of the Indus, started. As Kashmir had close cultural and political relations with Gandhara (Kabul Valley) in ancient times, it is quite natural that the Kaspapyros of Hecateus and Kaspatyros of Herodotus should refer to Kashmir. These early classical notes are valuable as they show antiquity of the name by which the land has been known in India and abroad from times immemorial.'

It is unfortunate that a historian of Bamzai's calibre doesn't quote any independent reference on his assertion that Herodotus mentioned Kashmir and described its surroundings.

Stein does not seem to be convinced by Wilson's argument referring Herotodus' Kaspatyros as Kashmir as he says, 'Wilson would scarcely have chosen to put forth such a derivation had the whole of the chronicle or other Kashmiri texts been at the time accessible to him. Extensive as this literature is, it does not furnish any evidence for Kasyapapura or a similar name having ever been used to refer to this country.'

Stein goes further to say that the fact is significant as allusions to the legendary origin of the country are otherwise so frequent. The philosophical impossibility of deriving Kasmira from Kasyapapura need scarcely be indicated in present times.

But, Stein thinks a reference to the theory above was however necessary, as it has found its way into works of historians such as Ritter,[14] Lassen[15] and Humboldt[16] and hence been reproduced even by recent writers.

Upinder Singh, head of the department of history, Delhi University, says Herodotus referred to Caspatyrus/Kaspatyros and Hecataeus mentioned a similar place (Caspapyrus).

Singh adds that scholars are divided in their view on the location of this place (many think it is a specific town and not a region). It is believed to be located in Kabul or Kashmir and has also been referred to as an ancient name of Multan.

It is clear from references to Herodotus and Hecataeus[17] that this region was located in Gandhara in the northwestern part of the subcontinent. According to Klaus Karttunen[18] (*India in Greek Literature*, p. 42), it was probably somewhere near the confluence of the Indus and Kabul rivers. Meanwhile, Wikipedia also refers to Herodotus and says the name 'Kashmir' means 'desiccated land' (from the Sanskrit: Ka = water and shimeera = desiccate). Kalhana's *Rajatarangini* states that the Valley of Kashmir was formerly a lake.

According to the Mahabharata, the Kambojas ruled Kashmir during the epic period with a republican system of government. Their capital was Karna–Rajapuram–gatva Kambojah nirjitastava, shortened to Rajapura, which has been identified as modern Rajouri.

But the *Encyclopedia of Islam*[19] categorically states that there is no mention of Kashmir by Herodotus or in the accounts of Alexander's invasion.

In my opinion, it is safe to go with Stein and leave it to the readers and future researchers to ensure the accuracy of these references.

PTOLEMY AND THE VALLEY OF UNMATCHED BEAUTY

Kashmir's unmatched beauty has been praised since time immemorial. It is difficult to say who was the first foreign traveller to have praised it and described its geographical contours. Claudius Ptolemy[20] had mentioned Kashmir and gave some information about Kaspeiria (Kashmir) and its topography.

Ptolemy wrote on geography, which was used as a textbook by successive generations. M.A. Stein[21] appreciates the significance of Ptolemy's mention of Kashmir as the oldest reference available. Stein says, 'It is significant we do not find any mention of the country in the first truly historical accounts of north-west India because the mountain barriers isolated Kashmir. In relation to Alexander's invasion, this isolation is further proved. The march from Taxila to the Hydaspes (Jhelum) took Macedonian forces along a route which lay comparatively near to the confines of Kashmir.'

Stein is correct that the mountain barriers didn't allow the Macedonian forces to enter Kashmir and therefore there is no reference of the Kashmir Valley in the accounts of Alexander's expedition. Stein says, 'On the contrary, the names of neighbouring territories on the west and south have been recognized, which clearly represents ethnic appellations derived from Urasa (Ptolemy's Ovapoa) and Abhisara.'

As Stein says further, 'The only reference to Kashmir that classical literature has preserved is found in Ptolemy's *Geography*. Undoubtedly, D'Anvile was correct in recognizing its name as the region of Kaoirpta situated below the sources of Bidaspes (Vitasta), Sandabal (Chandrabhaga)[22] and Adris (Iravati) rivers.'

Ptolemy correctly mentioned this territory between Dardnai or Dards on the Indus and Kylindrive or the land of Kulindas on the Hyphasis (Beas).

Stein explains further, 'Limits of the territory indicated this region would embrace a large portion of present-day Punjab with parts of the north-west provinces. Central India can have nothing to do with Kashmir. It has been suggested that Ptolemy's statement refers to a period when the power of the dynasty ruling over Kashmir extended widely over territories.'

Curiously, Kaoirpa was also in the long list of cities located within the region belonging to Kaspeirians. Its geographical position, as per Stein and Ptolemy's table, would bring Kaspeira close to Hydaspes and Zaradros (Satlej) that is, the neighbourhood of Multan, but, it seemed difficult to believe the information contained in this entry referred to any other locality but Kashmir.

Stein's assertion is correct when he says, 'Ptolemy's reference to Kaspeira is valuable because it presents an accurate transcription of that form of the country's name, which on independent phonetic evidence is an intermediate stage between the Sanskrit Kasmira and modern Kasmiri form, Kasir.'

Stein further describes the Sanskrit form of the name Kasmira used officially. But the country has been till date known abroad as Kasmir (Hindi) and Kashmir (Persian). The preservation of the popular Prakrit 'Kasvira' by Ptolemy deserves attention with regard to the original source of information. Stein also refers to a curious notice that Stephen of Byzance[23] has preserved from the *Bassarika*, a lost poem of Dionysios of Samos. Apparently, this passage was first noticed by M. D'Anvile, who mentions Kaspeiroi as a tribe famous among Indians for their fast feet.

The *Encyclopedia of Islam* mentions the word 'Kashmir' does not occur in Vedic literature. Its earliest reference is found in Panini's

Sanskrit treatise on grammar.[24] Later, the Mahabharata and some of the puranas also refer to it. The book says, there is no mention of Kashmir by Herodotus or in the accounts of Alexander's invasion, but Ptolemy's use of Kasperia definitely refers to Kashmir. The *Encyclopedia of Islam* also mentions that it is not clear when the Chinese mentioned Kashmir, but when Hiuen Tsiang visited this country in AD 631, he called it the Kingdom of Kiashimilo. Muslim historians and geographers such as Abu Fida and Ibn Batuta omitted this place altogether.

Almukaddasi[25] and Alidrisi[26] refer only to its geographical location. Almasudi's[27] account of Kashmir and its capital, the town of Kashmir, is long but not reliable.

However, Al-Beruni[28] gives a detailed and authentic account of Kashmir, although he never visited the region. He obtained information while he was in Pundhab (Punjab) and in Ghazna from reliable sources and describes the habits and customs of the people of Kashmir. He refers to the passes leading out of the Valley and traces the course of the Jhelum with considerable accuracy.

The *Encyclopedia of Islam* says nothing is known about the aboriginal inhabitants of Kashmir. It notes, 'Present population of Kashmir is thus a mix of different races—Aryans, Mongol, Turkish and Afghans. Their staple food is rice, which is also the most important crop. Early history of Kashmir is shrouded in legend till the era of Ashoka the Great, who, according to records of Chinese pilgrims, erected many monuments and stupas and Saivite shrines in the Valley.'

As per the book, it is Ashoka who laid the foundation of Srinagri, which was near present-day Srinagar. However, medieval Muslim chroniclers of Kashmir refer to Srinagar as the 'town of Kashmir' (Shahri-i-Kashmir).

Apart from Wikipedia and the *Encyclopedia of Islam* by E.J. Brill, we doubt whether we have access to any material that explains Ptolemy's reference to Kashmir. Stein's *Ancient Geography of Kashmir* is perhaps the only reliable source available which gives a comprehensive detail of Ptolemy's reference to Kashmir.

Stein makes many other interesting references. He says, 'Our sources for the early geography of Kashmir may be conveniently divided into foreign notices and indigenous records. As the information supplied by the former is earlier in date, though by no means more precise or important, we shall commence our review with them.'

Stein wanted to dovetail the records from the outer world on Kashmir with an array of Kashmiri authorities who possessed more detailed information (but not necessarily accurate) on Kashmir only to reach the real facts about Kashmir.

Therefore, Stein has done us a great favour with his in-depth study of the classical literature and to the best of my knowledge nobody before him told us the only certain reference to Kashmir which the classical literature has preserved is found in Ptolemy's *Geography*.

But then, as Stein concludes, 'Little reliance can be placed on the apparent exactness of Ptolemy's latitudes and longitudes in the Asiatic position of his work. None of the other city names in the same list can be connected to Kashmir.'

4

HOW FAR DID FA-HIAN TRAVEL?

Proceeding further in the study of ancient sources on the history of Kashmir, we must take notice of Chinese traveller Fa-Hian, who covered large parts of Ladakh without reaching Kashmir.

Although Fa-Hian's (AD 400) visit to India preceded Hiuen Tsiang's, it is the latter's description of Kashmir and other parts of India that are more accurate. Also, Fa-Hian travelled great lengths across India and visited far-flung areas such as Khutan beyond Ladakh, but did not make it to Kashmir.

Fa-Hian, who visited India during the reign of Emperor Chandragupta Vikramaditya, narrates a story of the construction of Kanishka stupa in Purushapura. Going southward from Gandhara, he arrived at the kingdom of Purushapura (Peshawar) in four days.

As Samuel Beal[29] mentions, there is no difficulty in tracing Fa-Hian's route as far as Khoten. From Khoten, he advanced towards Tsen-ho that is, Yarkand River and then proceeded through the country of Yu-hwui towards Kiancha. The former place cannot be Ladakh, but most probably correspond to a district in the neighbourhood of Chiltung Pass, bordering Tsung-ling mountains. Kiacha is certainly Kurtchon, to the east of which flows the Mng-Tsin River. Kartchou is placed on all maps to south-west of Yarkand. The kingdom (Kartchu or Han-Pan-to) appears to have been of considerable importance in the early period of our era. In Fa-Hian's time, the inhabitants were all Buddhists. From Kartchon, he proceeded westwards across the Tsung-ling mountains and after a month's travel reached the frontiers of northern India. Here, he came across a little kingdom called To-li. Judging from the time given, we may suppose the distance from Kartchon to To-li was about 100 miles in a direct course. Fortunately, we have been able to identify To-li with the Tha-li-lo (Dhalila) of Hiuen Tsiang.

The latest and most accurate description of the Indus in this part of its course is found in Sir Alexander Cunningham's[30] *Ladakh*, from which I quote the following: 'From Skardo to Rongdo and from Rongdo to Mkpio Shang-rong, for upwards of 100 miles, the Indus sweeps sullen and dark through a mighty gorge in the mountains which for wild sublimity, is perhaps unequalled. Pangdo means the country of defiles between these points the Indus raves from side to side of the gloomy chasm, foaming and chafing with ungovernable fury yet, even in these inaccessible places have daring and ingenious men triumphed over opposing nature.'

Cunningham adds, 'The yawning abyss is spanned by frail rope bridges and the narrow ledges on rock are connected by ladders to form a giddy pathway overhanging the seething Cauldron below. The Gilgit River is a mighty stream, perhaps not inferior to any of the mountain tributaries. From the junction of this river with the Indus, the course is south-west and distance to Attok is 300 miles.'

I believe Fa-Hian travelled west-south-west from Kartchou and south-west to the Gilgit River (which he calls the Sintou) over which he passed by one of the frail bridges referred to above, into north India.

If Fa-Hian had taken a route towards the Gilgit River, he would have entered Kashmir and hence marched to north India. Therefore, he touched only the frontiers of Kashmir.

5
HIUEN TSIANG: THE MOST CREDIBLE NARRATOR

Hiuen Tsiang is the first foreign traveller in Kashmir's history who visited it to study the people of the land and their lifestyle minutely. This Chinese pilgrim visited this ancient land to discover facts and didn't seem to be in a hurry. He remained in Kashmir from AD 631 to AD 633.

My own study of Kashmir's ancient history has led me to believe that Hiuen Tsiang's narrative is the most credible eyewitness record of facts and has no parallel as a document describing the people and their lives as he saw it. Although he describes the mythological aspects of their lives and beliefs also, he focuses his attention essentially on the lives of the people as he saw it.

It is before his arrival in Kashmir that Parversein had established the new capital as Parverseinpur in the north of Sulaiman hillock, which was earlier called Addisthan, and Hiuen Tsiang describes it with the same name but, then, the former capital Addisthan had become the old city. The world came to know of this name through Hiuen Tsiang's accounts only, who described Parverseinpur as Po-lo-wu-lo in the Chinese context.

Alexander Cunningham asserts in his book *Ancient Geography of India*[31] that when he wanted to study the Buddhist period of ancient

India and its geographical boundaries, he received inspiration from the following:

'My chief guides for the period which I have undertaken to illustrate are campaigns of Alexander in the fourth century before Christ, and travels of the Chinese pilgrim, Hiuen Tsiang, in the seventh century after Christ. The pilgrimage of the Chinese traveller forms an epoch of as much interest and importance for the history and geography of India, as the expedition of Alexander the Great.'

Cunningham elaborates the story further and says that actual campaigns of the Macedonian conqueror were confined to the valley of the Indus and its tributaries, but the information collected by himself and his companions and by the subsequent embassies and expeditions of the Seleucid[32] kings of Syria, embraced the whole valley of the Ganges on the north, the eastern and western coasts of the peninsula and some scattered notices of the interior of the country.

Cunningham asserts this information was considerably extended by systematic inquiries of Ptolemy, whose account is more valuable, as it belongs to a period midway between the date of Alexander and that of Hiuen Tsiang, when the greater part of north-west India was subjugated by Indo-Scythians.

This assertion of Cunningham is by itself a tribute to Hiuen Tsiang's travels across India, especially Kashmir.

As per Stein, 'The first reference to Kashmir was obtained from the account of an Indian envoy who reached China during the early Tang dynasty in AD 541.' He says further that the name of Kashmir is not mentioned, yet it is evident that M. Panthier,[33] who published the extract, was right in referring to Kashmir.

Stein goes further to say, 'The northern part of India is described as a country, situated at the foot of the snowy mountains and enveloped by them on all sides like a precious jewel. In the south, there is a valley that leads to it and serves as the gate of the kingdom. Ninety years after the date of the above notice, Kashmir was visited by Hiuen Tsiang.'

Although Samuel Beal[34] did considerable work in his two volumes of *Buddhist Records of the Western World*, it is Thomas Watters, who in his phenomenal work on Yuan Chwang's[35] *Travels in India*, has given vivid details of Hiuen Tsiang's travels across Kashmir. Watters says, 'The circuit which our pilgrim here assigns to the country of Kashmir is about 3,000 li,[36] given by Ma-Tuan-lin and other authorities and it is evidently much too great. The rocky pass "stone gate" through which he entered the country was the western pass which terminates near the town of Baramulla (Varahamula).'

The statement of Watters is correct as he refers to a ravine near Baramulla through which Hiuen Tsiang entered Kashmir. He mentions it as Al-Beruni's ravine, where the river Jailam (Jhelum) reaches on both sides. At the other end of the ravine is the watch station of Dvaz. Leaving the ravine, one enters the plain and reaches Addisthan, the capital of Kashmir, in two more days, passing on the road, the village of Ushkara, which lies on both sides of the valley in the same manner as Baramulla. The records show the pilgrim had horses and carriages and waited at the inner end of the ravine to be received properly.

Both Beal and Watters would not dispute Hiuen Tsiang to be the first person who mentioned Parvarseinpur and indicated its Chinese name as Po-lo-wu-lo.

As Watters certifies, among the products of Kashmir specified by the pilgrim in this passage is 'saffron', called Yuh-ching-hsiang in Chinese. That Yuh-chin-hsiang is saffron has been understood by comparing Tibetan and Chinese translocation of a Sanskrit passage, which tells of Madhyantika's (Arhat[37]) proceedings in Kashmir.

The valuable plant that this Arhat carried from the Gandhamadana mountain and introduced to Kashmir is called 'saffron' in the Tibetan rendering and You-chin in Chinese.

Watters says, 'The saffron plant, Crocus sativus, has been largely cultivated in this country from a very early period. Its flowers were long ago used to adorn the necks of oxen at the autumn festival and boiled in aromatic spirits to make perfume. The flowers of the saffron plant are still largely used in decoctions, both as a condiment and as a pigment by many inhabitants of Kashmir.'

Watters is surprised that Hiuen Tsiang, in his enumeration of some of the chief products of Kashmir, has no word about its grapes and wine. Yet, as Watters emphasizes, Kashmir was celebrated for its grapes and it was for long the only place in India where wine was made.

Watters dwelt extensively on the subject of the spread of Buddhism in Kashmir. He describes Kashmir as one of the most important and famous lands in history where Buddhism spread. In Buddhist texts, Watters found frequent references to the region that were praised and admired. Watters attributes the account to Hiuen Tsiang, who described the scene like this, 'The pious, learned and eloquent brethren of the region seemed to have had great reputation even at the time of King Ashoka, who called the disciples of Buddha dwelling in the charming city of Kashmir to come to his council.'

According to Watters, Emperor Ashoka had prophesied that Kashmir would become rich and prosperous as Uttaravat, and Buddhism would flourish there with innumerable disciples and it would become like the Tushita[38] paradise. The country would be like Indra's pleasure garden or the Anavatapta[39] lake and would make a great Buddhist congregation.

Hiuen Tsiang mentions as per the native records, Kashmir was originally a dragon lake. When Buddha having subdued the wicked dragon of Udyana,[40] arrived above Kashmir on his way through the air to Central India, he told Ananda[41] the following: 'After my death, Madhyantika, an Arhat, will establish a country, settle people and propagate Buddhism in that area. In the fiftieth year after Buddha's death, Ananda's disciple Madhyantika, perfect in spiritual attainments, having heard of Buddha's prediction, was delighted. He accordingly came here and took his seat in a wood at a great mountain.' It seems a story shrouded in mythology when Watters elaborates the detail regarding Madhyantika's miracles, saying, 'He (Madhyantika) made miraculous exhibitions and the dragon seeing these, asked the Arhat what he wanted. The Arhat said he wanted room for his knees in the lake, that is, he wanted to have as much dry land in the lake as would enable him to sit cross-legged. The dragon thereupon proceeded to grant his request by withdrawing water from the lake.'

Watters tell us further, 'Madhyantika through supernatural powers enlarged his body, until the dragon had drawn all the water from the lake. Then, the dragon was accommodated in a lake to the north-west of the old one and his relations and dependents wanted to live in a small place.'

Watters also explains what Hiuen Tsiang related about the

circumstances connected to the great Buddhist Council summoned by Kanishka, the king of Gandhara. He says, 'In the 400th year after Buddha's death, there was a great and powerful sovereign whose sway extended over a large population. In his month-long leisure, he studied Buddhist scriptures enjoying in the palace and giving instructions.' This information is shared by many other authors.

Watters paid rich tributes to Hiuen Tsiang for giving details of Kanishka's Buddhist Council, saying, 'It is to the statements made by our pilgrim (Hiuen Tsiang) about Kanishka's Council. Thus, Hiuen Tsiang is the first person to tell us about Kanishka's Buddhist Council in Kashmir.' There is no definite and acceptable information as to where this Buddhist Council was held in Kashmir. Some people say it was held at Harwan near Srinagar, while others assert the said council was held at Ushkara, near Baramulla.

Watters confirms from Hiuen Tsiang's accounts that after Kanishka's death, a native dynasty rose in Kashmir and its sovereign had become a persecutor of Buddhism. Here upon the king of Himatala, who was a Sakya by descent and a zealous Buddhist, was determined to dethrone the cruel Kritya king and restore Buddhism. By strategies cunningly devised and skillfully carried out, he succeeded in killing the king of Kashmir. He then banished the chief ministers of the court, reinstated Buddhism as the religion of the region and then returned to his own kingdom.

If we combine the information of Samuel Beal and Thomas Watters, we get a good picture of Hiuen Tsiang's narrative. Beal records what Hiuen Tsiang had to say, 'The kingdom of Kashmir is about 7,000 li, enclosed by high mountains on all sides. These mountains are very high with narrow and contracted passes. The neighbouring states that have attacked it have never succeeded in subduing it. The capital of the country on the west side is bordered by a great river. It (the capital) is from north to south 12 to 13 li and from east to west 4 or 5 li. The soil is fit for producing cereals and abounds with fruits and flowers. Here are the dragon horses and the fragrant turmeric and medicinal plants.'

Beal goes on to describe what Hiuen Tsiang said further in this connection. He says, 'The climate is cold. There is much snow but little wind. People wear leather doublets and clothes of white linen. They are light and frivolous and of a weak, pusillanimous disposition. As the country is protected by a dragon, it has always assumed superiority among neighbouring peoples. The people are handsome in appearance, but they are given to be cunning. They love lore learning and are well instructed. There are both heretics and believers among them. There are about 100 Sanghardams and 500 priests.'

Beal attributes this information also to Hiuen Tsiang and says, 'There are four stupas built by Ashoka Raja. Each of these has about a print measure of relics of *Tathagata*.'[42]

Both Beal and Watters agree that Hiuen Tsiang was the first person to tell the world about the Buddhist Council summoned by Kanishka.

The gist of the story of the Buddhist Council in Kashmir could be summed up as follows: The king summoned a holy assembly of men of learning from far and wide. Assembled for seven days, they made offerings of the four necessary things, after which, as the king desired there should be an arrangement of the law and as he feared the clamour of such an assembly, he said, 'Let those who have obtained the holy priest (as Arhats) remain, but those who are still bound by worldly influences, let them go.'

Kanishka gave many orders to lessen the number of the assembly. The final verdict was 'let those who are acquainted both with the three Pitakas and Vidyas remain, as to others, let them go.' Thus remained 499 men. Then, the king desired to go to his own country as he suffered greatly due to the bad weather conditions.

Watters and Beal agree that Kanishka after the Buddhist Council, referred these discourses to be engraved on sheets of red copper. He enclosed them in a stone receptacle and having sealed it, raised over it a stupa with the scriptures in the middle. He commended the Yakshas to defend the approaches to the kingdom so as not to permit the other sects to get these sastras and take them away, to allow those dwelling in the country to enjoy the print of this labour.

While there is need for a detailed study of Emperor Kanishka's Buddhist Council in Kashmir, Watters seems to have come to a definite conclusion. He says, 'This council, Yuan-chuang continues to say, composed 1,00,000 stanzas of Upadesa sastras explanatory of the canonical sutras,

1,00,000 stanzas of Vinaya-vibhasha-sastras explanatory of the Vinaya, and 1,00,000 stanzas of Abhidharma-vibhasha sastras explanatory of the Abhidharma. For this exposition of the Tripitaka all learning from remote antiquity was thoroughly examined.'

Watters elaborates further and says, 'The general sense and the terse language of the Buddhist scriptures were again made clear and distinct, and the learning was widely diffused for the safe-guiding of disciples. King Kanishka had the treatises, when finished, written out on copper plates, and enclosed these in stone boxes, which he deposited in a tope made for the purpose. He then ordered the Yakshas to keep and guard the texts, and not allow any to be taken out of the country by heretics; those who wished to study them could do so in the country.'

We may take some notice of what Sunil Chandra Ray says in his book *Early History and Culture of Kashmir,*[43] 'That Kashmir was a great centre of Buddhism under the Kusanas receives further corroboration from the fact that the fourth Buddhist Council took place in Kashmir under the auspices of Kanishka. At the end of the council, Hiuen Tsiang informs us, several expository commentaries were written on the Sutra, Vinaya and Abhidharma.'

Chandra confirms the original text and its explanation came to be known as Upadesa-sastra and Vibhasa-sastra. Kanishka had these treatises engraved on copper plates and deposited them at a stupa in Kashmir.

Mohammad Yusuf Teng, a scholar of Kashmir history, writing in *Sheeraza,* Vol-42[44] astonishes us by saying that Hiuen Tsiang's visit to Kashmir and the details of his eyewitness record was not available till 600 years after his visit when Tara Nath, a Tibetan scholar, certified the fact in the fourteenth century and said the council had been held in Kundal-Wan (in Kashmir). Surprisingly the most eminent scholar and chronicler of Kashmir's history, Kalhana, didn't mention Hiuen Tsiang's visit to Kashmir in his *Rajatarangini.*

Watters concluded that the discovery of copper plates which Yuang Chewang mentions, with the treatise inscribed on them, would help much to inform us about the spread of Buddhism taught in schools of Kashmir in or about the first century of our era. Without these plates, it is impossible to retrace how Buddhism flourished and then decayed or how the region was run at that time. There is consensus on the fact that these copper plates would have revealed a lot about the perfect message of Buddha, but unfortunately these have not been found.

Ibne Mahjoor, a respected scholar, was selected by the Jammu & Kashmir Cultural Academy in the 1960s to guide the excavations at Ushkara Baramulla to locate these copper plates, but the effort didn't yield any results.

6
AL-BERUNI'S KASHMIR

It is necessary to discuss Al-Beruni's description of certain important aspects of Kashmir's geography.

Abu-Raihan Muhamad Ibne Ahmad, popularly known as Al-Beruni, was born on 4 September AD 973 in the suburb of the old town of Kath (near the modern town of Khev) in Uzbekistan.

As per Hasan Askari Kazmi,[45] Ibne Ahmad got the title Al-Beruni appended to his name because he had spent the major part of his life outside the place of his birth, that is, Khwarizim. He had great respect for other religions. He took a rational view of Hindu thoughts and customs.

It would be interesting to know what Al-Beruni said of Kashmir, though he never visited it. As Kazmi writes, 'Kashmir is one of the examples he (Al-Beruni) cites which receives a lesser amount of rainfall by virtue of its mountain-locked situation.'

Al-Beruni notes Kashmir has no Vershakala (rainy season) and the meagre amount of precipitation during the two-and-a-half months, beginning with Magha and lasting up to the middle of Chaitra (April), is entirely in the form of snow. Just after the middle of Chaitra, Kashmir does receive a few showers, but that too are limited only to a few days. However, this is the season when Kashmir is washed and cleaned.

Based on my knowledge and that of other natives of Kashmir, what Al-Beruni calls a particular climate regime was known as 'Tsonth', which brought a lot of rains to Kashmir for a month or more mixed with sunshine, while heaps of snow lay on the ground with rows of icicles hanging on the rims of rooftops. Unfortunately, that situation is almost non-existent due to climate change.

Al-Beruni has also described the script that he identified as Siddarma Trikha. He has given the distance between Kanoj to Kashmir at 142 farsakh (1,136 km), which works out to be more than the present distance. The reason is Al-Beruni mentions a zig-zag route.

He takes us from Kanoj to Billawar in the north-west direction for a distance of 96 farsakh, then, he turns west for 21 farsakh and having reached Rajouri, turns north for Kashmir.

Al-Beruni gives a good description of the road system leading to Kashmir. He takes us from Babrahan, the best-known entrance to Kashmir, to the bridge on the confluence of Kasnari and Mahwi rivers. This distance is 8 farsakh (64 km). Then, from the bridge to Addisthan, the capital of Kashmir, Al-Beruni reckons the distance in marches. He said it takes five days to reach the gorge from where the Jhelum emerges and two more days to reach Addisthan. This total seven-day march comes to 147 km. Therefore, the total distance from Babrahan to Addisthan may be taken as 211 km. Al-Beruni mentions three road connections to mountain regions. Two were in the west, while one in the east. The two western routes joined Kanoj with Kashmir and Ghazna, respectively. He connects Kanoj first to the old kingdom of Jalandhar and then taking a piedmont course encircles the salt ranges, reaches Mangala Pass and following the course of the Jhelum finally reaches Addisthan. From Babarhan (identified elsewhere as Babar Khan) close to Mangala Pass to Addisthan, the road was difficult as it passed through ravines along the Jhelum. Other towns mentioned by Al-Beruni were Pinjaur, Ushkara and Dvar (in Kashmir) and Boteshar on Tibetan border.

Al-Beruni noted the importance of Babrahan as a town of great antiquity and his various references to it suggest it held a commanding position on the high roads to Kashmir lying halfway between the Jhelum and the Chenab. He did not write any comprehensive account on the historical and cultural aspects of Kashmir. However, he made a passing reference to Kashmiris being good pedestrians. Stein supports this concept saying, 'Natural conditions of an Alpine Valley enclosed by difficult mountains ranges are likely to develop the marching powers of its inhabitants.'

The *Rajatarangini* gives us several instances of very respectable marching performances. It shows riding animals were scantily used in these mountains.

The most surprising aspect of Al-Beruni's details regarding the geographical conditions of Kashmir has been accepted largely as accurate, although he never visited it.

7

KALHANA'S *RAJATARANGINI*:
COMPREHENDING KASHMIR

Kalhana's *Rajatarangini* is undisputedly the most valuable and relevant treatise for anyone studying the ancient history of Kashmir.

There is agreement among most historians and writers that of all the researchers who delved deeper into understanding *Rajatarangini*, it was Aurel Stein (1862–1943) who had successfully unravelled the comprehensive text. In 1889, he had obtained codex archetypes of all manuscripts of *Rajatarangini* and published in 1892, his critical edition of the chronicle. This edition is now published in three volumes by a local publisher of Srinagar.

According to Stein, Kalhana's *Rajatarangini* (river of kings) is the sole extant product of Sanskrit literature possessing the character of a true chronicle.

My own study on the subject has left me in no doubt that Stein's study of *Rajatarangini* is not only comprehensive, but also the most authentic source of information on Kalhana's understanding of the society in which he lived. Stein's merit lies in the fact that he made a strenuous effort to study the earlier translations of *Rajatarangini* and also went into the details of research undertaken by his predecessors.

Stein's understanding of *Rajatarangini* is, therefore, superb and he analyzes the research that went into the translation of Kalhana's chronicle into Sanskrit and Persian.

Stein has paid tribute to Buhler[46] for the accurate European account of the Valley, but he also admits that the Persian compilation of *Rajatarangini* by Haider Malik of Chadura,[47] prepared during Emperor Jahangir's time, was a remarkable work. Malik not just translated the chronicle, but also used it as a reference text.

Gladwin Francis[48] published the translation of *Ain-i-Akbari* of Abul Fazl in 1783–86, who had quoted Kalhana's chronicle as the authority on early Kashmir history. This work also came up for a minute study by Stein.

Stein believes that the history of Kashmir should be traced from Sanskrit authorities. The edition of *Rajatarangini* that appeared in 1835 under the auspices of the Asiatic Society of Bengal was mainly based on William Moorcroft's[49] manuscript, which in the opinion of Stein was not a reliable text. Many mistakes had crept into the translation from Sharda to Devnagiri characters.

Stein in his translation of *Rajatarangini*, however, considers Buhler as the most competent and fairest of the judges of Kalhana's work. Buhler found that M. Anthony Troyer's[50] text of 1840 was not authentic. Stein says, 'General (then Captain) Alexander Cunningham,[51] who came to Kashmir on political duty after the first Silk war and after the establishment of Dogra rule in the Valley, was able to elucidate with remarkable success a series of important questions which had a bearing on the chronological system of *Rajatarangini* and on the numismatic history of the country. With the help of information obtained through local inquiries, he correctly ascertained the era employed in Kalhana's chronological reckoning and thus he succeeded in fixing with fair accuracy the dates for almost all the kings from the advent of the Karkota dynasty. In the same paper, published in the *Numismatic Chronicle* of 1846, he communicated the results of his research for ancient Kasmirian coins and proved by his analysis the great value of numismatic evidence for the critical control of Kalhana's records.

'Equally useful for the study of Kasmirian antiquities was his survey of the most conspicuous architectural remains of the Hindu period still extant in the Valley. It threw light on the history of interesting temple-building mentioned in the chronicle and also enabled General Cunningham to identify a number of localities, which are important for the ancient topography of the country.'

Yet, Stein learnt that more trustworthy material was required to be obtained for antiquarian study and it was done very ably by B. Buhler (then of the Bombay Education Department) during 1875, when he visited Kashmir in search of manuscripts. His research yielded lucid details about *Rajatarangini* and that material helped to caution Stein to go into minutest details relating to the chronicle.

Stein quotes Buhler in his translation of *Rajatarangini*, saying, 'It was in 1805 that Colebrooke[52] secured an incomplete copy of Kalhana's work and twenty years thereafter he gave an account of it.'

Stein further says that Horace Hayman Wilson's famous essay on the Hindu history of Kashmir acquainted the European scholar (Colebrooke) with the general character of Kalhana's work and he gave an abstract of the contents of the first six cartons.

But, before him, the traveller Moorcroft made an attempt to obtain a copy of *Rajatarangini* in the Devnagiri script in 1823 from old Sharda manuscripts. Buhler got great help from Nilmatpurana, Maliatmyas of Kashmir tiraths and other Kashmir texts.

According to Stein, it was Cunningham who accurately found the dates for almost all the kings in Kalhana's chronological reckoning from the advent of the Karkota dynasty onwards.

Stein says Cunningham visited Kashmir for the second time in 1889 and laid his hand on manuscripts that Buhler had not been able to obtain. He then prepared the first Sanskrit text of *Rajatarangini*, published in 1892 and proceeded to prepare the present annotated translation in English. Stein admits he was closely assisted in this task by Pandit Govind Kaul,[53] a learned scholar, and also got great help from Buhler's research.

He lamented the loss of guidance in the demise of Buhler in 1888. Another loss for Stein was the demise of Pandit Govind Kaul in 1899.

Stein rejected the view that India of Hindus did not possess history. He said while it was true if people apply science and art of writing, the view generally held is correct, but as for historical development and the history for studying it, India has good records.

Stein also mentions Kalhana's *Rajatarangini* is interesting as it represents a class of Sanskrit composition which comes nearest in character to chronicles of medieval Europe and the Mohammedan East. Kalhana's narrative covers various dynasties that ruled till his time.

Stein has used this term in a broader sense. In his opinion, the *Rajatarangini*, even though containing lot of mythology, came closer to the Muslim historians of the East who had taken greater care of chronology.

Stein couldn't have given a long list of Muslim historians of the East, but this is a clear reference to great historians like Ibn Battuta (1369), Ibn Khaldun (1406) and others.

Stein tells us that nothing is known about the author except what his successor Jonraja tells us three centuries later. Writing in *Sheeraza* (Jammu, Kashmir & Ladakh in Ancient Chronicles and Travelogues, Vol. 45), Ghulam Nabi Khayal, a prominent writer of Kashmir, says that while Kalhana didn't say anything about his own self, historical records show that he was an educated Brahmin and his narrative proves his scholarship in ample measure. Khayal also says that the study of *Rajatarangini* itself shows that Kalhana visited every corner of Kashmir and what he wrote about the people and places shows his confidence in narrating the events.

Fortunately, the colophons that are attached to each book at the end give us his name as Kalhana and his father as Campaka, who held many responsible positions under King Harsha. Stein confirms these details are found in the codex, which is archetype of our extant manuscripts.

Kalhana wrote the introduction to his chronicle in 1148–49 and completed the work in the following year. Kalhana mentions Parihaspora as the birthplace of Kanaka (younger brother of Kampaka), showing Parihaspora as the original home of Kalhana's family, who were Brahmins.

Introductory verses prefixed to each book of the chronicle contain prayers addressed to Shiva. Kalhana was attached to Shiva worship. For centuries before Kalhana, Buddhism and orthodox creeds co-existed in Kashmir. Kashmir had embraced Bikhshus long before Kalhana's time. Nilmatpurana, the canonical authority for Brahmanical cult in Kashmir, prescribed celebration of Buddha's birthday as a great festival.

Kalhana considered himself a kav (researcher). He carefully studied the historical poems of his fellow countryman Balhana. He also carefully studied the well-known historical romantic novel by Harsha's court poet describing the exploits of King Harshvardhana of Kanauj and Thanseer. Kalhana also had an intimate knowledge of the Mahabharata. He often referred to this vast storehouse of traditional lore. His quotations from the Ramayana are less numerous. He had a lot of literary training as he refers to particular poets and scholars. A large portion of Kalhana's life passed in what was for Kashmir a long period of civil war and political disarray. Kalhana never held office with the ruling dynasty or enjoyed their special favour. He wrote in an outspoken manner. It seems he never expected any royal recognition.

Kalhana does not hide his contempt for the priestly class whose ignorance was equal to their arrogance and bitterly condemns their baneful interference in state affairs.

While Kalhana and his father were closely associated with Shaivism, Kalhana curiously displayed close attachment to Buddhism throughout his chronicle. Many rulers from Ashoka to his own time received his unstinted praise for the viharas and stupas they founded for the benefit of the Buddhist creed. Kalhana does not hesitate to refer repeatedly to the Bodhisattvas or to Buddha himself as comforters of everything, embodiment of perfect charity and nobility of feeling. To Kalhana, Buddhists are beings of absolute goodness, who do not feel anger against the sinner but patiently render kindness. Kalhana refers to images of Buddha with keen interest. While describing sacrilegious confiscations of Harsha, he names Buddha statues that were preserved, as the images of Hindu gods which shared that distinction. Kalhana takes care to show us on more than one occasion his thorough familiarity with the special points of Buddhist tradition and terminology.

But, Stein says the contrast that this partiality for Buddhist cult and traditions presents to the avowed Shavism of Kalhana is more apparent than real. For centuries before Kalhana's time, Buddhism and orthodox creeds had co-existed peacefully in Kashmir.

In Kalhana's time, every contemporary royal member or minister who is praised for his Buddhist endowments showed the same pious liberal views towards Brahmanical temples and establishments. That was a very heartening situation. Hiuen Tsiang too records this. He describes how Buddhists and Jains as well as Brahmins received equal honour and support at the royal court.

Kashmir had its married Bhiksus long before Kalhana's time. Buddha had centuries earlier been received into the orthodox pantheon as one of Vishnu's avatar and Buddhist worship had not failed to reap the practical benefits of such recognition. Hence, we find the Nilmatpuranas, the canonical authority for Brahmanical cult in Kashmir, directly prescribes the celebration of Buddha's birthday as a great festival. His statue is then worshiped according to Sakya rites by Buddhist ascetics; the latter themselves are to be honoured with presents and the Caityas to be decorated.

Kalhana's composition proves his studies in these departments of traditional learning had been both thorough and extensive. He carefully studied 'Vikramanka Devacarita', the historical poem of his fellow countryman Balhana, written in the eleventh century. Kalhana was thoroughly acquainted with the personal history of his fellow poet, as detailed in the latter's work. The strong resemblance in phraseology and style, which can be traced between the two works, is significant.

As Stein says, 'We can easily trace the connection between the close study of Sanskrit epic literature and Kalhana's work as a chronicle. To Kalhana as to the pandit of the present day, the legends clustering round the war between Kauravas and Pandavas and the life of Rama, with the mythology attaching to them, all appeared in the light of real history.'

Stein further elaborates this situation and says, 'What distinguishes these epic stories to the Indian mind from events of historical times is only their superior interest due to the glamour of a heroic age, and their record by sacred authority. We may safely surmise the study of sacred epics directly influenced Kalhana in the choice of his task.'

Kalhana's work deals with the history of his own country and a large portion of it is devoted to an account of events that Kashmir had witnessed within his own lifetime or within living memory. These facts place us in a very advantageous position. We are able to realize the political and social conditions in which Kalhana lived, with a degree of accuracy attainable for any old Indian author. His work gives us a detailed knowledge of the old topography of Kashmir. Kalhana's narrative, particularly where it deals with contemporary events, freely acquaints us with the author's opinion on many points related to his country and its representative men and classes.

Wherever, Kalhana got information of the past events of Kashmir history, he described these with interesting detail.

Stein quotes Kalhana on Rani Didda as follows:

'Insignificant as Ksemagupta was as a ruler, he was yet destined to influence materially the history of Kasmir during the next centuries by his marriage with Didda, the daughter of Sirhharaja, chief of Lohara.'

Ksemagupta's union with Didda, who ruled Kashmir from AD 958 to AD 1003, brought it under the rule of the Lohara dynasty, which continued to hold Kashmir as well as the Lohara kingdom till the times of Kalhana and later.

Rani Didda has played an interesting and important part in Kashmir history and was among the very few women rulers of her times.

Kalhana has also been quoted on Rani Didda by Archana Garodia Gupta in a magazine *Swarajya*[54]: 'Those treacherous ministers who for 60 years...had robbed sixteen kings, from King Gopala to Abhimanyu, of their dignity, lives and riches, were quickly exterminated by the energy of Rani Didda.

According to his own statement, Kalhana wrote during 1148–49, when he was not young. When describing the events that occurred in Srinagar in the spring of 1121, immediately before King Sussala's restoration, he speaks as an eyewitness of the treacherous conduct of the troops of usurper Bhiksacara.

The commencement of the twelfth century is marked in the history of Kashmir by an important dynastic revolution that brought about great changes in the political state of the country. Harsha, whose rule (1089–1101) seems at first to have secured a period of consolidation and prosperous peace in Kashmir, subsequently fell victim to his own Nero-like propensities. Heavy fiscal exactions necessitated by a luxurious court and cruel persecution of the Damaras who formed the landed aristocracy, led to a rebellion under the leadership of brothers Ucala and Sussala, two relatives of Harsha, belonging to the Lohara dynasty. Harsha succumbed in the struggle and was murdered. His territories got divided. Kashmir was to be ruled by elder brother Ucala, while the adjoining hill state of Lohara, the original home of the family, fell to Sussala.

Ucala seems to have held the throne merely by unscrupulous diplomacy by using one great feudal land-hold against the other and his alliance with the strongest of them, Gargacandra, the lord of Lohara. He was opposed by his brother Sussala and ultimately murdered by his trusted officials. Thus, the largest part of Kalhana's life passed in Kashmir was plagued by a long civil war and political dissolution. The dynastic revolution that had cost Harsha his throne and life had a lasting effect on the fortunes of Kalhana's family.

There is nothing to show that he wrote his poem by order of Jayasimha. The outspoken manner in which he judges the king's character and the undisguised allusions to the reprehensible nature of many of his actions make it very improbable that he ever expected royal recognition. The few passages where he praises Jayasimha or acknowledges his achievements were guarded. The same conclusion is indicated by his harsh remarks on the reign of Sussala, Jayasimha's father. He openly discusses grave defects of his character, his wanton cruelties, avarice, etc. He does not hesitate to record popular opinion that he was possessed by a demon. Significantly, Kalhana bestows the highest praise on the valour and heroism of the pretender Bhiksacara, who injured Sussala and his son. Bhiksacara's dynasty had brought no benefit to Campaka or his family.

The eventful period into which Kalhana's life was cast, with its rapid changes of royal and private fortune, had given him ample opportunities to study the character of his countrymen. So, it is not surprising his accounts are usually truthful and not always pleasing.

Kalhana realized the conspicuous need of physical and moral courage that is so characteristic of Kashmiris, particularly among the lower classes. He avails himself the opportunity furnished by historical incidents to expose with sarcasm the inveterate cowardice and empty bragging of the military of the state. We read of Kashmir's army that disperses at the sight or even the rumour of a resolute foe. We also get to know of the murder by a few guards, courtiers, ministers and troops. Kalhana more than once shows us in contrast, the bravery of the Rajaputras and other mercenaries from abroad, who in his own time were evidently the mainstay of the rulers of Kashmir. But his sarcastic allusions reflect the superiority assumed by these foreign adventurers was not to the liking of the chronicler. He bitterly refers to those in positions of influence and trust were ready to desert their master. Rare examples of faithfulness, on the other hand, find in him a warm eulogist even when it was displayed, for his country's or king's enemies.

By the side of the treason ever rife in the royal court and camp, Kalhana does not fail to notice the callous indifference with which Kashmiris were prepared to welcome any change. His graphic descriptions of the idle and disaffected city crowds and the feelings that swayed them show how thoroughly he understood the nature of his compatriots. Other weaknesses of the character of the Kashmiris are recognized by him with equal frankness.

Kalhana's attitude towards various classes of contemporary society and his open aversion and contempt for Damaras is clear. He holds these feudal lords responsible for people's sufferings. Kalhana called them *dasyu* (robber). The Damaras came from the agricultural class and were cruel and boorish.

Kalhana speaks of many petty land tyrants, who weighed heavily not only on cultivators but also on official class and the Brahmin population of the capital. The lands from which the latter drew their maintenance were in times of internal trouble at the mercy of the Damaras. This situation had saddened Kalhana.

Kalhana had nothing but hatred for the bureaucracy. In his book, *Kashmir and Its People: Studies in the Evolution of Kashmiri Society*, M.K. Kaw,[55] says, 'It (bureaucracy) consisted of all kinds of officials, both high and low, all of them being known by the general cover term "Kayastha", which did not denote any particular caste. Members of any caste or class could be recruited as Kayasthas, including the Brahmanas. Both Kalhana and Kshemendra have flayed them for their greed and for their cruel methods of exacting revenue and taxes from the people.'

We also know Kalhana's views about the influential class of old Kashmir, the Brahmin priests or purohitas. They played an important role in the internal politics of the country and often possessed endowments.

Kalhana does not hide his contempt for this priestly class whose ignorance was equal to their arrogance and bitterly condemns their baneful interference in state affairs. He describes several purohita assemblies and ridicules their combined self-assertion and cowardice, showing scant respect for their sacred character. Undoubtedly, there is much in Kalhana's detailed account of contemporary Kashmir's history as he was personally acquainted with various prominent actors. The high position of the family to which he belonged also explains this, but he himself never remained close to the power centres.

Historians, including Stein, agree that Kalhana was impartial in assessing the contemporary personages. He praises Rilhana, a minister and a faithful companion of Sussala, who held an influential position during Jayasimha's reign for his patronage of learning.

He was a keen observer and did not miss any important detail and hence wrote on facts that are very different from others. His chronicle was not written under the patronage of the ruling prince. Kalhana's independence of judgement on contemporary events and persons is amazing.

The chronicle is important as it furnishes detailed accounts of the conditions of ancient Kashmir. The narrative shows directness and simplicity of diction. Frequent references to epic literature must have been the need of the hour. Nothing is known of the literary personalities that preceded him. So, we cannot say Kalhana repeated the pattern.

The interest that attracts us to Kalhana's work is due to his character as a historian.

It is important to note that he was fully alive to the value of the historical record and we hold it to Kalhana's credit that he indicated materials that he had used for his narrative. He clearly accepts the subject matter of his work has been treated by others before him. In order to justify his own enterprise, he reviews these earlier compositions briefly, which is of considerable historical interest. He reveals that he had inspected eleven works of former scholars containing chronicles of kings besides Nilmatpurana.

Kalhana distinctly mentions the works of Kshemendra, who lived a century before him. Stein says, 'Kshemendra[56] (a poet and polyhistor) was a compiler rather than a writer.' Kalhana mentioned other two chroniclers also.

Kalhana describes his own work as an endeavour to give a connected account where the narrative of past events becomes fragmentary in many respects. He inspected inscriptions on temples. Stein mentions Kalhana as not only a poet but also an antiquarian and further adds that his chronicle contains unmistakable evidence of the actual use of such materials as his words indicate.

It cannot be doubted that a large portion of the detailed and exact data he gives regarding the foundation of temples and other religious buildings, the origin of particular sacred images, etc., was obtained from didactory inscriptions.

Inscriptions and written works, however, were not the only antiquarian materials that Kalhana used. Various allusions show historical information conveyed by the old coinage of the country had not escaped his attention.

The many detailed records Kalhana gives of the history of Kashmir in his own time were undoubtedly based on personal knowledge and accounts contemporary witnesses. It is this fact that makes the lengthy narrative of the eighth book so valuable.

Stein says in his accounts of Kashmir's ancient topography, he had endeavoured to show to what extent the great mountain barriers around the Valley have until quite modern times isolated its population from the rest of India. This isolation has exercised a decisive influence on the history of Kashmir. Its effects can also be traced clearly in Kalhana's chronicle.

The great natural ramparts that enclose Kashmir have assured to the land of Sharada not only long immunity from foreign invasions, but a historical existence of marked individuality. On this, no lasting impression was left even by those periods when the Valley was under the sovereignty of great foreign dynasties. Kashmir's history has thus borne a distinctly local character, which helped in preserving its historical traditions. We probably owe to it most of what is exact and reliable in Kalhana's narrative.

Stein says in this connection categorically, 'Kalhana's knowledge of the outside world was limited because of natural barriers. It is because of this isolation, superstitious beliefs exercised great influence on the population of Kashmir in comparison to India proper. Even Marco Polo heard in Central Asia that Kashmir was a land famous for sorcery and devilries of enchantment.'

It is interesting to know Stein's assessment of Kalhana's attitude on this aspect of the character of Kashmiris. He says, 'Kalhana's narrative proves how widespread the practice of witchcraft was prevalent in ancient Kashmir. He himself shares the belief in its efficacy. Hence he credits supernatural agencies with an important share in the events he relates.'

Kalhana's chronology also carries details that are problematic. For instance, the date of Yudhistra's coronation. He was prepared to accept a reign of 300 years for a single king (Ramaditya).

This is a fact on which not only Stein, but also many historians including Haidar Malik Chadurah and Pir Hasan Shah Khoihami[57] were genuinely bewildered.

This is also a grave defect in Kalhna's narrative. But he cannot be singled out. This has been the general trend. As Stein says, 'Al-Beruni's critical genius could read so deeply into the Hindu mind and he noticed saying unfortunately Hindus do not pay much attention to the historical order of kings; they are very careless in relating the chronological succession of their kings and when they are pressed for information, they are at a loss, not knowing what to say and they invariably take to tale-telling.'

Stein heartily accepts that Al-Beruni's blunt judgement is correct. But he gives some credit to Kalhana for restoring some semblance of chronology.

Stein speaks highly of Kalhana as a narrator and praises his honesty of purpose and impartiality. He does not hide the weaknesses and errors of the king under whom he wrote. He openly chastises the conduct of those holding important positions. He gives a clear picture of King Jayasimha's father and uncle as well as of his most dangerous adversaries, the pretender Bhiksacara. He was fair and just in his observations and his analysis was usually correct.

He was grateful to Harsha, who made his family influential, but pointed out the wrong deeds the king committed. Kalhana makes us feel the injustice of the fate that overtook this hero of Kashmir history.

The spirit of truthfulness pervades almost all situations that Kalhana describes. He gives large and disproportionate details, but they are graphic and interesting as he was in direct touch with the events.

This impression about Kalhana is true in description of events like Kalasa's[58] death, Queen Suryamati's[59] sati and King Susala's[60] murder. As Stein says, 'More often than not, Kalhana puts into the mouth of actors of his story words so characteristic and pregnant that we can scarcely doubt their authenticity. Everywhere we come across humorous anecdotes and expressions which bear the unmistakable stamp of contemporary popular origin.'

In judging the character of a chronicler's work, it is right to take into account the degree of precision he shows in matters of detail. Applying this test to *Rajatarangini*, we can't fail to note again a significant shortcoming in regard to chronology.

There is an artificial nature of chronology in the first three books, but later the length of individual reign is given. No real dates are stated. Kalhana starts giving proper dates only after the death of Cippata-Jayapida (AD 832–44). After the accession of the Utpala dynasty (Book V) the beginning and end of each reign is indicated by a statement of year, month and day. Sometimes, the details in respect of a dynasty's rule are not given accurately but the knowledge of events is correct. Kalhana's knowledge of topography was perfect.

Stein was impressed with Kalhana's knowledge of ancient Kashmir's topography. It helps us to establish a close relation between the study of the chronicle and ancient Kashmir's geography, yet the fact must not lead us to assume that Hindu chronicles could contemplate the records of the past without being influenced by certain general ideas. Ideas like spiritual merits (punya, yugas, etc.) have influenced the chronicler. It assumes progressive decay of all things spiritual and material in the present Kali Yuga. It naturally leads the Hindu mind to attribute more splendour and greatness to the past. Hindu chroniclers, therefore, accept in good faith the exaggerations of popular tradition. An equally characteristic feature is the unqualified belief in the power of fate.

A knowledgeable historian of Kashmir, Moti Lal Saqi, mentions in his book *Agur Naeb* the greatest drawback in Kalhana's narrative is that he mixes his faith with facts easily. Saqi also felt that Kalhana's attitude was that he couldn't discard mythology and, therefore, facts and fiction flow jointly.

It is fate to which Kalhana attributes the failing of all resolve and wisdom in Harsha yet Kalhana himself shows that fiscal oppression was there and Stein uses Kalhana's authority to show Kashmir suffered during Hindu rule as it did in more recent period. Kalhana demonstrates that avarice in a king defeats its own object and meets soon with due punishment. Stein speaks of Kalhana's reaction to social events based on superstitious beliefs such as presence of witchcrafts but, on different occasions he explains events logically. For instance, Kalhana does not hesitate to criticize the mistakes of policy by the opponents of Jayasimha and shows how the king succeeded due to their errors.

Kalhana dwells more than once upon the rapidity with which the great and the small in the land were ready to change their allegiance.

Popular attachment and loyalty is already a factor that he wishes his readers to exclude from serious consideration.

It cannot be denied that Kalhana often makes it difficult for us to follow exactly the purpose of his narrative. Particularly in the later portion of his narrative he often gives accounts of intricate affairs of the state, tangled intrigues of bloody incidents of the court life and administration.

Kalhana singles out Kakhemendra's list of kings for special mention. Kshemendra, the Kashmirian poet lived a century before Kalhana. His writings show him as a prolific compiler rather than a writer of originality. Regrettably, we have lost the text (Kshemendra's) to assess its worth properly. Kalhana describes his own work as an endeavour to give a connected account where the narrative of past events become fragmentary in many respects.

It is not only Stein but also many other historians and researchers who, while recognizing the merit of Kalhana's *Rajatarangini*, complain that it is unfortunate that Kalhana, in most cases, does not quote the authorities. None of the earliest chronicles that he had used are available to us for comparison. Miraculous stories and legends taken from traditional lore are related in a form showing that the chronicler fully shared the native credulity from which they had sprung. These scanty records are of doubtful value.

One of the critics of the style of Kalhana's recording of historical facts happened to be late Akhtar Mohi-ud-Din, who in his book *A Fresh Approach to the History of Kashmir*[61] says that there are so many facts and situations which have not been mentioned by Kalhana. For instance, the famous Dal Lake was not mentioned by him. But, in my opinion, this can happen with any writer as sometimes omissions remain.

I, however, wholly disagree with Akhtar Mohi-ud-Din who finds fault with Kalhana writing the *Rajatarangini* in Sanskrit rather than his own mother tongue. This seems to be wrong judgement as Kalhana produced his chronicle for a wider readership and it was Sanskrit that happened to be the language of the court and it is this language that was popular.

G.M.D. Sufi in his book *Kashir: Being a History of Kashmir* says that he was surprised that there were graves even in the graveyard of sultans in Srinagar that still bear inscriptions in Sanskrit.

Interestingly, R.S. Pandit in his book *Kalhana's Rajatarangini*[62] celebrates Kalhana's narrative in very chaste Sanskrit language. I didn't find anything special in Pandit's translation, which was not minutely studied and mentioned by Stein.

I differ with Pandit when he says that although Stein made a deep study of Kalhana's work, his main interest in the chronicle was archaeological and topographical.

After consulting various sources on *Rajatarangini*, I have a strong feeling that it is not correct to say that Stein's interest lay only in the topographical and archaeological situations only. In fact, he studied every aspect of the people and their life as portrayed by Kalhana.

Stein, however, is not satisfied with Kalhana's chronological order given in his chronicle. He says categorically, 'Our inquiry will show the artificial nature of the chronology adopted by Kalhana in the first three books of his work, that is, up to the beginning of seventh century of our era.'

Stein elaborates further, 'We cannot expect critical judgement in matters of chronology from an author who based his reckoning on a legendary date like that of Yudhisthira's coronation and is prepared to accept a reign of 300 years for a single king (Ramaditiya).'

In this connection, Stein makes an interesting comment that the exact dates which Kalhana mentions both at the beginning and end of his chronicle assure us that the work couldn't have undergone any material change after its completion by the author.

Stein agrees with Buhler's conclusive analysis that Jonaraja, who wrote his continuation of *Rajatarangini* about 200 years after Kalhana, distinctly states the work of his predecessor ended with the reign of Jayasimha, that is, the one described at such length in Book VIII.

We assume Kalhana never finished the revision of his work.

The grave defects of Kalhana's chronology for the so-called Gonanda dynasties were duly recognized by Wilson, Cunningham and Lassen, who first subjected it to a critical analysis. We must attribute it to the want of more reliable historical materials at the time when each of the scholars was tempted to a conjectural readjustment of Kalhana's dates with a view to using them for the elucidation of early Indian chronology. Needless to mention it here that Kalhana had indicated that on the whole 2,330 years had passed since the accession of Gunanda-III and 1,266 years were believed to be comprised in the sum of the reigns of fifty-two kings. Stein made an assessment that Kalhana had professedly obtained information from the works of earlier chroniclers.

Stein found great merit in Buhler's assessment that conjectural adjustments are useless.

After all this analysis of chronological order in *Rajatarangini*, Stein says finally, 'Kalhana's chronicle at present is our earliest accessible record of historical traditions of the country and is likely to remain so hereafter.'

There is no doubt in my mind that Stein is right in his final assessment of Kalhana.

It is with great pleasure that I bring to the notice of my readers what Jawaharlal Nehru has to say on Kalhana. In his foreword for R.S. Pandit's translation of *Rajatarangini*, Nehru writes, 'And, yet Kalhana's book is something far more than a record of kings' doings. It is a rich storehouse of information, political, social and, to some extent, economic. We see the panoply of the middle ages, the feudal knights in glittering armour, quixotic chivalry and disgusting cruelty, loyalty unto death and senseless treachery.'

Nehru further writes, 'We read of royal armours and intrigues and of fighting and militants and adulterous queens. Women seem to play quite an important part not only behind the scenes but in the councils and the field as leaders and soldiers. Sometimes, we get intimate glimpses of human relations and human feelings, of love and hatred, of faith and passion.'

Not many in Indian subcontinent know that Nehru happened to be one of the most well-read scholars of Kashmir history. Hence, I feel confident to say that his comment on Kalhana, as narrated above, is a decisive assessment of *Rajatarangini* and it is so close to what Stein thought of the historical chronicle.

SPREAD OF ISLAM IN KASHMIR

A large part of Kashmir's population adopted Islam during the latter half of the fourteenth century. G.M.D. Sufi[63] observes in his book *Islamic Culture in Kashmir* (a phenomenal work on Islam and Islamic institutions in Kashmir) that the influx of foreign adventurers both from South and Central Asia prepared the ground for this situation. He writes, 'From the beginning, spread of Islam has been, on the whole, peaceful. Islam was never introduced in the Valley by a conqueror like Mahmud or a warrior like Shahabuddin nor a general like Mahmud Bin Qasim. It was introduced by a simple faqir (Bulbul Shah) whose simplicity and piety impressed the then sovereign, Renchan Shah. The work was taken up by the faqirs though occasionally stimulated by a sultan like Sikandar. Islam's widespread penetration was due to the piety, purity and simplicity of rishis and saints who denied any pleasure for themselves and worked for others.'

Though Islam spread, the administration remained in the hands of Brahmins. According to M.A. Stein,[64] 'Jonraja and Srivara's chronicles frequently refer to Brahmins holding high positions under sultans. It is also a fact that Sanskrit continued for a considerable period as the mode of official communications and records in Kashmir, even after the end of the Hindu rule.'

Sufi's observation on the use of Sanskrit, even among Muslims, is borne out by the Sanskrit inscription on a tomb in the cemetery of Hazrat

Bahaudd in Srinagar. The existence of a vast majority of Muslims among the population of Kashmir is due to the fact that the message of Islam was spread by Muslim messengers.

The greatest push for the spread of Islam came from Renchan Shah, who adopted Islam under the guidance of saint Bulbul Shah, whose original name was Syed Abdul Rahman. Renchan adopted the name of Sultan Sadruddin and became the first Muslim ruler of Kashmir. He hailed from Tibet and wanted to change his religion.

It is widely believed that one evening Renchan decided he would adopt the religion of a person whom he would see first next morning. It so happened he spotted Bulbul Shah next morning and, therefore, Renchan adopted Islam. The spot where Renchan met Bulbul Shah is still known as Bulbul Lankar in Srinagar.

The conversion of Renchan to Islam was the primary reason for mass conversion of Kashmiris to Islam. Continuous influx of Syeds, particularly the visit of Mir Syed Ali Hamdani (Shah Hamdan) a devout Muslim scholar and preacher from Iran helped Islam to spread all over Kashmir.

Mir Syed Ali Hamdani through his strenuous efforts spread the spiritual message of Islam in Kashmir, which was given to many superstitious beliefs imbibed from deep-rooted mythology. Hamdani and his companions invited people to value-based teachings of Islam. The basic message was that in the eyes of God all were equal and they had to be good human beings. Belief in one God was the basic tenet of Islam and people were taught to believe they were answerable to God for their deeds. So, many started giving up their superstitious beliefs and developed a trait of togetherness and harmony.

The message that all human beings were equal brought a kind of solidarity among the people. The caste system had no place in Islam and the concept that anybody is high in society by birth lost relevance.

The Rishi cult of selflessness was born from the teachings of Islam propagated by Mir Syed Ali Hamdani and his son Mir Mohammad Hamdani and a host of Syeds who had accompanied them. While masses got converted to Islam, a minority continued to be Hindus but they also became wedded to a social philosophy of togetherness that was the essence of the teachings of Mir Syed Ali Hamdani. Even today, all shrines of Muslim saints and rishis attract members of both communities, despite religious divisions.

Over a long period of time, a tolerant social behaviour of humanism, togetherness, respect for each other's beliefs evolved, which became a unique feature of the life in Kashmir and got ultimately recognized as Kashmiriyat.

Ishaq Khan in his book *Kashmir's Transition to Islam: The Role of Muslim Rishis*[65] speaks about the conceptual framework of conversion to Islam. He says, 'Conversion to Islam in the Indian subcontinent, though a subject of vital importance, has not yet received the scholarly attention it deserves. Among scholars who have rejected the theory of forcible conversion in India are Thomas Arnold,[66] Tara Chand,[67] Muhammad Habib,[68] A.B.M. Habibullah,[69] S.M. Ikram,[70] I.H. Qureshi,[71] Khalid Ahmad Nizami,[72] Aziz Ahmad,[73] Abdul Karim,[74] Momtazur Rahman Tarafdar[75] and Richard Maxwell Eaton.'[76]

One can expect future researchers will examine the findings of these luminaries to appreciate the subject in further detail.

An earlier attempt to introduce Islam in Kashmir took place by a Syrian Arab Hamim, whom Mohini Qasba Raina quotes in her book *Kashur: The Kashmiri Speaking People.*[77] She writes, 'According to evidences, in AD 677, a person named Hamim, son of a Syrian Muslim Sama, was the first follower of Islam to enter the Valley in the company of Jaisiya. The ruler of Kashmir, as per inherent culture of hospitality, gave Jaisiya a place to stay called Shakalha. After Jaisiya's death, his accomplice Hamim took control over Shakalha, converted a few locals to Islam and founded a masjid. The Hindu majority declared them as untouchables and hence they were forced to live separately. They were called Mallechas. The king of Kashmir gave him and the Mallechas a colony to settle in a part of Srinagar which was known as Mallechamar (Ali Kadal of present Srinagar).'

Sufi in his book *Kashir: Being a History of Kashmir* mentioned about Syrian Hamim visiting Kashmir and trying to spread Islam. But there is no comprehensive account of Hamim staying in Kashmir with his mission to spread Islam and having succeeded in that.

Bhattacharjea in his book *Kashmir: The Wounded Valley*[78] writes, 'It was a unique period of cultural synthesis that shaped on ground and promoted understanding and mutual trust between Muslims and Hindus. This mutual understanding was symbolized by two powerful spiritual personalities—Laleshwari (popularly known as Lal Ded) and Sheikh Nooruddin, also known as Nund Reshi.'

Lal Ded was a Hindu, Sheikh Nooruddin was a devout Muslim. But they had much in common.

Bhattacharjea says, 'One must delve into the long history of Kashmir to comprehend the positive and negative aspects of the relationship. It is deeply rooted in the cultural and political forces that have influenced the Valley over centuries and in the native resistance to them. These forces have been guided by unique geographic situation of the Valley at the northern extremity of the landmass of the Indian subcontinent.

Kashmir's surrounding mountain ranges induced insularity, while the passes enabled positive interaction with surrounding cultures. But they also became routes of foreign domination and subjugation, leaving a deep impression on folk memory. This, in turn, promoted a sense of Kashmiriyat; a distinct vision of their future, common politico-cultural identity, which continues to dominate the people.'

G.R. Malik says in his article 'Cultural Heritage', 'Kashmiri culture is composite. It is not exclusive and rigid but inclusive and flexible. Its elasticity has always enabled it to synthesize various cultures to form a composite cultural current ever widening and evergreen. Every other cultural stream trying to impinge upon it has to submit to the terms of the temperament of this culture. In other words, the genius of Kashmiri culture assimilates all influences and converts them to its own character so that these are integrated with it.'

Kashmiri culture is multi-dimensional. Kashmir presents a unique character of preserving its cultural and historical legacy, which has never been impaired by the religious affiliation of the people.

Malik rightly mentions, 'The ruins of Harvan, Martand, Pattan, Awantipora and some other historical sites stand witness to the antiquity of the rich Kashmiri culture. The name of Anandavardana, Abhihav Gupta, Kalhana, Ghani, Sarfi and Anwar Shah Kashmiri are amongst the most distinguished contributors to arts and letters.'

Mirza Muhammad Haider Dughlat gives interesting details of Kashmir's heritage in *Tarikh-i-Rashidi*.[79] 'The first and foremost wonder of Kashmir is its temples. There are more than 150 temples in and around Kashmir, built of blocks of hewn stone, fitted so accurately, that no cement was used. They are so carefully placed in position without plaster or mortar that even a sheet of paper could not be passed between the joints.

'The blocks are 3–20 gaz[80] long, 1 gaz in depth and 1–5 gaz in breadth. The marvel is how these stones were transported and erected. The temples are mostly identical. There is a square enclosure, which in some places reaches a height of 30 gaz, while each side is about 300 gaz long. Inside this enclosure are pillars, with square capitals on the top. These capitals have supports and mostly made of one stone block. On the pillars are fixed supports of the arches and each arch is 3–4 gaz wide. Under the arches are a hall and a doorway. On either side of the arch are pillars of 40–50 gaz in height having supports and stone capitals. On the top of this are pillars made of 1–2 stone pieces. The inside and outside of the halls appear like two porticos and are covered with one or two stones. The capitals, the ornamentations in relief, the cornices, the dogtooth cover and the outside are crowded with pictures and paintings. Such a building is not found anywhere in the world. How wonderful sight it is!'

This period of harmony was a marvellous time in Kashmir's history. Even when the sultans established their rule, Sanskrit continued to be used for a considerable time, even though an overwhelming majority had converted to Islam. There is evidence to show great care was taken to preserve temples and other relics as these were considered to be a great heritage of Kashmir.

Mir Syed Ali Hamdani realized that the usual tenets of Islam would not go so easily with the unique ideology of Kashmiriyat that people of this land followed. Kashmir had its own spiritual leaders like Lal Ded, and her disciple Sheikh Nooruddin and others represented a blend of Hinduism and Islam. This universal acceptance of religions with leaders from different religious groups was unique to the basic concept of Kashmiriyat. Nooruddin accepted Lal Ded as his guru and led to the development of a culture of togetherness and unique pluralism.

This pluralism of Kashmir is far bigger than mere secularism. A value system special to Kashmir is reflected in everything they do, the way they treat and welcome strangers and guests, how they respect them irrespective of their caste, colour and creed. This ideology is embedded in their psyche.

This was possible as mass conversion to Islam was not under any coercion. When the king of Kashmir accepted Islam under the guidance of the saint Bulbul Shah, a major part of the population automatically converted to it. Syed Ali Hamdani authored and prepared *Awrad-e-Fathiyya* (the attributes of God) where praises of God were recited in a similar style to Hindus singing bhajans at temples. The praises of God are in Arabic and are loudly recited. When these praises are recited from mosques, it creates an emotional aura that is fascinating. This unique and integral part of pluralism of Kashmir defines the most important element of Kashmiriyat.

An eminent scholar, Showkat Hussain Keng, who described Syed Ali Hamdani as the architect of Islamic identity in Kashmir, explained to me that Syed Hamdani imagined that even though people had converted to Islam they would like to recite something in mosques that was similar to bhajans and feel psychologically comfortable.

Keng also told me that the Awrad is recited from that very time in Kashmir's mosques every day after the Fajr (morning prayer). It is something traditional and unique to Kashmiris and Kashmiriyat. Nowhere in the Islamic world is Awrad-e-Fathiya part of the prayers.

9

TWO TORCHBEARERS OF KASHMIRIYAT

Lal Ded and Sheikh Nooruddin are names unique to Kashmir. Even though age separates these saints, they represent Kashmir's spiritual and cultural personality, Kashmiriyat. Lal Ded was much senior to Sheikh Nooruddin though her date of birth is not decisively known. Sheikh Nooruddin, it is believed, was born when she was around forty years old. This was around 1335. B.N. Parimoo, a scholar of Kashmir history, has accepted the date certified by Abdullah Baihaqi and Baba Kamal (two eminent scholars and historians) as 1375. Several manuscripts mention the same date.

Parimoo's conclusion is on the basis of a legend that after leaving home on her wanderings, Lal Ded came by chance to the house of Sheikh Sladin where Nooruddin was born and was not taking his mother's milk. On entering the house Lal Ded said to the newborn:

Zena yale Mandchokh Na,
Te Chana Kiyazi Chukh Mandchaan
(You were not shy to take birth,
Why then are you shy of taking mother's milk?)

As per legend, on hearing these words, the baby started to suck milk and everybody was surprised. Such was the spiritual power of Lal Ded.

Later in life when they came close spiritually, Sheikh Nooruddin paid a tribute to her and said:

That Lalla of Padmanpore,
Who gulped elixir to her full;
She is our prophetess in our bosom,
O, God bestow such merit upon me!

Ajit Bhattacharjea says, 'Lal Ded abandoned her family and worldly desires and wandered through the Valley, dressed in rags, singing her verses and depending on local hospitality to survive. While wandering, she met a Shaivite teacher, Sidh Bayu, who introduced her to the philosophy of Trikha. She held discussions with Shah Hamdan, when he came to Kashmir with his followers and learnt the philosophy of Islam from him. Thus, her personal philosophy was a blend of the best of both religions and she was revered by Muslims and Hindus equally. Hindus remember her as Lalleshwari, while to Muslims she is Lal Ded or Lalla Moj, but the most popular name by which she is known throughout the Valley, is Lal Ded.'

The Valley still resounds with her verses (wakhs), preaching religious integration:

Shiva lives everywhere,
Do not divide Hindu from Muslims.
Use your sense to recognize yourself,
That is the real way to God.
And;
Truth is not a prisoner of mosques and temples and is all pervading,
Idol is of stone, temple is of stone,
Above and below is one
Which of them wilt thou worship,
O, foolish Pandith,
Cause thou the union of mind and soul!
The time is coming when seven generations will sink to hell,
When ultimately showers of rain and dust will fall,
When plates of flesh and wine cups,
Brahmins and sweepers will take together.
By overeating you will not achieve anything and by not eating at all you will become conceited by considering yourself an ascetic.

Lal Ded had considerable influence on Sheikh Nooruddin (Nund Rishi) founder of the Rishi order of Kashmir. Sheikh Nooruddin was born on 8 April 1375 in Kaimuh, Anantnag. Even as a child, he showed exceptional traits. At the age of twelve, he retired to the caves and spent his time in contemplation. His saintly teachings were conveyed through a form of poetry called shruks. He was not interested in poetry, but in the message he wanted to spread.

Mirza Arif Beg in his article 'Role of Mystics & Sufis', elaborates the Rishi order in Kashmir founded by Sheikh Nooruddin: 'Rishis abandoned worldly life, gave up family life and stayed in seclusion, fasting most of the time or living on vegetables, wild fruits or what little they got from their surroundings. The rishi appeal was more effective and gathered momentum. All this happened after Mir Mohammad Hamdani, who initiated him (the Sheikh) to higher degrees of mysticism and gave him the title of Nooruddin Noorani.'

I do not subscribe to this theory that Mir Mohammad Hamdani initiated Sheikh Nooruddin to higher forms of mysticism and gave him the title of Nooruddin Noorani, as Mirza Arif did not quote the source of his information. Sheikh Nooruddin was recognized as the founder of the Rishi order even while Mir Syed Ali Hamdani was preaching Islam in Kashmir.

However, it is universally acknowledged that Sheikh Nooruddin was given to contemplation from his young age. He came into contact with the mystic saint Lal Ded at birth and by adolescence he had become her disciple. The message in their poetry is a blend of the best of both religions and Lal Ded was revered by both Hindus and Muslims.

Same was true of Sheikh Nooruddin. Surprisingly, though both spiritual luminaries professed different religions, their message was fundamentally same.

Historian Ishaq Khan writes in an article published in *Cultural Heritage of Kashmir* (published by Kashmir University in 1997), 'Some of Lal Ded's great advisers were venerated Sufis themselves. Among them was Lal Ded's spiritual offspring, Sheikh Nooruddin, who immortalized her name as an Awatara of Kashmir.'

Bhattacharjea has chosen some shruks representing Sheikh Nooruddin correctly. He says, 'The Sheikh was popularly known as Nund Reshi, founder of the austere, tolerant Sufi order of Rishis and his mystical teachings had spread as widely as his mentor, Lal Ded's. Like Lal Ded, he is revered by Muslims and Hindus alike. His teachings are virtually untranslatable because of their devotional fervour.' Here is an attempt:

> The love is he who burns with,
> Where self doth shine like gold,
> When man's heart lights up with the flame of love,
> Then shall he reach the infinite!

> Or, more simply and humanely;
> Sow thou the seed of friendship for me everywhere,
> And, slay not even my enemies.

Nund Rishi was no admirer of the priestly class and drew attention to their greed.

> The rosary is like a snake
> Thou beedest it on seeing the disciple,
> Thou hast eaten six platefuls, one like another,
> If thou art a priest, then who are the robbers?

And, he advised his disciples,

> Do not go to the Shaikh and priest and mullah;
> Do not feed the cattle on ankhor leaves.
> Do not shut thy self up in mosques or forests;
> Enter then own body with breath controlled
> In communion with God!

The great Sultan Zainul Abideen was the chief mourner at Sheikh Nooruddin's funeral. His grave at Charar-e-Sharief continues to be a place of pilgrimage for followers of all religions.

10

SULTAN ZAIN-UL-ABIDIN: THE BUDSHAH

There is one sultan whose name has to be mentioned whenever anybody writes anything on history and culture of Kashmir. It is Sultan Zain-ul-Abidin.

Shahi Khan, one of the five sons of Sultan Sikander, assumed the title of Zain-ul-Abidin after a very difficult contest with his brothers. The date of his ascension to the thrown was June 1420 and he was nineteen years old then. He reigned for more than fifty years and that period is described as the golden period of Kashmir.

Zain-ul-Abidin's reign can only be compared to that of Lalitaditya. Kashmir never experienced the kind of peace and prosperity that it enjoyed during his fifty-year rule. Kalhana believes Lalitadatiya was one of the greatest kings who ruled in different parts of India during that time. This is supported by Chechenama, the only historical document about how Sind was conquered by Muhammad-Bin-Qasim. The same is true of Sultan Zain-ul-Abidin.

Muhammad-ud-Din Fauq in his book *Tareekh-e-Budshahi*[81] mentions even the King of China recognized Lalitaditya as the king among kings of India and they established a relationship with him (*The History of Medieval Hindu India* by C.V. Vaidya). Zain-ul-Abidin gained the same reputation as the most popular sultan of Kashmir.

Sir Walter Lawrence in his book *The Valley of Kashmir*[82] accepted Zain-ul-Abidin (Budshah) did not rule Kashmir only but his kingdom extended to Peshawar and Punjab, Poonch, Rajouri and many other areas of Jammu.

Muhammad-ud-din Fauq did a commendable work by producing opinions of prominent historians who wrote on the history of Kashmir and on the character of Zain-ul-Abidin. Here are some opinions:

1. Shri Vara, author of *Zona Rajatarangini* says, 'It is not only that Budshah died but with him promotion of arts and crafts and the esteem that men of letters received from him (Zain-ul-Abidin) also died. Nobody spoke of art and craft, or promoted them after his death.

2. Mirza Muhammad Haidar Dughlat in *Tareekh-e-Rasheedi* says, 'Sultan Zain-ul-Abidin ruled Kashmir and other areas for 50 years and was benevolent to all, irrespective of caste, colour and creed. The sultan treated Muslims and non-Muslims equally and this was a period of peace and prosperity in Kashmir.'

3. Muhammad Nizamuddin, author of *Tabaqqat-e-Akbari*, Muhammad Qasim, author of *Tareeq-e-Farishta* and Jahangir's *Tuzki Jahangiri* support what Mirza Haider Kashgari and Sharivara said about Sultan Zain-ul-Abidin's generosity, liberalism, his love for promotion of arts and crafts and respect for men of letters and artisans. All respected Zain-ul-Abidin for his culture of providing equity and justice.

Fauq briefly describes what other prominent authors said about Zain-ul-Abidin's life and his governance. He mentioned a galaxy of authors such as Narayan Koul Aajiz, Khawaja Muhammad Aazam, Dewan Kripa Ram, Pandit Birbal Kachroo, Pandit Hargopal Koul and Wolseley Haig, who agreed Zain-ul-Abidin's rule was the best period of peace and prosperity in Kashmir.

In addition to Zain-ul-Abidin's innate quality of creating an atmosphere of piety, peace and prosperity and a system of true justice, he was also a great builder who built several historical monuments in Kashmir:

1. He had ensured the completion of the famous architectural masterpiece, the Jamia Masjid of Srinagar, which was conceptualized

by Mir Syed Ali Hamdani and its construction started by the sultan's father, Sikander. This mosque also opened for prayers during Zain-ul-Abidin's time.

2. He built a mausoleum on the tomb of Sheikh Nooruddin at Charar-e-Sharief.

3. He built Jamia Masjid at Baramulla and the famous Zaina Kadal bridge.

4. He also constructed many small bridges to connect remote areas. These included Naid Kadal, Bahori Kadal, Saraf Kadal, Kadi Kadal, Rajori Kadal, Kawdar Kadal, etc. He built Sona Lank and Ropa Lank in the middle of Dal Lake, Srinagar. He laid the foundation of the small town named Sanangiri near Sopore and built two temples named Martand and Amarnath on a hillock. He built a famous palace on the Wullar Lake called Zaina Lank.

5. Zain-ul-Abidin is also remembered for constructing many irrigation canals such as Lal Kool (Lal Canal) and Nala Puhroo that starts its flow from Lolab and after a 40-mile journey, flows into the Jhelum. Zain-ul-Abidin connected Sopore through small canals to irrigate the land. This water irrigates the entire Zainagir area, set up by Sultan Zain-ul-Abidin himself.

6. Some historians say Shah Canal (Shah Kool) was earlier constructed by King Lalitadatiya around Martand Temple. Zain-ul-Abidin recreated this canal which had got defunct.

7. Nalamar was developed from the waters of Dal Lake that promoted transport by boats and facilitated communication.

G.M.D Sufi[83] in his book writes, 'Zain-ul-Abidin received early education from Maulana Kabir, a reputed scholar. Early in life, he showed his abilities and noble qualities as a minister. His accession was, therefore, hailed with joy both by Hindus and Muslims... Shortly after assuming authority, Zain-ul-Abidin engaged his brother Muhammad Khan in the prime minister's office and associated with him Halmat Raina and Ahmad Raina.'

Zain-ul-Abidin exhibited farsightedness, liberal outlook, piety and a sense of justice. N.K. Zutshi[84] in his book *Sultan Zain-ul-Abidin* writes, 'One of the earliest teachers of the Prince was Syed Muhammad Hamdani from whom he took lessons on the Quran. But he remained unaffected by the Syed's narrow religious outlook.' We have the testimony of Jonaraja that Shahi Khan's mother, Meraj, was a virtuous lady and her righteousness stamped the impressionable mind of the young prince with all that was noble during his formative years. He received his formal education from Maulana Kabir, a reputed scholar. Kabir was liberal and his influence on Shahi Khan must have been decisive in cultivating a humanistic outlook, sagacity, fortitude and the liberal outlook. He had later gone to Herat and settled there.

N.K. Zutshi quotes Haider Malik Chadurah to say that in the later part of his reign, Zain-ul-Abidin recalled Kabir and appointed him as the principal of a prestigious school founded in the newly established capital city—Noushahra.

Zutshi's reference to Syed Mir Mohammad Hamdani as a scholar with narrow religious outlook is not supported by either Muhammad-ud-Din Fauq or Sufi, who wrote comprehensively on the sultan. Undoubtedly, he was a very liberal king and his liberalism is described, in some detail, by Hyder Malik of Chadoora in his *History of Kashmir*.

He writes, 'Although Sultan Zain-ul-Abidin was not as pious and upholder of the Sunnat as his father was, he looked after his subjects well. Because of his noble character and good qualities, the subjects became prosperous. He built a few qaryas (villages) of which Zainagir, Zainapur, Zainakot and Zainadab are some. He also built a bridge on the Behet (Jhelum), which is famous as Zaina-Kadal. Then, he built an island on the Ular (Wular) lake and a palace which is now known as Zaina Lank.'

The exodus of the Pandits took place during Sultan Sikander's time at the behest of a Kashmir Pandit Sehdev, who had converted to Islam and assumed the name of Malik Saifuddin and was a minister with the sultan. Saifuddin Malik committed atrocities against Kashmiri Pandits. Some say Malik committed cruelties at the behest of Sultan Sikander himself. The migrant Pandits settled in Delhi, Lukhnow, Banaras, Allahabad and Deccan. Budshah paid attention to this problem and created an atmosphere conducive for the return of Pandits whose properties were returned, and they settled for peace and togetherness in Kashmir.

Fauq describes how some Muslims became critical of Budshah for getting back the Kashmiri Pandits. Fauq rejects their criticism saying critics happened to be ignorant of the fact that there is a code for governance for every king who has to treat all people equally, with all facilities for promoting religious freedom. Narrow-minded critics didn't understand how the king had to be a custodian of the rights of his subjects, irrespective of religious denominations to which they belong.

This trait made Zain-ul-Abidin a Budshah (great king) for all the people of Kashmir. Budshah laid great stress on the necessity for Pandits to learn Persian language, since it was the official language. So, Pandits started learning Persian and subsequently surpassed even the majority community as they were already well-versed in Sanskrit. They got higher positions in the system.

Some of the Pandits who became courtiers of Budshah included Shiv Bhat, Zoona Raja, Yodh Bhat, Sadashiva Gopal Kaul, Madhav Kaul, Ganesh Kaul, Sonu Pandit, Tilak Charya, Roopa Bhat, Taripot Seema, Shri Bhat and Shivara (historian). These prominent persons of the Pandit community not only adored Budshah's court, but also looked after separate departments and exercised considerable influence on the king.

Surprisingly, the Budshah succeeded in attaining the perfect stature as a liberal king and did everything he considered necessary for the welfare of Pandits such as:

Cancelling Jazia: Tax on Pandits that was in vogue for a long time. The cancellation brought great joy to them.

Setting up Jogi Lanker: While educated Pandits got positions in the government, there remained a section who engaged only in religious activities. For them, Budshah set up a place in Rainawari in Srinagar called Jogi Lanker, where they could live and have food and other requirements at the government's expense. They also received education.

Visiting Sharda Temple: Jonaraja mentions the king braved all hazards to visit the Sharda Temple (beyond present-day Gurez) only to ensure the ancient temple was maintained properly and worshippers faced no difficulty. Budshah had also visited the historic Amarnath shrine.

Establishing special courts for Hindus: Jonaraja's *Rajatarangini* mentions Budshah even set up special courts for Pandits so that disputes related to temples and Hindu shrines could be decided speedily. A Pandit was the judge of such courts. Khawaja Muhammad Azam proudly mentions this in his book *Tareekhi Waqaat-e-Kashmir*.

Fauq rejected Birbal Kachroo's criticism of Budshah's emphasis for Pandits to learn Persian language. Kachroo while lavishing praise on Budshah for many qualities in him, criticized him for asking Pandits to learn Persian as an inducement to them to neglect their religion. This was decidedly Kachroo's narrow understanding of the Budshah's character, as a king, who was essentially interested to provide a dispensation based on equity and justice. Many writers and historians found Budshah was unique in his dispensation of liberalism and justice. His earnest plea to Pandits for learning Persian language was to help them to get jobs in the system, as Persian was the official language of the time.

Narain Kaul, a renowned historian, described how the king respected the learned for their knowledge and promoted arts and crafts. He got many Sanskrit books translated into Persian, including the Mahabharata.

Dewan Kripa Ram in his book *Gulzar-e-Kashmir* pays rich tributes to Budshah for his patronage of knowledge and his special treatment of Brahmins.

Pandit Hargopal, author of *Guldasta-i-Kashmir*, said the Budshah established perfect peace and harmony among communities and meted out equal treatment to people irrespective of their religion.

Wolselcy Haig writes in *The Cambridge History of India* that Budshah respected the learned and promoted arts and crafts like his father, but in other matters, he did not follow his father and ensured welfare to all on the basis of equality and justice. Wolseley thought he was rightly compared to Akbar the Great.

11

MARCO POLO'S CURIOUS VIEW

M arco Polo's travelogue on Kashmir is very important because he was one of the first foreigners to visit the region and shared many details of its topography and people.

Marco Polo (1254–1324) is believed to have travelled more extensively than any man and it has largely been accepted that even among Arab globetrotters, Marco Polo had no serious competitor, till Ibn Battuta, two generations later. He revealed to Christendom a world that was unknown to it. But it is also a fact that the western world had some knowledge of India and trade routes since Alexander the Great.

In his book *Exploration and Adventure*,[85] Clifford Collinson writes, 'It was purely a trading venture that led two men from Venice, named Niccolo and Matteo Polo, to make their way in 1255 through unknown Persia and Afghanistan to the Court of the Great Khan (Kublai Khan) Emperor of China, at Peking. Sixteen years later, they repeated the journey, this time taking with them Niccolo's son, a boy of fifteen, whose name was Marco.'

Now, if we look back, that journey will certainly seem to be incredible for the three men, including Marco Polo, who passed through unknown regions which have been penetrated again, with great difficulty and effort, by Europeans and others within the last 100 years or so.

In her book *Kashmir Crisis: Unholy Anglo–Pak Nexus*,[86] Saroja

Sundararajan mentions Marco Polo's visit in the last quarter of the thirteenth century, as described in his travelogue *II Milione*, known in English as the *Travels of Marco Polo*.

I find a lot of merit in Sundararajan's book as far as two issues are concerned. One was the presence of saracens in Kashmir during Marco Polo's visit and the other was the existence of evil practices such as sorcery and devilries. The mention of these issues have found their way in almost all accounts describing Marco Polo's visit. The presence of evil practices seems to have developed in Kashmir due to irresponsible and cruel kings, who used these methods to fulfil their greed. Many accounts regarding Kashmir show that practices such as sorcery were prevalent in Kashmir as Marco Polo has described.

Sundararajan says sorcery and devilries added to the moral decadence and economic decay of the Hindu state that was on the brink of collapse when adventurers were hovering around like vultures on a dying beast.

Many statements that Marco Polo made, such as Kashmiris being idolaters, speaking a language of their own, a reference to their diet of fish and rice and reference to the climate of Kashmir, have not been contested. But, when Marco Polo asserts that Kashmiris practised magic, and through magic they made their idols speak or created clouds through magic, which caused rain, many scholars don't agree with him at all. Therefore, some people believe that Marco Polo had heard about these situations and not seen these with his own eyes.

In *Sheeraza*,[87] researcher Arjundev Majboor says that the details of Marco Polo's travels were mentioned by Sir E. Delison Ross and Eileen Power, the translation of which was published in 1939.

The same book makes a mention of Keshimur. It carries the following details: 'Keshimur is a province where people who are idolaters live and they have a language of their own. They can change the weather by magic and create darkness. They also perform miracles through magic. The men are strong skinned and the women are very beautiful. They take rice, meat and milk. The weather here is very temperate and this land can be reached through very narrow gorges.'

Majboor has an impression that Marco Polo never made it to Kashmir and he wrote what he heard from people. But, I feel since Majboor has not quoted any authority on his presumption that Marco Polo may not have visited Kashmir, his assumption seems to be incorrect.

Henry Yule, who translated *Travels of Marco Polo*, mentions the following: 'There are in this country eremites who dwell in seclusion and practice great abstinence in eating and drinking. They observe strict chastity and keep away from all sins forbidden in their law so that they are regarded by their own folk as very holy persons. They live to a very great age.'

Yule seems to have done a minute study of Marco Polo's understanding of Kashmir and explains the details clearly. He says that the people of Kashmir didn't kill animals and spill blood. Kashmiris had left the job of slaughtering animals to saracens who lived in the region. Yule tells us one more wonderful thing and it is that Marco Polo saw that coral was carried to Kashmir from other parts of the world, but it sold in Kashmir better than in any other country.

Although Yule's translation has made many things clear for readers, there was a need for further research as, for instance, the reference to eremites practising seclusion and abstinence is, perhaps, a clear reference to rishis, who practised strict abstinence and seclusion and the Rishis also did not kill animals and lived on whatever nature had offered them in vegetation.

I have a feeling that Marco Polo's visit to Kashmir needs further research.

12
FRANCOIS BERNIER'S VIVID ACCOUNT

French national Francois Bernier visited India in 1656 and lived here till 1688. His travelogue, which is covered in his letters to the king of France, throws tremendous light on the history of Kashmir.

Bernier had set sail for Egypt, but later decided to travel to India and reached Surat during the reign of Emperor Shahjahan. He was witness to the fact that each of Shahjahan's sons laid claim to the empire. Bernier got closely associated with the court for eight years. It took him seven weeks to reach from Surat to Agra and Delhi. He accepted a salary from the great Mughal in the capacity of a physician. He also got help from Dewan Chand Khan, who was rated as the most powerful among the courtiers.

Of the sons of Shahjahan—Dara, Shuja, Aurangzeb and Murad—Dara was well-versed, polite and liberal, but he thought he did not need counsels. He remained ignorant of the conspiracies of his brothers. He deterred his sincerest friends and didn't accept advice. Aurangzeb declared him a kafir and got him ultimately beheaded. Sultan Shuja resembled Dara, but he was discreet. Unfortunately, he was a slave to his pleasures—numerous women, dancing, singing and drinking. He imbibed the Persian cult of sympathy to Ali. Aurangzeb was not as enlightened as Dara, but possessed sound judgement and skill. He was reserved and subtle and was completely a master of dissimulation. He professed selflessness, but he was clever. Shahjahan praised him, but Dara would say that he was suspicious of that Nemazi bigot (Aurangzeb).

Murad Bukhsh was inferior to all and he took to enjoyment and pleasures, but he was generous. He was courageous but did not accept advice.

The eldest daughter, Begum Sahib, was beautiful and close to Shahjahan and courtiers suspected mutual affection. No dish was served without her approval. She was very rich with gifts. She was close to Dara and had promised to watch his interest. Dara had promised that when he got the throne, she would get married.

Shahjahan was afraid of his sons and divided his empire into four parts. The three acted independently but Dara, expecting the throne, did not leave his father's court. The father gave him a small throne below him. Shahjahan was not cordially attached to him and he continued secret correspondence with Aurangzeb, of whose talent he was convinced.

The sons of Shahjahan fought for the throne. Shahjahan's advice did not matter to any one of them. Finally, Aurangzeb made it to the throne.

After having settled on the throne, Aurangzeb wanted to improve his health through a visit to Kashmir. Bernier gives graphic details of this visit.

Aurangzeb left the city on 6 December 1664. He had 35,000 cavalrymen and infantry was manned by 11,000 men. It was rumoured that he was going to attack Kandahar. Bernier also accompanied him. At that moment he was receiving a salary of 150 crowns a month.

Explaining the travel to the king of France through his letters, Bernier said that it was a slow march. The grand quartermaster selected the place in advance for the king's tents and then paid attention to the symmetry of the whole camp. The tents were not lofty and watchmen prevented robberies.

'The first and largest tent erected in the royal camp being the place where the king and all the nobility will meet; that is where they assemble at nine o'clock in the morning for the purpose of deliberating on affairs of state and for administering justice.

'The second tent little inferior in size and somewhat further within the enclosure, is called the place of bathing. It is here that all the nobility meet every evening to pay their obeisance to the king, in the same manner as when the court is at Delhi.

'Adjoining the royal tents are those of the begums, or princesses and of the great ladies and principal female attendants of the seraglio. These tents are also enclosed on every side by rich kanats and in the midst of them are tents of the inferior female domestics and other women connected with the Seraglio, placed generally in much the same order, according to the offices of the respective occupants.

'The arrangements are elaborate. The king goes for hunting sometimes. The shikar is distributed among omrahs (nobles). In this journey, there were 1,00,000 horsemen, 1,50,000 animals and 50,000 camels and as many oxen. Simple habits of diet have to be observed. Rice and vegetables constitute the common food. Shops were also available in transition.'

It took the large caravan eleven days to reach Bimbar from Lahore. The days had started becoming hotter. On the eighth day of March, they reached from Bimbar to the entrance to Kashmir, the terrestrial paradise of the Indies. The king would stay there for three months.

Bernier translated Hyder Malik's chronicle from Persian to French. 'Kashmir is thirty leagues in length and twenty leagues in breadth. There is a variety of mountains which have no serpents. There are high mountains with snow. There are innumerable streams and springs. The land is fertile and flowers and fruits are in plenty. Two hillocks, Hariparbat and Takhte Suleiman, are worth a visit. There is no evidence that Solomon ever visited here. The most beautiful garden is Shalimar.'

Bernier recorded that the kingdom surpassed in beauty all that his warm imagination had anticipated. It is probably unequalled by any country of the same extent.

When Aurangzeb entered Kashmir, he received poems praising Kashmir. These were written in hyperbole.

In every March, the king was accompanied by a great number of omrahs and rajas, who followed him closely on horseback, placing themselves promiscuously in a body, without much method or regularity.

Many mansebdars or inferior omrahs came next, well-mounted and equipped with swords, quivers and arrows. This body was much more numerous than that of omrahs, which followed the king.

The princesses and great ladies of the Seraglio had also different modes of travelling. Some preferred chauldaries (like palanquins), which were borne on men's shoulders.

'Truly, it is with difficulty that these ladies can be approached and they are almost inaccessible to the sight of man. Woe to any unlucky cavalier, however, exalted in rank, who meeting the procession, is found too near. Nothing can exceed the insolence of the tribes of eunuchs and footmen which he has to encounter and they eagerly avail themselves of any such opportunity to beat a man in a most unmerciful manner. I shall not easily forget being once surprised in a similar situation and how narrowly, I escaped the cruel treatment that many cavaliers have experienced.'

Then Bernier moves further to say, 'I shall now speak of the field sports of the king. I could never conceive how the Great Mughal could hunt with an army of one hundred thousand men, but there certainly is sense in which he may be said to hunt with two hundred thousand or with any number of which his army may consist.'

Then Bernier gives other details of the situation like this:

'But, of all the diversions of the field, the hunting of the lion is not only the most perilous, but is peculiarly royal; for, except by special permission, the king and princes are the only persons who engage in the sports. As a preliminary step, an ass is tied near the spot where the gamekeepers have ascertained the lion retires.'

Then Bernier describes, 'I observe that the great rivers are commonly without bridges. The army crossed them by means of two bridges of boats, constructed with tolerable skill, and placed between two or three hundred paces apart.'

Then Bernier moves to give further details: 'As to the number of people, whether soldiers or others, which the camp contains, it is not easy to determine this accurately; so various are the opinions on this point. I may venture, however, to state generally that in this march, there are at least one hundred thousand horsemen, and more than one hundred and fifty thousands of animals, comprising horses, mules and elephants; that besides these, there cannot be much less than fifty thousand camels.'

The details given by Bernier in his letters to the king of France make his narrative very interesting. In one of his letters, he says, 'There is a curious fact respecting the king which I had almost forgotten to relate.

He enters the camp sometimes on one side, sometimes on another that is, he will today pass near the tents of certain omrahs and tomorrow near the tents of others.

'It is not without reason that the kingdom of which Lahore is the capital, is named the Penje-ab (Punjab) or the region of the five waters because five rivers do really descend from the great mountains which enclose the kingdom of Kashemire, and, taking their course through this country fall into the Indus which empties itself into the ocean at Scymdi, near the mouth of the Persian Gulf.

'To ensure a scarcity of food doesn't take place, in the small kingdom of Kashemire, the king was followed by a very limited number of individuals. Of females, he took only ladies of the first rank, the intimate friends of Raushan Ara-Begum and those women whose services cannot easily be dispensed with.

'The king had a few of the choicest elephants for his baggage and the women of the Seraglio. Though heavy and unwieldy, these animals are yet very sure-footed, feeling their way when the road is difficult and dangerous and assuring themselves of the firm hold of one foot before they move another.'

Then, Bernier describes the detail of an accident which occurred near the entry to Kashmir Valley. He says, 'A strange accident cast a gloom over these scenes and damped all our pleasure. The king was ascending the Pir-Penjale Mountains, the highest of all the mountains, and from which a distant view of kingdom of Kashemire is first obtained. He was followed by a long line of elephants, upon which sat the ladies in their mikdembers and embarys. The foremost, appalled, as is supposed, by the great length and acclivity of the path before him, stepped back upon the elephant that was moving on his track, who again pushed against the third elephant, the third against the fourth, and so on until fifteen of them, incapable of turning round or extricating themselves in a road so steep and narrow fell down the precipice. Happily for the women, the place where they fell was no great height; only three or four were killed; but there were no means of saving any of the elephants.'

Describing the beauty of Kashmir Bernier says, 'There are many beautiful gardens in Kashmir. The most beautiful of all these gardens (in Kashmir) is one belonging to the king, called Shalimar. The entrance from the lake is through a spacious canal, bordered with green turf, and running between two rows of poplars. Its length is about five hundred paces and it leads to a large summer house placed in the middle of the garden.

'You have no doubt discovered before this time that I am charmed with Kashemire. It should be as in former ages, the seat of sovereign authority, extending its dominion over all the circumjacent mountains, even as far as Tartary and over the whole of Hindustan, to the island of Ceylon. It is not indeed without reason that the Mughals called Kashemire the terrestrial paradise of the Indies; or that Akbar was so unremitting in his efforts to wrest the scepter from the native princes. His son Jahangir became so enamoured by this little kingdom as to make it the place of his favourite abode, and he often declared that he would rather be deprived of every other province of his mighty empire than lose Kashemire.'

'The Kashemirys are celebrated for their wit and considered more intelligent and ingenious than other Indians. In poetry and science, they are not inferior to the Persians. They are also very active and industrious.

'But, what may be considered peculiar to Kashemire, and the staple commodity, that which particularly promotes the trade of the country and fills it with wealth, is the prodigious quantity of shawls which they manufacture and which gives occupation even to the little children. These shawls are about an ell and a half long, and an ell broad, ornamented at both ends with a sort of embroidery, made in the loom, a foot in width. The Mughals and Indians, women as well as men, wear them in winter round their heads, passing them over the left shoulder as a mantle. There are two sorts manufactured: one kind with the wool of the country, finer and more delicate than that of Spainish (Ibex); the other kind with the wool, or rather hair (called touz) found on the breast of a species of wild goat which inhabit Great Tibet. The Touz shawls are much more esteemed than those made with the native wool. I have seen some, made purposely for the Omrahs, which costs one hundred and fifty roupies; but I cannot learn that the others have ever sold for more than fifty. They are apt, however, to be worm-eaten, unless frequently unfolded and aired. The fur of the beaver is not as soft and fine as the hair from these goats.

'The people of Kashemire are proverbial for their clear complexions and fine forms. They are as well made as Europeans and their faces have neither the Tartar flat nose nor the small pig-eyes that distinguish the natives of Kcheguer and which generally mark those of Great Tibet. The magnificent cascades between the rocks increase the beauty of the scene.

'In regard to my excursions in the different parts of this kingdom, I shall begin by informing you that we no sooner arrived in the city of Kashemire than my Navab, Danechmend-kan, sent me to the further end of the country, three short journeys from the capital, that I might witness the wonders, as they are called of a certain fountain. I was not sorry for another little excursion and set out with my former companions, the trooper and the native of the country.'

Bernier travelled to Baramullah and visited the shrine of Syed Mohammad Janbaz at Khanpora and saw a large bowler filled with rice and meat which was distributed among the people.

It is unfortunate that Bernier does not give any detail of what tasks Aurangzeb accomplished in Kashmir for three months.

The graphic detail of Aurangzeb's visit was however, given by Brigid Keenan in her book *Travels in Kashmir*.[88] The following paragraphs narrate the entire situation: 'The Emperor Aurangzeb visited Kashmir only once, in 1665 and left nothing there to be remembered by, except rules—rules which harassed the Hindu population and rules which forbade music, dancing and drinking which were particularly painful to the exuberant Kashmiris.'

Keenan goes further to say, 'For most of his reign Aurangzeb was preoccupied with problems far away from Kashmir, at the other end of his kingdom in Deccan, where he spent the last years of his life campaigning ceaselessly against turbulent local chiefs, trying to keep his empire intact. He succeeded, more or less, but his heirs were weak and quarrelling men and after Aurangzeb's death in 1707, most of the power of the Mughal emperors was simply frittered away.'

Keenan laments and says, 'In Kashmir, a golden age had come to an end. No longer was the valley of Jewel in the Mughal crown, the cherished retreat of the great emperors to be favoured and protected above all other parts of their empire.'

The author further describes the sad situation, 'After Aurangzeb's single visit, the Mughal court never made the long journey there again, and the governors appointed to rule Kashmir could now rarely be bothered to go to the Valley themselves but appointed representatives to rule in their places—something that would have been unthinkable under Akbar, Jahangir or Shah Jahan.'

Keenan laments further saying, 'Once again Kashmir became isolated from the rest of the world and at the mercy of greedy local officials who could behave as they pleased, and the all-too familiar story of corruption, oppression and civil strife began all over again. It was at around this time that the Nehru family, forebears of three Indian prime ministers, emigrated from Kashmir to Uttar Pradesh.'

I see it as a fortunate situation that a few early European travellers visited Kashmir and their visits conveniently coincided with the three main periods of foreign rule in the Valley and so we have eyewitness accounts of Kashmir under the Mughals, the Afghans and the Sikhs.

13

GEORGE FORSTER'S ACCOUNTS OF AFGHAN TYRANNY AND BEAUTY OF KASHMIR

George Forster who visited Kashmir in 1783, started his narrative on Kashmir saying natural beauties of the Valley (Kashmir) perhaps stand unparalleled for its air, soil and picturesque variety of landscape.

In his journey from Bengal to England, he has given graphic details of the beauty of the Valley, besides sharing his experience of meeting the people of Kashmir.

In his second volume, he describes his journey across Kashmir. This travelogue was first published in London in 1798. This happened to be the first account of Kashmir after Bernier wrote in 1684.

Forster travelled all by himself and met people of Kashmir very closely. When he was descending the heights of Banihal, he was struck by the beauty of Kashmir, especially the snow-clad mountains which presented to him an unparalleled spectacle of beauty. He first arrived in Veernag. His first experience was that he was subjected to severe search of his possessions by the customs house. He saw people wearing shoes made from grass called 'Pullahoor'. He praised Veernag, particularly, its trees, streams, forests and mountains. It was summer and he found flowers and fruits of all kinds in plenty. He saw red and white roses and was immensely happy and said it was like travelling in a land inhabited by nymphs. He was surprised that a difference of just 2 degrees in longitude makes such a big difference that the earth in Kashmir produces great variety of fruits and flowers. He praised 'Door' (Duroo-Shahabad) for the courtesies that the people offered to guests. Next day, he arrived in Anantnag, where he hired a boat to travel to Srinagar.

While Forster was deeply impressed by the beauty of Kashmir, he felt distressed by the stories he heard of the extreme atrocities committed by the Afghan rulers. He narrates what he saw himself and heard from the people during his stay in Kashmir.

'The Afghan rule proved to be one of extreme tyranny and cruelty and the beauty of this land and the nobility of its people has been brutally ravaged by the Afghans.' Forster records this tyranny saying, 'Governor Azad Khan, of the Afghan tribe, succeeded his father Hadji Kareem Dad, a domestic officer of Ahmed Shah Duranni. On the death of Duranni, he was made governor of Kashmire, by Timur Shah (son and successor of Ahmed Shah Abdali), as a reward for quelling the rebellion of Amir Khan. Though the Kashmirians exclaim with bitterness at the administration of Hadji Kareem Dad, who was notorious for his wanton cruelties and insatiable avarice; often for trivial offences, throwing the inhabitants, tied by the back in pairs, into the rivers, plundering their property and forcing their women of every description; yet they say he was a systematical tyrant and attained his purposes, however atrocious, through a fixed medium; they hold a different language in speaking of the son, whom they denominate the Zalim Khan, a Persian phrase which expresses a tyrant without discernment and, if the smaller charges against him are true, the appellation is fitly bestowed.'

Forster laments the fact that Kashmiris had themselves invited Afghans to rule over them in the following words: 'Little did the Kashmiris know that the Afghans whom they invited to rule over them were not a refined race like the Mughals.'

Forster assessed that entering Kashmir stealthily was much more compatible than seeking proper permission. He describes how his chance of meeting with the governor of Kashmir helped him to continue his travel from Anantnag towards Srinagar by boat.

Forster described Srinagar as a cut-built on both sides of the

Jhelum River and it is spread over three miles on both sides and the city is connected by three bridges. He found roofs of the houses laden with earth where flowers would be grown and this kind of roof kept houses warm during winter. Forster found lanes narrow and littered with dirt and Kashmiris themselves remained dirty. He praises the habit of building wooden bathrooms on the banks of river so that people take bath in private and women also used these bathrooms.

He found the lake in Srinagar called Dal presenting a beautiful show. He thought it was 5–6 miles long and it remains connected with the Jhelum through a narrow canal.

Forster did not use the expression Shankar Acharya for the hillock on the earth of Srinagar but connects it with Solomon and said that people of the Valley called it Takhte-Sulaiman. He also talked of Hari Parbat where people pay obeisance at the tomb of Makhdoom Sahib, a saint who is a household name in Kashmir. Forster has made a mention of Mughal gardens and an island within Dal lake called Char Chinar as four Chinar trees stood there one of which had become dry. He lamented the fact that Afghans did not maintain the heritage sites as liberal Mughals had done. But, he mentions the name of Amir Khan who came to Kashmir as governor and promoted preservation of heritage sites and developed good relations with local people. The first bridge was named after him as Amira Kadal and people loved him for his human qualities.

Forster described Chinar and its leaves comparing it with the palm of human hand. He also mentioned roses of Kashmir which were famous in the East for their beauty and fragrance and oil produced out of these flowers was famous in the world.

When roses appear in spring time, the Kashmiris celebrate the season as a festival and they sing and dance in groups. It is astonishing that nowadays, Kashmiris don't celebrate the season as a festival.

Describing Jhelum as a unique river, Forster says it is perhaps the only river that flows within Kashmir from one end to another.

Forster observed before Muslims conquered India, Kashmiri Pandits had established themselves as men of learning and the temples of Kashmir were famous. He described the art and crafts of Kashmir especially the world famous Kashmiri shawls.

He said that the word 'shawl' came from Tibet and Kashmiris rub rice flour on it and later mix colours on it. At that time, an ordinary shawl could be bought for rupees eight, but he had seen a shawl that fetched rupees forty (which when compared to present time meant an enormous amount of money). The embroidery on the shawls was exquisite.

He showered great praise on Kashmiris who could make the best paper and emphasized that if they are provided patronage, they can afford to be the best artisans in the world. But, he lamented that Kashmiris did not receive fair deal from any of their rulers.

He felt Kashmiris looked like Jews. This was also noted by Bernier earlier. He wrote that women of high classes are not accessible but the common women did not look attractive. He also testified the presence of women dancers and sex workers in one part of Srinagar city but their number had grown small by his time in Kashmir.

He describes the presence of fish as an important element of food for Kashmiris.

He thought the word Kashmir was derived from Sanskrit and its colloquial language compared favourably with Marathi. He described Kashmiris as people full of life and they are ingenious about earning wealth and spending it as well. He was surprised that the tyranny of the Afghans failed to check this trait of Kashmiris.

But, he does not hesitate to say that once a Kashmiri gets some authority, he teases his fellow Kashmiris and indulges in pocketing as much money as possible. A Kashmiri could be both a great friend and the worst enemy. Corruption was rampant as money worked wonderfully everywhere. During his time, the currency was produced at Muradabad of Rahailkhand.

He also mentioned river Kishanganga, which people crossed on the hides of sheep filled with air. Forster was enormously moved in favour of Kashmiris due to cruelties perpetrated over them by the rulers.

14
VICTOR JACQUEMONT AND THE SIKH REGIME

Victor Jacquemont (born in Paris in 1801) grew as a person who ultimately settled for deeper studies of natural history.

He was very much given to false theories of a visionary republicanism and indulged in wildest theories of metaphysics and had a variety of political dreams, but, finally he landed at the Museum of Natural History in Paris, where he was employed to investigate the natural history of India and collecting materials wherewith to enrich the museum and promote the progress of science.

His letters to his family and friends throw light on the life of the people of those countries that he visited.

He first came to London in 1828 and delivered the letter of introduction to Sir Alexander Johnston (Rt. Hon'ble chairman of Royal Asiatic Society) who helped him by introducing him to Governor General of India and others.

In India, he was allowed to attend meetings of the Asiatic Society of which Johnston was the chairman. The English and French governments, equally conscious to promote scientific inquiries on India, helped Jacquemont to a great deal and allowed this eminent naturalist to remain in India for seven years.

While in India, he also visited Kashmir in 1831 and chose to enter it through Punjab and reached Mirpore and on the way he received lavish hospitality. Needless to mention it here that it was part of the system that had evolved around Maharaja Ranjit Singh's government that foreigners, particularly the English and the French, were offered lavish hospitality by Ranjit Singh himself and his governors in the provinces.

Sheikh Bodu Bochs, the Mehmandar and Mirza, the lieutenant of his (Jacquemont) escort, kept his company. The first village after Mirpore he mentioned was Berali where they reached after a hazardous journey. The governor of the area Neal Singh appeared on the scene and wanted to use Jacquemont as a kind of hostage to receive favours from the king, but Jacquemont succeeded to proceed; but, not before he (Neal Singh) got assurance that Jacquemont would report to the king. Neal Singh also made Jacquemont agree to give 500 rupees (as if willingly, although it was a ransom), a bottle of wine which Jacquemont later sent to him.

When he left Berali, he met Sheikh Noor Mohammad who was leading an army of about 3,000. They were to report back at Lahore. Thereafter, Jacquemont reached Kotli.

On his way to Srinagar, he described certain scenes depicting the miseries that the Kashmiris suffered at the hands of the Sikh administration. He says in his book *Letters from India,* describing a journey in the British dominions, 'I mention to you a man hanged at Kotli. A dozen were suspended from trees near my camp, on the banks of the river. When the governor visited me, he told me, with an air of indifference that in the first year of his government he had hanged two hundred, but that now, one here and the other there was sufficient to keep the country in order. Now, mark that the country is a wretched and almost desert province. For my part, if I had to govern it, I should begin by putting in irons the Governor and his three hundred soldiers, who are the greatest thieves of all and I would make them work in the formation of a good road. They now live in idleness upon the labour of the poor peasant; they should continue to subsist on the same rice, but then they should earn it.'

On the other hand, Jacquemont describes Kashmiris as very clever people. The Hindus thought themselves to be of a superior caste. He said they ate everything but beef and drank arrah.

Jacquemont said that he had never seen anywhere such hideous witches as in Kashmir. He described the female race to be remarkably ugly. He meant the common folk. The women belonging to the high class kept themselves indoors. He thought that the prettier girls were sold at the age of eight years to Punjab. Jacquemont maintained a distance from the people and tried to remain polite.

He described in detail how generously he was treated by Ranjit Singh and the governor of Kashmir and imagined this kind of generosity was possible under a feudal system of the East only. He said that one can imagine the advent of the English administration had brought much needed relief to the local population whose condition happened to be bad under local administration.

He also wrote to friends in France about the lavish treatment at the hands of Ranjit Singh and his provincial governors. Sometimes his narrative became satirical as he described various aspects of feudal life. In one of his letters he wrote, 'I must have eaten four or five sheep, thousands of fowls at the Raja's expense.'

He also referred to the number of the sick who were brought to him. Once a crowd of diseased people gathered around him who could not be treated. In one of his letters, he described to his father that he found blindness of all descriptions. He lamented that there were no medical facilities. He wrote of giving some alms to those who could not be treated.

Jacquemont, in one of his letters described the panorama from Shalimar across Nishat, Charchinari, Hazratbal to the throne of Solomon.

He is, however, not happy with manners of the Kashmiris. Writing bitterly he says, 'With the system of constant seclusion of women, their degradation is seen; love is as rare as you may easily suppose.'

He wrote to his father that the people of Kashmir have not learnt good manners as they believe in a set of immutable laws.

It seems Jacquemont suffered ignorance on the immutable law that he refers to as there was none to explain to him the reality.

Jacquemont has thrown light on several other aspects of social life in Kashmir.

He observed that throughout the whole viceroyalty of Kashmir, there is no tribunal to settle private disputes upon a basis of equity.

Since he had been introduced to the viceroy and through him to Ranjit Singh, he experienced unimaginable sights during his visit. He wrote to his father, 'I am truly ashamed of the enormous bale of Kashmir shawls with which my luggage has been increased during the last seven months; though if my money should happen to run short during the remainder of my journey, they would prove an important resource. I really do not know what I shall do with them. I should like to be able to take them with me to Europe, with my animals, plants and minerals. They would serve as presents which I should like to make to the wives of my friends. But, how could I get them passed through the custom house?'

On return from Kashmir, he had an audience with Ranjit Singh without witnesses and in this meeting Ranjit Singh offered to him viceroyalty of Kashmir. He narrated all this to his father in a letter and told him that now instead of the title Sahib Bahadur, he was now known to be Aflatoon-e-zaman, that is, somebody with great wisdom and, therefore, with great stature.

After crossing the Sutlej for his onward journey, he realized that he was no more Plato of the world, the Socrates, the Aristotle of the age, the high and mighty Lord Victor Jacquemont. He says, 'I shall never again be treated as I was by Rajah of Mandi, who received me as if I had been Ranjit Singh himself. On crossing Sutlej, I lost all my lordly privileges.' Jacquemont was now walking about alone when he found that he had no other escort than his walking stick.

Jacquemont boasted, 'Ranjit Singh, a monarch absolutely independent and possessing the greatest power in Asia after the British, always received me barefooted.'

It appears that Ranjit Singh considered Jacquemont as a powerful European with enormous contacts and so deserving good hospitality.

15
HUGEL AND THE IMPOVERISHED KASHMIRIS

Charles von Hugel, a German national, was fascinated by the beauty and grandeur of Kashmir. He visited it in 1835 and initially, he felt sad to find Kashmiris not only living in poverty, but also in extremely dirty conditions. He found old dilapidated houses, narrow lanes full of filth and dirt—the quality of life totally incongruous with the bounty of nature.

He thanked God for the opportunity he got to visit Kashmir and enjoyed the breathtaking grandeur of the snow-clad mountains surrounding the Valley of Kashmir, considered widely as a paradise on earth.

Hugel met Mian Singh, who was the governor of Kashmir during the Sikh rule from 1834–41. Hugel found Mian Singh a courteous person who helped the poor. He reported this to Maharaja Ranjit Singh.

Hugel had recorded that a canal connected Dal Lake to the Jhelum River. He also described the gate on the lake near Takhte-Suleiman, which according to him happened to be three miles away from Bagh-e-Dilawar Khan where he resided during his stay in Srinagar.

Describing the level of poverty of the people, Hugel said that barring a small number of shawl weavers, the common people were not better off than beggars.

Hugel crossed all the seven bridges of Srinagar which he thought were made of ordinary wood. He visited Shah Hamdan's mausoleum,

Hazratbal, Tomb of Badshah and Hariparbat. He praised Emperor Akbar for building a wall around the city with minarets. Hugel, however, found the city maintained in poor conditions.

He found that Sikhs had only two army battalions which were enough to control the people who were non-violent and meek.

Hugel felt sad that Kashmir had lost its charm due to subjugation. With the permission of the governor, he went to Islamabad (Anantnag), and on the way he found a huge number of crocks at Panderathan.

He realized the importance of saffron which was grown at Pampore. He visited Awantipora, Kashmir's ancient capital which had lost all glamour and he felt sad to see the ruins of two old temples which the majority of archeologists accept as Hindu temples, dedicated to deities Shiva and Vishnu.

Hugel was surprised that there was no mention of Awantivarman in *Rajatarangini*. He mentioned that the Prophet had written a letter to King Dein (Awantiverman) for accepting Islam. It was said that the letter was received in the fourth century of Hijra and it had not been explained as to where this letter had been kept hidden for all that long time.

While travelling to Islamabad, Hugel saw a master beating his servant for indulging in theft. Meanwhile, a Sikh soldier passed by and the master and servant became friends instantaneously. This explained that against the callous attitude of the rulers, they could accept anything.

On reaching Bejbehara, he did not see anything worth mentioning about this ancient capital except a garden that had been laid by Dara Shakooh. Then, he went on horseback to Islamabad. He discovered that Anantnag was built by King Salkhan in 3200 BC. Then, he went to Mattan where he found people begging at the temple. He paid a rupee to a person who refused to accept it as he demanded fifty rupees.

Hugel described Mattan and the adjoining caves. His guide told him not to go inside the caves, but not caring for the advice, he entered the caves and found a room 20 feet long and 12 feet wide and behind this, he found a temple and the wooden door which was closed. Then, he sought permission from officers to enter a temple, but, there was nothing worthwhile there. He went to Aishmuqan and a Bodh temple nearby.

According to Hugel, Kashmiris were superstitious and surrendered to their fate. Hugel also set off to see the relics of Korwas and Pandwas. He went into a deep valley which dated back to 2000 BC. When he reached there, he found a small house and a garden owned by a saintly person.

After some days, he left Islamabad for Srinagar by boat. He suggested to his English friends to commemorate earlier visitors to Kashmir. They placed a plaque at Char Chinari with these words, 'Three visitors –Baren Hugel, T.G. Vigne and John Hunderson who decided to inscribe names of those persons who visited Kashmir before them, on a plaque.'

Vigne found Srinagar (the city of sun) divided into zilas as in the time of Pathans (Afgans) each under a kotwal or mayor. There was night patrol to stop thefts and people lived in peace.

'Peasants differed from city inhabitants, but the latter were more civilized and better-looking. There were Musalman and Hindus. The Musalmans were mostly Sunnis, the number of Shias being very inconsiderable. Hindus saluted each other with Rama Rama. A Kashmirian Hindu of the rank to a Musalman of the rank said "Sahib Salamat". A Musalman stranger saluted a visiting Hindu with "Daulat Zeada" and the answer would be "Umar Daraz" (may your age be long).

'Independent of the forehead mark, there is little difference in the style of living between Hindus and Musalmans. The Hindu smoothens the turban over the right temple and the Musalman on the left.

'The complexion of the Musalman Kashmiri is generally not so dark, certainly not darker than that of the natives of the south of Europe, the Napoleans, for instance, to whom they may also be compared on account of the liveliness and commonalities of their disposition, but his features are large and aquiline, like those of the Afghans and, I don't know, I can better describe them by calling them subdued Jewish; whilst a Hindu may often be distinguished by the fairness of their complexion.

'I was told this was attributable to their eating a less quantity of animal food than Musalmans. I have heard that the natives ascribe their own beauty to the softness of the water of the valley.

'Nine out of 10 Kashmiris eat oil with their food instead of ghee or clarified butter. It is chiefly extracted from apricot and almond, but there are other kinds also.

'I have remarked that the water in Kashmir softens a shawl better than any other thing and there is undoubtedly a peculiar softness in the air within the Valley. The horns of cattle, sheep and goats, never attain any extraordinary size and, in fact, are smaller than otherwise.

'The broad Herculean built and main features of the Kashmirian peasant, contrasted with his whining complaints and timid disposition, if considered apart from the effects of a long continued subjugation, tyranny and despotism. I think it would now be difficult to induce Kashmiris to rise in revolt and be assisted against their oppressors.'

Mehmud failed twice to take Kashmir, but got it later. Akbar made two unsuccessful attempts before he succeeded. Hugel knew that Akbar had tried to reduce their (Kashmiris) martial spirit.

Hugel was advised by some people as in the following:

'If you meet a snake do not put it to death, but do not spare a Kashmiri. Do not admit a Kashmiri to your friendship or you will be forced to hang him on a hatchet over your doorway. It is in this spirit that the neighbouring nations make remarks, when speaking of a Kashmirian. But, this is a case that gives the dog a bad name and hangs him. They are certainly lying and deceitful race of people, but when detected in a fault their excuses are so very ready and profuse.'

He goes on to say further, 'Many women are beautiful. They wear a red gown with large loose sleeves. The hair is collected in separate plaits, then gathered and a long tassel of black cotton is suspended from it, almost down to the ankles. The Hindu women usually wear a white rolled cloth tied loosely round the waist. In Kashmir, there is no pardah or concealment of features, except among upper classes. Usually, women are gifted with a figure which would entitle them to be compared with handsome women of European society.

'I have also been much struck with the beauty of the Watul tribe who are perhaps gypsies. They raise tents or small huts of thatch. They are looked down upon both by Musalmans and Hindus, with the greatest contempt. Many of their beautiful children are sold and sent as slaves to Punjab and I believe many of the prettiest of dancing girls are born of Watul parents.'

The whole space which intervenes between the Manasbal and Wullar lakes, is nearly covered with the wild indigo plant that grows in the marshy land, the left of the Jhelum are the ruins of Parihaspura built originally by Laltadiyya in AD 714 where according to *Ain-i-Akbari*, there was a Hindu temple destroyed by Alexander.

The river next enters Wullar Lake which again leaves it at Sopur on its way to its exit at Baramulla. But, the visitor must first visit the sacred lake of Gangabal on the mountain of Harmukh.

16

SIR RICHARD TEMPLE'S GRAPHIC DETAILS

Sir Richard Temple, who was at one point of time secretary to the Government of India and held many positions, described Kashmir the way he thought better in his two travelogues. Temple later became the Lieutenant-Governor of Bengal.

He visited Kashmir twice—first, on 8 June 1859 and then on 9 April 1871. He found time to appreciate its beauty and studied the characteristics of Kashmiris. Although Temple was a guest of the government, he tried to be impartial. He has described the milestones of his travel on Mughal Road in June 1859.

Temple went to see Mattan and visited temples there. He went to Martand to see the Sun temple and visited various other temples built during Lalitaditya's time.

He appreciated the taste of Mughal kings who laid beautiful gardens in Kashmir. On his second visit to Kashmir, he travelled via Pirpanjel and reached Veernag on 2 April 1871 and then proceeded to visit Wullar for the second time and went up to the hill to see the shrine of Baba Shukruddin.

Temple found the greatest characteristics of Kashmir are that it is surrounded by snow-clad mountains.

In his letter to Lord Lytton on 30 September 1876, Temple said that Kashmir could be reached through three ways—one through Cart Road (which later became Jhelum Valley Road); the other two roads through Bhimber and Banihal.

Temple's description is unique in the sense that there is hardly any place of importance which he has not mentioned.

He did not forget to mention that half of the produce had to be passed on to the Dogra ruler Ranbir Singh and the excesses that the officials of Wazir Pannu, who was the governor during the Dogra rule in Kashmir, perpetrated on the common people.

Temple has given graphic details of the characteristics of Kashmiris in his book *Journals Kept in Hyderabad, Kashmir, Nepal and Sikkim.*

'The Kashmiris, if we accept the weakly shawl makers, are one of the finest races physically in all India; robust, broad-shouldered, muscular, and well-featured but of not more than middle height as a rule. In character they are credited with exceptional cowardice, and the concomitants of this failing—lying and deceitfulness, wrangling and weeping on occasions. But, they are intellectually superior to all their neighbours, talkative and cheerful. They are divided into Hindus or Pandits, which term in Kashmir does not by any means imply Brahmanical rank—and Muhammadans, the latter forming six-sevenths of the population.

'The large and important class of boatmen is, of all those inhabiting Kashmir, best known to European travelers, because the great highways of the country are the Jhelum River, the canals and the lakes. They are called Hanjis and possess alike the best and worst traits of the Kashmiris. Powerful, well-developed and exceedingly skilful in the management of their boats, their cowardice in a storm on one of their lakes is a source of danger to themselves and their passengers. Good-humored, energetic and versatile, they will yet lie with extraordinary readiness and are greedy and importunate to a degree.

'The Kashmiri Muhammdans are split into some twenty tribes or classes of which the most important are the Chaks, originally the warrior class, the Maliks and the Bats. The chief religionists are the Rishis, who seem to be celibate monks of a type not uncommon in the East, but are nevertheless, as a class, peculiar to Kashmir. The shawl-weavers, too, are Muhammadans, ill-paid and malnourished and badly housed and, therefore, physically and morally wretched.'

After this graphic detail, Temple didn't forget to mention the use of the long loose garment, pheran and a portable brazier known kangri which Kashmiris invariably used to protect themselves against cold.

17

DIARY OF A PEDESTRIAN IN KASHMIR AND TIBET (CAPTAIN KNIGHT)

Captain Knight, a British army officer, decided in 1860 to visit Kashmir along with another British officer.

Knight had acquainted a Kashmiri Hindu who was his domestic help who happened to be an adventurer whom he took to Kashmir as a trusted guide. They started their journey on 21 May 1860.

They adopted the route through Bhimber and entered Kashmir from Mogul Road. Knight would maintain a diary of events and places that he had visited and the same was published in a book form in June 1863.

Knight was a keen observer and while travelling he saw a body hanging from a tree at Chingus in Rajouri, half of which had already been eaten up by wolves. On enquiry, he was told that it was a sepoy who had killed another armyman and was punished for the crime this way. But, he found this dispensation of justice unacceptable.

Knight saw an army parade at the Parade Ground in Srinagar where every armyman was wearing a turban. Maharaja Ranbir Singh visited the parade on horseback.

He described the parade as a disorganized one. The uniforms did not match. The maharaja appeared to be thirty-eight years old.

There was a separate cemetery for the English in Srinagar and whenever the English died, the maharaja would send a shawl to be laid on the coffin.

On Knight's arrival, the maharaja organized a concert and a dance in which chosen women danced and a guard of honour was presented. Many military men and prominent citizens were present. All this was followed by a sumptuous dinner. When guests started eating, the maharaja withdrew and he appeared again with a troupe of dancing girls.

Knight noticed that good shoes that were placed on steps of stairs were replaced by old and torn ones. This he heard had been happening in Kashmir.

Knight admitted that in its beauty, Srinagar could rightly be called the Venice of the East. He noticed wooden houses on both sides of the river. He saw many mosques and temples. He enjoyed Shalimar garden and its numerous fountains.

He found a lot of dirt in the market place and cheap varieties of shawls. But, a good piece of shawl could be purchased for a price between Rs 300–1,000. He described the paper market of Srinagar as inferior. He saw Srinagar connected through seven bridges over the river and water transport in full swing. During his visit to places of attraction, he appreciated the taste and culture of the Mughals.

While he appreciated the beauty of Kashmir, he described how swarms of flies and mosquitoes attacked visitors and put them to discomfort.

After spending one and a half months in the Kashmir Valley, Knight left for Tibet via Ladakh.

18

LIEUTENANT ROBERT THORP'S
TRUTHFUL ACCOUNTS

Robert Thorp will go down in Kashmir's history as a person who was deeply involved in understanding the misery that Kashmir suffered through what he called misgovernment. He wrote in his famous book *Kashmir: Misgovernment* how Kashmiris were treated inhumanly and how the outside world remained ignorant of what was the nature of atrocities committed by the rulers against the common people.

Thorp's father, a British army officer, visited Kashmir in 1833. He fell in love with a Kashmiri girl named Jana from Sugen village near Khag (Beerwah), married her and took her to England. Robert Thorp was their third son. He came to Kashmir in 1865 when Ranbir Singh was ruling the state. He witnessed the helplessness of Kashmiris and described their plight through his letters to friends and relatives in England.

So, Thorp made it his business to study and expose the pattern of misrule unleashed against the people by Ranbir Singh and his agents. Those days Englishmen were allowed to stay in Kashmir only for summer months—from April to November. So, Thorp was constrained to visit Kashmir for a longer duration to complete his research on *Kashmir: Misgovernment*. Later, he brought the miserable condition of Kashmiri Muslims to the notice of the governments of India and England by publishing his findings. His research titled *Kashmir: Misgovernment* continues to be a major historic document of what happened to Kashmiri Muslims during the 1860s.

Thorp came to Kashmir, like many other British officers, to shoot big game on the mountains, but his mind was soon directed to a more important matter namely, the sorrows of the Kashmiris under maladministration. He found the peasants, who were Muslims, suffering terribly under the rule of Hindu officials, who sucked the very lifeblood out of them. They paid their taxes in kind, the state claiming half the crops, and the state officials who collected the grain taking a quarter or more. There was such an army of Hindu officials whose duty was to collect the grain that, when supplied, both lawfully and unlawfully, there was very little left for the zamindar and his family who had farmed the land. Often it happened that the farmer and his family had to live on roots, or anything they could find on which to exist.

Thorp goes further to say: 'Tehsildar reported directly to the governor. Those days the governor of Kashmir was the dreaded Kripa Ram, the author of Gulabnama, and Gulzari-Kashmir. He also was a bigoted Hindu and is credited with the authorship of an anti-Islam book titled *Radde-Islam: The Rejection of Islam*. It was at his (Kripa Ram's) behest and support that Pandit Raj Kak Dhar, Daroga of Dagshal, Chief of Shawl Department drowned twenty-eight shawl workers at Zaldagar in Srinagar on April 29, 1865 for demanding permission to buy more rice to eat. They were expected to work and pay huge taxes but at the same time not allowed to buy sufficient rice to feed their families.'

Thorp published the details of how the shawl industry worked and of the extortionate taxes levied on it and also of shawl workers' massacre to the outside world.

F.M. Hassnain, who reset Thorp's *Kashmir: Misgovernment*,[89] quotes Thorp lamenting the fact that shawl weavers who were taxed heavily, were not allowed to purchase food with their little money and were made to starve. When new regulations were issued by the raja by which they were allowed to purchase food, the occasion became a celebration for them.

Thorp describes this in the following words: 'At some of their spring fairs this year, I was struck with the increased number of people as compared with the year before, and, on enquiry, was told that this year they have been allowed to buy food enough to eat and are consequently able to come out and enjoy themselves a little. The poor wretches, so accustomed to oppression and misusage of all kinds that they look upon this as a concession deserving of the utmost gratitude.'

Thorp was particularly disgusted with the atrocities that were committed by the 'Dag-e-Shall' as under the system, the weavers had to pay high taxes and they could not keep their bodies and souls together.

The weavers would run away to Punjab. Many of them were caught at Pirpanjal, brought back and incarcerated. The system of taxation was so severe that the victims preferred death to life under such a cruel system.

Thorp lamented the fact that his own people (the British) were responsible for the extreme hardships that Kashmiris were suffering as it was the British government that had set up the Dogra rule in Kashmir.

A system of making people of Kashmir work free of charges and carry load on their backs to far-flung borders in Gilgit was known as 'Begaar'. Whenever the load had to be carried, men of all ages were caught and sent on this duty against their will. It was a system of tyranny, perhaps prevalent only in Kashmir. Many people sent to Gilgit on 'Begaar' never returned home as they were never given provisions and died of starvation and undernourishment.

Thorp attracted the attention of British government towards the atrocities that were committed against the people from whom the government collected taxes and these atrocities included life imprisonment for the person who would slaughter a cow. The person was thrown in the jail and had also to bear burns from hot iron rods. What was dehumanizing was that the Hindus were either set free for the same crimes or given a very light punishment. This caused deep disgust in Thorp's mind. He felt sad that the Muslim peasants suffered extreme hardships at the hands of government's representatives who were invariably Hindus. Half of the produce would go to the government; and the rest to the government's functionaries and at the most, one-fourth would be left to the peasants. Thorp saw people starving and eating barks of trees.

Thorp was given two months to stay, but he extended it and spent some more time stealthily and then tried to cross the Pir Panjal mountains.

He was caught and since the government was extremely annoyed with him for writing against it, he was brought to Srinagar. Next day, Thorp's body was found on the Shankar Acharya Mountain on 22 November 1868. It became common knowledge then that he had been poisoned at the behest of the rulers.

The *Friend of India* newspaper published from Calcutta (now Kolkata) stated in its publication of 11 May 1875 that the people of Kashmir suspected foul play and the common people thought he was poisoned.

After *Kashmir: Misgovernment* was published in 1870, the British government paid some attention to Kashmir and there was a little improvement in the situation.

During the 1865 famine, three Kashmiri Muslims were sighted by an English traveller on the bank of the Jhelum where they had been kept for three days and nights wearing stinking fish around their necks in the shape of garlands. Their crime was that they had violated the ban on fishing (p. 30, *Wrongs of Kashmir*, Kashmir Papers, Arthur Brinkman).[90] The net result was that population of the Kashmir Valley progressively dwindled throughout Ranbir Singh's rule (1856-85) as his coffers swelled.

Paying a tribute to Thorp, Tyndale Biscoe wrote in his book *Kashmir: Sunlight and Shade*: 'In the European cemetery at the Sheikh Bagh, which is situated near the first of the seven city bridges, is a grave which I never pass without taking my hat off, for in it are the mortal remains of Lieut. Robert Thorp, who gave his life for the Kashmiris in the year 1868. The grave lies under the shadow of one of those beautiful chinar trees, which are a continual comfort to those seeking shelter from the summer sun, and a joy to behold when the leaves take on their glorious autumn tints of pink-scarlet.'

Ranbir Singh was a devout but a zealot Hindu. For Hindus he opened Sanskrit schools and raised temples in and around Jammu city, the most prominent among them being the Ragunath temple with its Sanskrit school. S.S. Charak in his book *Maharaja Ranbir Singh*[91] gives a graphic description of what Ranbir Singh did with public money raised through taxes on a very large scale in Kashmir. Charak says, 'He spent large sums of money on maintenance of Hindu religious establishments at Haridwar, Kashi, Prayag, Badrinath, etc.

'For the miniscule Kashmiri Pandit minority he built temple complexes throughout the Kashmir Valley including Martand, Bijbehara, Pampore, Khir Bhawani, Gadadar, Sharika, Sharda, etc. The huge expenses thus incurred were collected mostly from Kashmiris.'

Thorp's account on Kashmir had definitely a strong element of his compassion for the people of Kashmir. However, Thorp's description of the tax burden on Kashmiris receives good support from Charak. He had been tasked by the University of Jammu and the Dharmarth Trust to write a comprehensive book on Ranbir Singh and he must perhaps, have been expected to deal with the subject with a certain amount of restraint. But, then, facts are facts and, therefore, Charak respected his own scholarship and gave details of the taxes that the Maharaja imposed on the people of Kashmir. In this way, Thorp's description of the tax burden on Kashmiris received full support from Charak in his said book, where Charak gives the details of the taxes imposed by Ranbir Singh.

He says: 'It has been truly said that no product is too insignificant, no person too poor, to contribute to the state. This literally applied to the taxation conditions in the Kashmir Valley where every person had to pay to the state under some name, and every product thinkable was taxed. The tax on shawls which was called Dag-i-Shawl dated back to 1197 Hijri.'

Moorcroft who visited Kashmir in 1824 describes how heavily the shawl trade and other trades were taxed in Kashmir from time immemorial. Most of these taxes had continued for many early years of Ranbir Singh's reign. The shawl industry was taxed in various manners.

The wool was taxed as it entered Kashmir, the manufacturer was taxed for every workman he employed; again he was taxed at various stages of the process according to the volume of the fabric; and lastly, the merchant was taxed before he could export the goods. Under the circumstances it was 'a marvel how the industry could have outlived the impositions to which it was subjected. Other callings were exposed to exactions of the same sort. Even coolies who were engaged to carry luggage of travellers, had to surrender half their earnings. Butchers, bakers, carpenters, boatmen and even prostitutes were taxed.

Agricultural products were similarly taxed, and where "kind rates" prevailed the apportionment of rice, maize and pulse products was to the tune of half the gross produce to the government, whereas the half remaining with the cultivator was further burdened with various exactions, leaving a balance of about one-fourth to the zamindars.

There were custom duties, and cesses collected on the movement of the trade goods from one region to the other which have been in force for quite a long time. These Rahdari (movement) taxes were charged at seven places in Jammu province and at twelve places in the Kashmir Valley. The taxes imposed included temple tax, Sanskrit tax and other taxes.'

Charak mentions that three-fourths of the fruit produce was appropriated by the government. One anna was also charged annually per sheep and goat. Milk, honey, water nuts and reeds used for thatching were also brought under taxation. There was also a cess from 4 to 20 annas levied on each house in the villages. Every tiller, trader, craftsman labourer and every citizen was taxed in some form or the other. The revenue accruing from such a policy of taxation was considerable.

Even sex workers and grave-diggers were taxed heavily. A sex worker was disallowed to change her profession because she earned taxes for the government as a prostitute.

Of the Dag-i-shawl, which yielded highest revenue to the raja, but left the weavers high and dry, Charak says: 'The Dag-i-shawl, or shawl tax on old rates brought to Ranbir Singh's treasury annual revenue of twelve lakhs. As soon as a shawl had been commenced on the loom, the contactor put his stamp on it, and the duty was to be paid at once at a rate of about 12 per cent of the value of the shawl.'

If a starved coolie carried the luggage of a traveller in the Kashmir Valley, he had to surrender half his earning to the maharaja's coffers. Likewise, houses, marriages, cattle, beasts of burden, grazing, were taxed to the maximum.

19

CHARLES ELISON BATES AND HIS ACADEMIC PURSUITS

Charles Elison Bates did a commendable work of preparing a 'Gazetteer of Kashmir' at the behest of the British government. He started this stupendous work in 1870 and completed it in three years.

Since the British government had entrusted this task to Bates, the maharaja of Kashmir extended all help to him.

A galaxy of Kashmir scholars working in the Bureau of Translation and the Department of Archaeology and Research was asked to render help Bates.

The main focus of Bates happened to be Kashmir etymology. In this connection, Bates consulted valuable and authentic sources.

Bates' reference to the findings of Wilford[92] and Humboldt[93] regarding Kashmir is mentioned in his book as follows: 'The etymology of the name of this celebrated region has singularly perplexed antiquarians. Wilford derives the name from Chasas, a very ancient and powerful tribe, who inhabited the Himalaya and Hindu Kush, from the eastern limits of India to the confines of Persia. They are mentioned in the institutes of Manu and other sacred books of the Hindus, and still hold large tracts in northern Hindustan.'

According to others, it is derived by Brahmins from kas (light) and mira (sea). Humboldt states its primeval name was Kasyapamar, signifying 'the habitation of Kasyapa, a mythological personage by whose agency the valley was drained'.

Bates also found Ptolemy's *Geography* had referred to Kashmir as Kaspeiria and the people of Kashmir as Kaspeirians. According to Bates, Kashmir's length from north-west to south-east was 118 miles while the length of the plains on average was 89 miles and width 17 miles. He also mentioned two divisions of the Valley as Maraz (South) and Kamraz (North). Bates is recognized as a person who gave correct figures about the population and its social status.

According to him, the population of Kashmir was twenty lakh in 1885 which had got reduced to eight lakh due to usual atrocities of the administration, famines and earthquakes.

Bates quoted Elmslie[94] saying that the population of the Valley happened to be 402,700 and the community-wise distribution was the following:

Muslims (Sunni): 312,700

Shais: 15,000

Hindus: 75,000

Bates noted the following situations as part of his research:

1. No non-Muslim paid any taxes to the government.
2. There were 5,573 persons in Maharaja Pratap Singh rule who served as government servants. None among them happened to be a Muslim.
3. Out of 403 jagirdars only five were Muslims.
4. Out of 7,500 petty government servants 285 were Muslims. Bates recorded that while 95 per cent of the population in the state was Muslim, their share in the administration was almost nothing.

Bates found religious leaders of the Hindus and the Muslims were equally ignorant of the philanthropies others were promoting.

He recorded that rishis were popular among people. They led a saintly life and ate vegetables and cereals only. They planted trees and gave food to hungry and water to quench people's thirst.

He listed eleven varieties of fish and found that most Kashmiris ate fish and vegetables.

Speaking about the character of Kashmiris, Bates says, 'Kashmiris were poor but were generous and offered food, etc. to even strangers. In rural areas, Kashmiris served food, etc. and helped those in the neighbourhood who were old and sick.'

Bates realized Kashmiris were intelligent people and wherever certain people found shortcomings in their behaviour, it was due to the circumstances in which they have lived for a long time. He accepted the categorization of Kashmiris as East's Napoleans. He rated Kashmiris as hardworking, alert and witty just like Napoleon.

But, then, having lived lives of slaves for centuries, they could not get rid of habits like lying and indulging in deceit.

20
W. WAKEFIELD'S CRITICISM OF THE TREATY

W. Wakefield, who visited Kashmir in 1875, referred to it as a happy valley and was fascinated by its beauty. His description of the beauty of Kashmir is really and, in large measure, quite different from others. Almost in his first breath on seeing Kashmir, he described it as a happy valley, 'the scene of the poet Moor's inimitable Lalla Rookh'.

Says Wakefield, 'Nowhere in Asia, nor even perhaps in the remaining quarters of the globe, can the parallel be found of such an earthly paradise; a paradise in itself as formed by nature, but made doubly beautiful by its surroundings.' He calls Kashmir Be-Nuzir, that is, without equal.

Then, Wakefield describes another aspect of the Kashmir Valley. He says, 'Apart from its acknowledged claims to picturesque beauty, Kashmir has others no less important, and equally interesting alike to the scholar, the antiquary and the prospect-hunter; for its recorded claim to be considered a place of the highest antiquity will, I am sure, be conceded by any who have studied its history and have seen or heard of the noble ruins, relics of past days, standing yet in various parts of the Valley, testifying alike to its former greatness and prosperity.'

One can imagine the lavish treatment towards foreigners, especially the British, by the governors under the Sikh rule and then under the Dogra rule, from the following statement: 'A curious, but a very polite, custom prevails in Kashmir, that on the day following one's arrival, the native agent, attended by a number of servants, in making his first visit, presents an offering of food and fruit and a sheep or a goat from the maharajah, at the same time bidding you welcome in his name to the capital of his country. This politeness of the ruler of the state to strangers is frequently extended not only to the living, but also to the dead; for if an English officer is so unfortunate as to come to his death during his stay in the Valley, this attentive prince, to show his sympathy with the melancholy event, usually sends a shawl of price to wrap the body in before burial.'

Wakefield seems to have been struck by the helplessness of Kashmiris and he pitied their fate due to the cruelty of various kinds that the authoritarian rule inflicted on the natives. He criticized the English people for having entered into the Treaty of Amritsar with Maharaja Gulab Singh. He makes a graphic reference to it by saying, 'The huckstering spirit that so often pervades our national policy and which caused the great Napoleon to apply to us term of a nation of shopkeepers was dominant in this case (Kashmir) for relinquishing all the advantages that accrued to us from its possession. The supreme government sold this fair province to Gulab Singh for a paltry and insignificant sum of 75 lakhs of rupees and under the treaty by which it was assigned, known as the Treaty of Amritsar.'

Wakefield tried his best to understand Kashmir's topography, its geographical contours, its history, its language, its culture and, above everything else, the character of Kashmiris. He found out of 4,20,000 inhabitants, more than a third lived in this city and its environs, the population of Srinagar being estimated at 1,50,000 souls but, as no census was taken, it was difficult to fix the number of the people dwelling either in the towns or in the Valley generally.

Wakefield's describes the Kashmiris as undoubtedly a fine race, the finest perhaps existing in this part of Asia and the type of the old Aryan race, the stock from whence they have sprung. He described them to be tall, strong and stoutly built, the features of the men were large and aquiline, with a wide, straight-up and high forehead, a well-shaped head and a cast of countenance somewhat like the Afghans but Jewish in character, although there is nothing known that would connect their origin with any of the tribes, lost or otherwise, of that celebrated nation. The beauty of the women of Kashmir was of ancient and worldwide reputation; and certainly, as a well-known author remarks, many of them were beautiful enough to induce a man to exclaim, as did the Assyrian soldiers when they beheld the beauty of Judith, 'who would despise this people that have among them such women?'

Wakefield, one of the greatest admirers of Kashmir's beauty, was however, dismayed to see many weaknesses in the demeanour of Kashmiris. He describes them as 'Personal working is unknown and from childhood to old age, they never so employ it; and instead of a people that one would expect to find the cleanliest of the clean, a short glance at their visible condition suffices to inform the spectator that he sees before him human beings fashioned in the image of their creator, but alas! for their manners and customs veritably the dirtiest of the dirty.'

It is so tragic that one, who called Kashmir as a virtual paradise on earth, should feel hurt on knowing various traits of Kashmiri character. He laments these characteristics.

Unfortunately, Wakefield found the failings and faults outnumbered the good qualities of Kashmiris. He found that Kashmiris were inveterate liars without a parallel in the East.

Coming to women of Kashmir, Wakefield said, 'This is a part of the world where the inhabitants generally seem to imbibe the talent of lying with their mother's milk. They are also a race decidedly cowardly, ever made to wrangle, but never to fight; and, if threatened by their superiors in any way, cry and act after the manner of children and consequently are not to be depended on to bear themselves well against any physical danger. They are decidedly clever and ingenious and talkative and cheerful in disposition but their selfishness, ignorance and their intriguing, false and dishonest qualities have caused hard things to be said of them by other nations which undoubtedly they in measure richly deserve.'

While it is not possible to find fault with Wakefield's assessment of Kashmiri character, a question will always lurk in the mind of every reader of this account, especially the researchers, as to why the accounts of M.A. Stein and Walter Lawrence are, generally, at variance with the statements of people like Wakefield.

21

ARTHUR NEVE AND A PHYSICIAN'S ASSESSMENT

D r Arthur Neve's travelogue started in 1882 and ended in 1910. He arrived in Kashmir in 1882. He was a physician who was deputed to Kashmir by the English Church's Missionary Society. He first joined the mission in Amritsar and then moved to Kashmir.

He described in those days one could travel on a tonga up to Koh Mari, that too in summer and during the winter one had to travel on horseback. He described his travel to Mari in detail and he found it to be a habitation buried under snow. Beyond Mari, he had to travel on horseback, but the terrain was very difficult. Those were the days when Jhelum cart road was being constructed into Jhelum Valley road and the construction had enhanced difficulties in travel. When he reached Uri, he spent the cold night at a dilapidated rest house. When he entered the Valley, he saw the snow-clad Harmokh mountain shining in the sunshine and he travelled by boat to Srinagar.

He settled down at Mission Hospital at the foothills of Kohi Sulaiman (Solomon mountain). It was he who unfurled the flag of the Red Cross in Kashmir. He described how there was no female doctor or nurse for treating women in Kashmir.

When Neve reached Srinagar, the traces of famine were still visible. He thought with a little effort, the famine could have been avoided as there was plenty of water. But, he thought floods could be a danger in Kashmir as it happened in 1877. Wazir Panno wanted to punish Muslim peasants who had not paid revenue in kind. The grains got spoiled in godowns and the seeds were not allowed to be distributed. Peasants ran away to other areas. Kashmir witnessed a severe famine while Jammu remained safe. There was a rumour that many of famine-stricken people were sunk in Wullar Lake. The person who saw it happening died in a few hours. Neve didn't believe it to be true, but since the rulers had no sympathy with Muslim peasantry, everything was seen with suspicion.

When Neve arrived on the scene, the impact of famine was visible and people had hardly any clothing available and they were physically weak, especially shawl-making people.

The Mission Hospital became a source of hope, but there were no arrangements for surgery.

A Hindu officer who had perpetrated great miseries on the people during the famine two years earlier, and now was himself ill, called Neve an angel when he went to treat him and he offered lavish courtesies to the doctor.

After Ranjit Singh's demise, a political agent was upgraded to a resident who met many foreign travellers.

Neve was fully privy to what a disaster had taken place due to a dangerous earthquake in 1885. That year, rains continued to pour till end of Magh (February) and there were landslides on a large scale. Then came the devastating earthquake on 30 May, which created disaster all around. Neve saw houses crumbling down and people, particularly women and children, crying. Many houses that were made of timber suffered minor damage but the ones having clay on roofs crumbled down.

It was a widespread devastation and the Mission Hospital did what it could do under the circumstances. Neve went to Sopore and Baramulla by boat and saw the devastation that these areas had suffered. He treated the injured people in tents. The earthquake tremors continued to occur in various parts of Kashmir. Many villages had sunk into depths. Laridora (a village in Baramulla tehsil) had sunk with forty-seven persons living there, only seven persons had survived. After a few days, Neve reached Laridora and he found heaps of fallen trees in the jungle. The stink of dead animals reached a distance of at least half of a mile.

The 1,000-feet high plateau between Gohan, Muran and Laridora was fully stricken by the earthquake.

A shrine on a hillock was completely devastated. When a companion of Neve asked people why the saint had not saved them, he was told by the people that some fools had covered the saint's grave with earth and he (the saint) took a turn in the grave and the earthquake occurred. This is the level to which superstitions can go.

After some time, Neve came again to Baramulla with supplies of relief and he noticed selfishness, greed, so it became difficult for him to cover all the affected villages. Neve had medicines and ferans (Kashmir gowns) and all his ferans got distributed among three villages only. He felt discouraged and thought that they (the English) should not take much interest in the people's mutual relations and keep contented with what they can do by way of relief.

Neve says that Maharaja Pratap Singh was given to paying obeisance at various shrines and he had been to Amarnath twice. His father had wanted Jammu to be second Banaras but that had not happened as the resources of Banaras happened to be far greater, but Jammu had changed for the better.

Neve visited Jammu during Pratap Singh's time and an elephant was sent to receive him at a distance of three miles from Jammu. This indicated that he would be treated as a guest of the government. Neve described how Jammu's life had changed for the better due to the rail engine, western goods, system of education and the maharaja's kind treatment of his subjects. For some years, the administration of Jammu & Kashmir was run by the British government, but Lord Curzon restored all powers to the maharaja in 1905. When the Prince of Wales, King George, came to Jammu, a camp was set up at Satwari and Rs 40,000 was spent on the reception.

The people in the East, Neve thought, do not consider this kind of expenditure as extravaganza. During Basant (spring), a durbar would be organized with great pomp and show and all invitees had to wear yellow dress with turbans of same colour. All invitees paid nazrana to the maharaja, which was equal to 3 per cent of their salary. Durbars were held on Nauroz and Dussehra. The maharaja entertained Neve in Jammu till the road was repaired and Neve went to Srinagar by Banihal road on which no European was allowed to travel till then.

Banihal road was fit for horseback only. Neve stayed with a Muslim Sufi at Banihal who Neve found to be large-hearted and very liberal.

Neve was impressed and admitted that in the West people got knowledge through books whereas the people of the East learnt through meetings and exchange of ideas and that knowledge through this route was better.

The Muslim saint told Neve that he had met people of all the seventy-two sects of Muslims and people of other religions and told him further that whatever faith people held, he was kind to all.

On reaching Kashmir he decided to go to Gurez where he reached after facing so many odds. Neve found that although people of Gurez spoke Kashmiri, they were different people who belonged to the tribe of Dards. He found the people of Gurez were living in difficult conditions. They lived in unhygienic conditions and many a time he found humans and cattle living together.

Neve's accounts are a comprehensive detail of his travels to Ladakh, Baltistan, Gilgit, Kazakistan and other distant territories. He was greatly attracted by the Nanga Parbat, which was accessed through Gilgit.

Neve's book *Thirty Years in Kashmir*[95] is full of interesting details of his long stay there.

22

SIR WALTER LAWRENCE AND KASHMIR

Sir Walter Roper Lawrence happened to be a member of the British Council and served in British India. He wrote several travelogues. The most prominent among these is on the Kashmir Valley. He was appointed as a settlement commissioner for Jammu & Kashmir during the rule of Maharaja Pratap Singh. He started his work in 1887 and completed the stupendous task in seven years' time.

Lawrence, who was thoroughly prepared for the work and invested time to select experienced, motivated men of friendly demeanour as his companions in the field. This task was accomplished through consultation with government functionaries.

The task that had been entrusted to Lawrence took him to villages in the Kashmir Valley and after the hard work of seven years; he had known almost everything about Kashmir and its people. His report got published as a book *The Valley of Kashmir*,[96] and was first published in 1895. Thereafter, many reprints were produced, the latest one having been produced by a local publisher in Srinagar in 2011.

Lawrence wrote about every aspect of the life that Kashmiris lived and his book is a great treasure of information for the general readers, especially for researchers for all times to come.

In *The Life of Napoleon Buonaparte*,[97] William Hazlitt gives a fair idea of Kashmir before the settlement commenced. 'The peasants were overworked, half-starved, treated with harsh words and hard blows, subjected to unceasing exactions and every species of petty tyranny, while in the cities a number of unwholesome and useless professions, and a crowd of lazy menials, pampered the vices or administered to the pride and luxury of the great.'

Once he had started his work, he got into a kind of romance of working with Kashmiris directly. What helped him most in the field was his deep study of the history of Kashmir and his effort to learn the Kashmiri language to understand the populace perfectly.

Lawrence had encountered two major difficulties initially—one was the lavish treatment extended to him by the maharaja's government as that was customary for all the rajas in the region who had developed a culture of treating the English, the French and other foreigners with utmost courtesy. But, Lawrence saw to it that this treatment from the maharaja didn't get him swayed into any kind of compromise on the requirements of his job. The second difficulty was that some of the government servants who were in the field with him were not prepared to work sincerely. As per G.N. Aatish,[98] a well-known writer, Lawrence faced these difficulties with utmost patience. He went close to the people and talked to them in their own language and didn't accept any intermediaries beyond what was required.

M.Y. Teng, a very prominent historian of Kashmir rightly says in his article 'Lawrence of Kashmir: Kal Bhi Aur Aaj Bhi',[99] 'Lawrence rejected the infamous Treaty of Amritsar with contempt and in practical terms transferred the ownership of land from the maharaja and mutated all lands into the hereditary ownership of the peasants. This was the first step in history to restore the dignity of a devastated people through a worst kind of subjugation for centuries. Kashmiris called Lawrence "Laran Saheb" with utmost affection.'

Teng goes on to say, 'By the time Lawrence had finished his job to his utmost satisfaction, he had become the greatest friend of Kashmiris in history and he became an important part of Kashmiri lore.'

In another article on Lawrence and his understanding on Kashmir, published in *Sheeraza*, Vol. 43,[100] Teng says, 'Lawrence did a meticulous planning on seeking consultation and help directly from the sources that he found to be relevant to his task. He invited a competent historian

Hassan Khohihami and many others to help him to understand the entire situation.'

When Lawrence established a meaningful contact with the people directly, he was thrilled to find that Kashmiris had knowledge of their history and they knew their earlier relations with China and other neighbourning countries and they had a deep understanding of ancient rulers like Lalitaditiya, whom they held in high esteem. He was further surprised that Kashmiris talked of Kalhana as a matter of pride.

Since Lawrence had established a direct relationship with the peasantry and the revenue records were presented to him, apart from government functionaries, directly by the peasants and since he had learnt the language, he could manage his job through direct commands. Lawrence is the only person among the foreigners who lived in the villages with the Kashmiris and got into a situation of knowing their day-to-day activities, their good habits, their good qualities, their weaknesses and he felt satisfied that he had known things that needed to be learnt.

It was, therefore, possible for Lawrence to repudiate all the foreign travellers who had criticized Kashmiris for certain traits in their character as they had only wanted to know their virtues.

To critics making sweeping remarks, Lawrence gave the following retort in his book, *The Valley of Kashmir*, 'It is not reasonable to look for virtues among an oppressed people, nor is it fair to descant on their vices. When one has been for some years living in the village and seeing the Kashmiris as they are, one cannot help feeling pity for their lot and being a little blind to their faults.'

Lawrence finally elaborates his assessment of the character of Kashmiris whom he had known better than anybody else and he wrote, 'I have tried to make the best and not the worst of them and it is possible that in the remarks on the character and disposition of the Kashmiri cultivators, I may not be expressing the views usually held on the subject. I can only urge that my work has given me opportunities, which no Europeans have previously enjoyed, of becoming acquainted with the people of the villages.'

Lawrence, therefore, saw many virtues in Kashmiris such as their simplicity, their good neighbourly relations, their spirit of togetherness and above everything else, their courtesy to strangers, whom they offered food and other comforts, irrespective of caste, colour and creed.

Teng rightly characterizes Lawrence's book as the most authentic encyclopaedia on Kashmir and the life of its people. He is also right when he says that nobody before had ever put in such a sustained and meticulous effort to understand Kashmiris.

This author agrees with Teng's observation that ultimately, Lawrence established his position as one of the greatest benefactors of Kashmiris.

This author knows the fact himself that Kashmiris remember Lawrence even to this day and they affectionately called him 'Laran Saheb' and it is an established fact with them (Kashmiris) that he was the man who tried to understand the agony of Kashmiris in the periods of their long subjugation.

While studying the history of Kashmir, Khushwant Singh[101] came to realize the great contribution of Lawrence towards assessing character of Kashmiris and Singh felt thrilled and described *The Valley of Kashmir* as a magnum opus on Kashmir.

Lawrence vehemently refutes writers such as Moorcroft, Fredric Drew and Hugel who criticized Kashmiris for fraudulent and deceitful practices in trade and their habit of telling lies. He reminded them that the vices in Kashmiris were not innate but were due to the government under which they lived.

He says, 'The natives of Kashmir have always been considered as amongst the most lively and ingenious people of Asia, and deservedly so. With a liberal and wise government they might assume an equally high scale as a moral and intellectual people, but at present a more degraded race does not exist. The vices of the Kashmiris I cannot help considering, however, as the effects of his political condition rather than his nature, and conceive that it would not be difficult to transform him into a very different being.'

23
MAJOR T.R. SWINBURNE'S HOLIDAY

Major T.R. Swinburne visited Kashmir via Baramulla, having started the journey from Lahore via Rawalpindi in 1905. His book, *Kashmir: A Holiday in the Happy Valley*, gives a day-to-day account of his engagements in Kashmir. The book, written in first-person narrative, gives even minuscule details of the journey in an easy-to-understand style. After a tiring journey on a tonga, Swinburne settled in Nedou's Hotel in Srinagar, which he didn't find more comfortable than he had found the dak bungalow in Uri.

Unfortunately, Srinagar was facing floods and there was a chance that his holiday would finish in that kind of climate but after sometime, the weather improved and he started moving around the Valley.

He had been told in England that Srinagar was called 'Venice of the East' but he refuted that description saying, 'In as much as waterways from the main thoroughfares in both, there is a certain resemblance.'

He says further, 'Shikaras are first cousins to gandolas, rather poor relations perhaps; both are dingy and clumsy in appearance and both are managed with an extraordinary dexterity by their navigators. Both cities are smelly, though Venice, even at its worst, stand many degrees above the incredible filth of Srinagar.'

Then Swinburne, further elaborates, 'The charm of Venice lies in its architecture, its art treasures, its historical memories and its interesting people. Srinagar has no architecture in particular, being but a picturesque chaos of tumble-down wooden shanties.'

Swinburne seems to have gotten fed up while he was invited to shops. So he writes, 'Shopping in Srinagar is not pure and unadulterated joy. Down the river, spanned by its seven bridges, amidst a network of foul-smelling alleys, you are dragged to the emporiums of the native merchants whose advertisements flare upon the river banks and who, armed with the cards and possessed of a wonderful supply of the English language, swarm around the victim at every landing place and almost tear one another in pieces while striving to obtain your custom.'

He gives a graphic detail of the Kashmiri art and says, 'Certainly the Kashmiris are exceedingly clever and excellent workers in many ways. Their modern embroideries (the old shawl manufacture is totally extinct) are beautiful and artistic. Their wood-carving, almost always executed in rich brown walnut, is excellent; and their old papier-machie lacquer is very good.'

Swinburne goes further to describe the character of artisans in Srinagar saying, 'The tendency, however, is unfortunately to abandon their own admirable designs and assimilate or copy western ideas as conveyed in very doubtful taste to English visitors.'

He says further, 'Their colours almost invariably obtained from native dyes, are excellent and they rarely make a mistake in taste. The workers of silver, copper and brass are many, but their productions are usually rough and inartistic. Genuine old beaten metal-work is almost unobtainable.'

Swinburne was left with a bad taste in his mouth while he found that one had to go through the process of haggling when purchasing anything from the market. In his own words, 'Bargaining is an invariable necessity in shopping in Kashmir, as everywhere else in the East, where the market value of an article is not what it costs to produce, but what can be squeezed for it out of the purse of the, usually ignorant purchaser.'

Swinburne adds, 'Three things are essential to the successful prosecution of shopping in Srinagar: 1. Unlimited time. 2. A command of emphatic language, sufficient to impress the native mind with the need for keeping to the point. 3. A liver in such a thorough working order as to insure an extraordinary supply of good temper.'

Swinburne documented that the rishis of Kashmir didn't marry and were considered by one and all as pious. He had cared to read Abul Fazl's[102] remarks about rishis and then said that during Akbar's time, rishis were considered to be the respected people and he (Abl-Fazl) had said that there were 2,000 of them in Kashmir during Akbar's time.

However, Swinburne's praise of the snow-covered mountains, flowers and the greenery of Kashmir, the beauty of lakes of Kashmir and its valleys is superb, but his minute study of traits in the character of the Kashmiris is also unique.

But, then, there are other areas that earned his praise. He visited numerous places in Kashmir and maintained his diary and recorded his impressions almost on a daily basis. He describes Lolab Valley as: 'The sloping snow melting into little rills which trickled through the fresh-springing flowers-strewn grass; the extraordinary blue of the hillsides overlooking the Lolab valley seen through the sloping boughs of the pines; the crows hopping audaciously around or croaking on a dried branch just above our heads; and above all, the glorious sense of freedom, of aloofness from all disturbing elements of utter and irresponsible independence, in a lovely land (Lolab) unspoiled by hand of man?'

Describing the beauty of Pahalgam, Swinburne notes, 'The road towards Pahalgam is a charming woodland walk, where wild strawberries, still hardly out of flower, grow thick amidst a tangle of chestnut, yew, wild cherry and flowering shrubs. Overhead and to the right of rocky steeps rise abruptly until they culminate in the crags of Kohinar, and on the left, the snow-fed Lidar roars through the cloven ravine in cataract after cataract.'

Swinburne enjoyed the beauty of Gulmarg and called it a meadow of flowers and one thing that attracted his attention, among many things while walking through the valleys in Gulmarg, was that he could see clearly the lofty peak of Nanga-Parbat.

He also said, 'Gulmarg is the most frequented resort in summer of the English colony and contingent from the broiling plains of the Punjab. Here the happy fugitive from the sweltering heat of the lower regions will find a climate as glorious as the scenery.'

He describes further, 'He (visitor) can enjoy the best of polo and golf, and if he be not a misogynist, he will vary the daily round with picnics and scrambles on foot or on horseback, in exploring the endless beauty of the place, coming home to his hut or tent as the sun sinks behind the great pines that screen the Rampur Road, to wind up the happy day with a cheery dinner and game of bridge.'

He goes on to describe the beauty of Gulmarg, 'But, if Gulmarg does not appeal to him, let him go with his camping outfit to Sonamarg or Pahlgam—he will find neither polo nor golf nor the gay little society of Gulmarg, but he will find equally charming scenery and, perhaps, a drier climate—for it must in fairness be admitted that Gulmarg is a rainy place.'

Swinburne seems to have enjoyed Gulmarg best of all places and he goes on to count the advantages of visiting and staying at Gulmarg. He says, 'Likewise his (the visitor's) pocket will benefit, as his expenses will surely be less, and he will still find neighbours dotted about in white tents under the pine trees.'

Swinburne seems to have been deeply impressed by the beauty of Gangabal and Wullar lakes. Of Wullar, he says, 'The Wullar lay like a burnished mirror reflecting the buttresses of Haramok on our right, and the snowy ranges by the Tragbal ahead, its silvery surface lined here and there with the wavering tracks of other boats, or broken by bristling clumps of reeds and tall water plants. Our transit was perfectly peaceful, and by lunch time, we were safely tied up to a bank, purple with irises, just below Bandipur.'

24

PEARCE GERVIS: THIS IS KASHMIR

Pearce Gervis, an Englishman, visited Kashmir in 1948 and stayed here for nearly four years. He seemed to have realized he had seen Kashmir dispassionately and was confident his conclusions were borne out of his deep study of facts and by meeting a wide variety of people.

Finally, he focused on the people of Kashmir. He strongly contested those who had described Kashmiris in bad light. He thought it was due to the fact that such visitors had only a superficial understanding of the character of Kashmiris.

Gervis took the position as to why Kashmiris had imbibed certain shortcomings in their character. He analyzed the reasons as follows.

First of all, he described in detail the calamities that had been occurring in Kashmir since time immemorial. In this connection, he mentioned the devastating earthquakes. As per his knowledge, the first earthquake had occurred during Sudar Sena rule that had lasted from 2082-2041 BC. The middle of the river formed a rift and water gushed from the river. The whole city had submerged. Another earthquake occurred in AD 1552 which lasted for two months. Another occurred in 1662 followed by another in 1735 which had lasted for three months and destroyed 1,000 houses. Another earthquake occurred in 1778. An earthquake took place in 1803 in which the spire of the Shah Hamdan Mosque was destroyed. The most terrible earthquake took place on 30

May 1884 whose epicentre was at Laridur (Arthur Neve, however, gives the date of this earthquake as 1885) where most of its population along with the houses were destroyed. The total number of people who died in the Valley was 3,390. Thousands of cattle had died.

The earthquakes were followed by floods. A flood occurred in 1379 in which 10,000 houses were destroyed. Another flood came in 1746 and the same number of houses again got destroyed and all the bridges on the Jhelum were carried away. Another devastating flood occurred in 1787 when the gateway at Dalgate and whole of the eastern part of Srinagar was submerged.

After the floods, Gervis mentions the famines that continued to occur for a long time. One such famine was in 150–114 BC when the snow fell in the month of August, destroying all the rice crops. Then Gervis comes straight to a recent famine in Kashmir's history that occurred in 1832 when Ranjit Singh came to Kashmir from Lahore and ordered his governor to collect sufficient supplies for his camp. He did collect and left very little for the peasants. Then, a very bad famine occurred in 1864 followed by another in 1877 which was ghastly. It is said that two-thirds of the population died of starvation. The famine went on for two-and-a-half years.

One of the natural calamities has been the dreadful epidemic of cholera in 1604. There was a plague in 1089. The period of cholera lasted for forty days. A severe cholera occurred in 1910, when thousands of people died. Another occurred in 1892.

Gervis reminds people that alongside the calamities, there were ever present conquerors, oppressors and masters who had held authority on the land without serving them. So, the people always starved at the hands of the rulers. So, Gervis justifies Kashmiris telling lies because they had historically been deprived of the food which they had produced in plenty. The trait of hiding and telling lies remains with the tormented and subjugated people. No wonder, therefore, that the people had fallen into a trap of most shocking degradation with a fear which had become nothing short of cowardice.

Says Gervis, 'It is a terrible state for the people of any nation to have fallen into, but, there is not the slightest doubt that they have been forced down to it through generations until their morale has almost, but not quite, disappeared, for they had not even been taught how to defend themselves; they did not know how to fight and protect their loved ones, they had not learned how to kill even when driven to it by temper, as is proved by the very few murders which take place in the Valley.'

Gervis seemed to have developed a very intense interest in understanding the miseries of Kashmiris and he derived support to his analysis from Moorcroft.

Moorcroft, who made his travels through Kashmir between 1819 and 1825 said, 'The people were suffering from the most loathsome diseases brought about by scant and unwholesome food, dark, damp, and ill-ventilated lodgings, excessive dirtiness and gross immorality. Kashmiris were selfish, superstitious and false and his transactions are always conducted in a fraudulent spirit, equalled only by the effrontery with which he faces detection. These must be effects of his political condition rather than his nature and would not be difficult to transform him into a very different being.'

Also referring to their ingenuity, he says, 'With a wise government they might assume an equally high scale as a moral and intellectual people'.

Gervis quotes G.T. Vigne, Frederic Drew, Wilson, Lawrence, Ernest Neve and others only to explain that Kashmiris have both good and bad qualities in their character. But, finally, he concludes, 'Though the character of the Kashmiris leaves much to be desired, I think that it is to their credit that it is not worse, considering the few chances they have had for becoming truthful, manly and self-respecting. A man, who can be beaten and robbed by anyone with a vestige of authority, soon ceases to respect himself.'

Gervis likes Lawrence bluntly declares, 'The Kashmiri is what his rulers have made him, but I believe and hope those two generations of a just and strong rule will transform him into a useful, intelligent, and fairly honest man.'

And, finally, being extremely sympathetic to Kashmiris, Gervis says, 'He (Kashmiri) still has to learn that after all these years, he can tell the truth and start life anew without fear of the past creeping up behind and strangling him.'

Gervis in his sympathy for Kashmiris gives the following advice, 'He still has to learn to forget all the dark and terrible years in which he suffered nothing but degradation, fear and shame, little of which was of his own making, and regaining his self-respect, look to the future which, if only he will make the supreme effort, holds so very much for him!'

25

THE AFGHAN RULE IN KASHMIR
1752–1819

Most historians describe the Afghan and Sikh rules as a bleak period in Kashmir's history. G.M.D. Sufi wrote in detail about their rule in his phenomenal book *Kashir: Being a History of Kashmir.*[103] Unlike the Mughals, the Afghans organized their invasion of Kashmir from Herat, Qandahar and Kabul. Ahmad Shah Durrani conquered Kashmir in 1752. He was Mohammad Zaman Khan's son and belonged to the Sadozai clan, a branch of the Abdali tribe living in Herat. The Sadozai clan's chief obtained some concessions from Shah Abbas of Iran in the sixteenth century. Khan migrated to Multan, where Ahmad was born.

The exact date of Ahmad's birth is not known. The *Encyclopedia of Islam* gives it as 1722, while the *Encyclopedia Britannica* says 1724. The Sadozais were Shias, but later became strict Sunnis. Before the advent of Nadir Shah, there was trouble in Iran, and around this time, Khan and his sons Zulfikar and Ahmad returned to Herat from Multan.

Later, the Afghans revolted against Nadir Shah, but lost the battle. As punishment, he pushed the Ghilzais inhabiting Kandahar to Herat and forced the Sadozais to move from Herat to Kandahar. During this transfer of tribes, Zulfikar and Ahmad were taken prisoners, presumably as they had protested. The elder brother was asked to command a large clan in 1737 and was made the governor of Herat, where he lost his life in a fight with the Ghilzais. Ahmad was enlisted in the personal staff of Nadir Shah because of his bright features, keen intelligence and conspicuous gallantry.

Nadir Shah was murdered near Mashhad in eastern Iran on the night of 19 June 1747.

In the confusion that ensued, Ahmad seized a major part of Nadir Shah's territory and obtained the famous diamond, Kohi-Noor—the 'mountain of light'. Then, he hastened to Kandahar. The Afghan chiefs elected him their leader and called him Ahmad Shah. Ahmad Shah was crowned at a Kandahar mosque with the pouring of wheat on his head, a symbol of prosperity. He laid the foundation for the Afghan kingdom.

Ahmad Shah became Ahmad Shah Durrani due to his Pir, Mohammad Shakir Shah, who called him Duri Dawrain or 'pearl of the age'. Later, he became Durri-Durrain or 'pearl of pearls'. Ahmad Shah claimed the provinces that Nadir Shah had wrested from Emperor Mohammad Shah as part of the Durrani kingdom, which included Kandahar, Ghazni, Kabul, Hazara, Peshawar, Multan and Sindh. He invaded India ten times. During his fifth invasion, he defeated the Marathas in the Third Battle of Panipat in 1761, while Kashmir was annexed in 1752. Ahmad Shah died on 7 October 1772. He was highly revered by the Afghans, who treated him as a saint.

It was Kashmir's misfortune to have fallen to the Afghans. The Mughal rule was weakening and some notable Kashmiris such as Mir Muquim Kanth and Khawaja Zahir Dedamari wrote to Ahmad Shah to invade the region. Ahmad Shah sent his commander Abdullah Khan Aishak Aqasi, who arrested Abul Qasim, a noble, and established the Afghan rule in Kashmir in 1752.

Kanth and other prominent Kashmiris thought that the Afghans were like the Mughals, but soon Aqasi revived the persecution of Zulchoo.[104]

Aqasi showed enough of his cruelty during his rule. He plundered Kashmir for more than five months and left for Kabul with a crore of rupees and many valuables. He appointed Abdullah Khan Kabuli as the governor and Sukhjivan Mal as the sahib kar (executive officer).

In his book *Kashmir: Its Aborigines and Their Exodus*,[105] Colonel Tej K.

Tiku says something important about Aqasi's rule: 'Though Aqasi himself ruled only for five months, he left behind a trail of terror and destruction. He handed over the charge of Kashmir to Abdullah Khan Kabuli, with Sukhjivan Mal, a Hindu Khatri adventurer, as his chief adviser.'

It is a very interesting story as to how Sukhjivan Mal came to rule Kashmir later for a long time.

In *A History of Kashmiri Pandits*,[106] Jia Lal Kilam describes the rise of Sukhjivan Mal, saying, 'Sukhjivan, a native of Gujrat, was serving in the army of Ahmad Shah Abdali when he was deputed to serve under Aqasi in his Kashmir campaign. Aqasi appointed him as sahib kar to Abdullah Khan Kabuli.'

Kabuli tried to rule justly, but Mal did not support him. After five months, Mal got him killed along with his son. He appointed Abul Hassan Bande as prime minister and brought the situation under control. Ahmad Shah heard the story but due to expediency, he accepted Mal and appointed Khawaja Kichak as deputy subedar to establish his authority. Mal remained silent for some time. Then, he revolted by refusing to pay tribute to Ahmad Shah. Mal confronted him in connivance with Abul Hassan Bande.

In his book *Kashir: Being a History of Kashmir*, Sufi describes an important aspect of Mal's defiance of Kabul. He says, 'Sukhjivan was the first to assert his independence with the aid of Abul Hassan Bande, a Kashmiri noble. The reason, it is said, was a heavy financial demand by Ahmad Shah Durrani for his campaigns, which Sukhjivan felt could not be met with.'

Sufi gives further details on why Mal revolted against Kabul, saying that as Abdullah Khan Aqasi had already drained off from the Valley as large a sum as one crore of rupees, Sukhjivan refused to pay money to Ahmad Shah Durrani. Some notables such as Khawaja Kijak, Malik Hassan Khan Irani, Azam Khan and Mirza Khan opposed him, but were defeated at Baramulla by Mal, who established touch with Alamgir II at Delhi.

Now, Mal ordered to include the king of Delhi in the sermons. He ultimately suffered, as he had a rival in Raja Ranjit Dev of Jammu who was induced by Ahmad Shah to come to Lahore and guide an expedition to recover Kashmir. This mission failed, but the second expedition organized in October 1762 was a success. The Durrani army entered Kashmir through Tosamaidan. Mal organized 50,000 troops, but was deserted by his general, Bakht Mal, and was easily defeated. Thus, his eight-and-a-half-year rule ended. He was blinded and brought to Lahore, where Ahmad Shah got him trampled to death.

Nooruddin Khan Bamzai, who was appointed governor, tried to improve the situation. Buland Khan was appointed as his successor, who remitted unjust taxes and treated Muslims and Hindus alike. Around this time, Kailash Dar got Mir Muquim Kanth killed.

Meanwhile, Nooruddin left for Kabul and put his nephew Jan Mohammad Khan in his place. Lal Khan Khatak displaced Jan Mohammad Khan and indulged in oppression. Then, Khuram Khan was sent as governor to Kashmir in Nooruddin's place, but his entry was resisted by Lal Khan Khatak.

Nooruddin was appointed governor for the third time in 1769. He ruled for two years and was replaced by Khuram Khan. He did not rule properly and Amir Mohammad Khan Qazilbash, his commander-in-chief, displaced him with the help of some boatmen. Amir Mohammad Khan built the fort of Shergari, the bridge of Amira Kadal and a small island in Dal Lake called Sona-Lank. However, he pulled down Akbar's memorials such as Darshani Bagh and the Jarokhahi-Shahi at Dal.

The death of Ahmad Shah Durrani on 13 April 1772 emboldened Amir Mohammad Khan to declare independence and he ruled for six years. As Sufi says, 'He was cruel to both Muslims and Hindus and avenged the death of Mir Muqim Kanth by killing Pandit Kailash Dar. Pandit Dar happened to be a notable at that time.'

Ultimately, Ahmad Shah's son Timur Shah appointed Karimdad Khan Bamzai as the governor of Kashmir. He defeated Amir Mohammad Khan and sent him in chains to Kabul, where he remained in prison and was finally pardoned by Timur Shah.

Karimdad also defeated Raja Ranjit Dev of Jammu. He was a heartless ruler, killing Hindus and Muslims on the smallest provocation. He avenged the death of Khawaja Kamaluddin Naqsbandi, who was killed during Amir Mohammad Khan's rule, who was a Shia. Karimdad treated

Shias very strictly. He died in 1783. His son Azad Khan succeeded him.

English traveller George Forster visited Kashmir during Azad Khan's rule and gave vivid accounts of his atrocities.

Forster writes in his book *A Journey from Bengal to England,*[107] 'Though Kashmiris exclaim with bitterness at the administration of Hadji Kareemdad, who was notorious for his wanton cruelties and insatiable avarice, often for trivial offences, throwing the inhabitants, tied by the back, in pairs into the river, plundering their property and forcing their women of every description, yet they say he was a systematical tyrant and attained his purposes, however atrocious, through a fixed medium. They describe the son, Azad Khan, as Zalim Khan (most cruel Khan). At 18, he had few vices of youth. He was not addicted to the pleasures of the Haram, not to the hookah. But, his acts of ferocity exceed common belief. The ferocity seems to have originated in the wildest caprice and to display a temper rarely seen in the nature of man.'

Forester describes Azad Khan's atrocities further and writes, 'While he was passing with his court under one of the city's wooden bridges, on which a crowd had assembled to observe the procession, he levelled his masquet at an opening which he saw in the pathway, and being an expert marksman, shot to death an unfortunate spectator soon after his accession to the government.'

Forster describes the pathetic atrocities of Azad Khan being a tyrant and cruel person, saying, 'He (Azad Khan) accused his mother of infidelity and in defiance of the glaring absurdity which appeared in the allegation as well as the entreaties of the woman who had borne him to save her from shame; she was ignominiously driven from the palace. He even killed one of his wives.'

Forester goes on further to say, 'A film on one of his eyes had baffled many operators and being impatient at the want of success, he told the last surgeon called in, if the disorder was not remedied within a limited time, his belly should be cut open. The man failed in the cure and Azad Khan verified his threat.'

Forster mentions, 'Azad Khan, in first three months of his governance, became an object of terror and a casual mention of his name produced involuntary supplication of the aid of their Prophet.'

Interestingly, with all sympathy for Kashmiris, Forster, however, found their character disgusting. 'I never knew a body of men more impregnated with vice than natives of Kashmir. When invested with official power, supported by an authority which prescribes no limits to its agents, in the accumulation of public emoluments, the Kashmiri displays genuine composition of his mind.'

Forster describes the traits in Kashmiri character further, 'He (Kashmiri) becomes intent on immediate aggrandizement, rapacious and arrogant, he evinces in all his actions, deceit, treachery and species of refined cruelty which usually actuates the conduct of a coward. A shopkeeper rarely acknowledges possession of a commodity, until he is apprised of the quantity required.'

Even though his criticism of Kashmiris seems convincing, he ignored that a long period of slavery and abject subjugation and tyranny, particularly under the Afghans, had snatched away their zest for life.

Lawrence's description of their traits is more realistic as he gave allowance for some weakness in their character due to a long period of subjugation, neglect and deprivation.

Moorcroft also felt Kashmiris were selfish, superstitious, dishonest and false. Drew said they were false-tongued, ready with a lie and given to various forms of deceit. Hugel has nothing good to say about Kashmiris. But, Moorcroft admits that the vices of Kashmiris are not innate but due to the government under which they lived. He added that the natives were considered among the most lively and ingenious people of Asia.

The Afghan rule was undoubtedly a disaster for Kashmir. They were capricious and plundered as much wealth as they could. Kashmiris remained terrorized. Twenty-six governors were sent by Kabul to Kashmir in turns and were exceptionally cruel and remorseless rulers.

As James Ferguson says, 'While Azad[108] was described as the cruelest of Afghan governors, Atta Mohammad Khan was comparatively better.'

The miseries suffered by Kashmiris under the Afghan rule have aptly been described in a Persian couplet quoted by Sufi:

Purseedam Az Kharabiye
Gulshah Ze Bagban;

Afghan Kasheed, Gulft Ze
Afghan Kharab Kard!

(I asked from the gardener as to why the garden was desolate; he raised a lament and said—the Afghans had destroyed it.)

Ferguson mentioned that unable to secure relief from such tyranny by their own efforts, Kashmiris appealed to the Punjab ruler Ranjit Singh to come to their help. An expedition was organized by the Sikhs. Diwan Chand, the most competent Punjab general, was in command of the Sikh force that expelled the Afghans in 1819 and brought Kashmir under the Sikh rule.

During the Afghan rule, a prominent Kashmiri Muslim, Abdul Qadoos Gojwari, made the supreme sacrifice of laying down his life for the sake of his Kashmir Pandit friend. When Birbal Dhar earned the wrath of the last Afghan governor, Azim Khan, and left Kashmir to personally appeal to Ranjit Singh to conquer Kashmir, he left his wife and daughter-in-law under the care of Gojwari. Birbal Dhar's son-in-law informed Azim Khan about this, who got Gojwari killed along with his family. Birbal Dhar's wife committed suicide and his daughter-in-law was abducted.

When the Sikhs came to power, Birbal Dhar got a prominent position as a revenue collector.

26
THE SIKH RULE IN KASHMIR
1819-46

The establishment of Sikh rule in Kashmir has a very interesting background. The tyrannical rule of the Afghans had mauled Kashmiris to such an extent that they decided to invite the Sikhs to rule over Kashmir.

In his book *Kashmir Under the Sikhs*,[109] Dewan Chand Sharma mentions, 'Early years of the nineteenth century saw power of Afghans on the decline. The Sikhs were encroaching on their Cis-Indus[110] territories. Earlier attempts of Sikhs in 1812 and 1814 failed. But, then an opportunity arrived, when Pandit Birbal Dhar (a Kashmiri nobleman) escaped to Lahore and urged Ranjit Singh to drive away Afghans from Kashmir. The Sikh forces led by Devan Chand and guided by Dhar, successfully invaded the Valley in 1819. The conquest of Kashmir was a significant addition to the Sikh kingdom.'

Since the stories of Afghan extortion in Kashmir had spread all around, the Sikhs decided to continue this onslaught to the best of their advantage. Kashmir soon became the richest province in terms of revenue receipts of the Sikh kingdom.

Baron Von Hugel, in his book *Kashmir under Maharaja Ranjit Singh* says, 'The conquest of Kashmir was a significant addition to the Sikh kingdom as Kashmir was the richest province of the Sikh kingdom next only to Multan.'

Ranjit Singh deputed nine governors to Kashmir within a short span of twenty-seven years and many of them held office only for a short duration. Moti Ram, the first Sikh governor, celebrated the change from Muslim rule by forbidding the killing of cows and put to death several people who were found guilty of this practice. Mosques such as Jamia Masjid were closed and call to the prayer was banned. In his book *Kashir: Being a History of Kashmir*,[111] Sufi gives graphic details of the suffering of Muslims during this period.

Sufi describes that it was Diwan Moti Ram who had closed down the Jamia Masjid of Srinagar for public prayers. William Moorcroft[112] saw it closed when he visited Kashmir during Moti Ram's time. Many other mosques were turned into Nazul property. Jagir grants attached to mosques and shrines were resumed. Muslims were forbidden to utter the azan .

Sufi mentions that the shrine of Shah Hamdan, the well-known Khanqahi-Mualla, was ordered to be razed to the ground. The plea advanced by Sikh commander Phula Singh was that it was the site of the Kali Shree temple twelve centuries ago. In fact, guns were levelled at the shrine from the Patthar or Shahi Mosque Ghat on the opposite bank of the Jhelum.

Sufi says further, 'But, the order was not executed in fear of a rebellion. When a deputation of Muslims headed by Sayyid Hasan Shah Qadiri Khanayari approached Birbal Dhar to dissuade the Sikhs from the destruction of the Khanqah, he used his influence and saved this historic structure from vandalism.'

As Sufi elaborates further, 'Cow slaughter, prevalent for centuries, was declared a crime punishable by death and Muslims were hanged, dragged through the city of Srinagar and even burnt alive for having slain cattle. Thus oppressed in this and various other ways, hundreds of Muslim families left Kashmir. Their descendants are found in Punjab and the united provinces.'

Then, Kirpa Ram who had followed Hari Singh was sent as governor. He happened to be the most interesting among Sikh governors. As Ferguson describes, 'His pleasure-loving reign was like Jehangir. He was devoted to lavish enjoyment the Valley offered, and was referred to as "Kirpa Shroin" sound of the boat paddle. Wherever he (Kirpa) went, he was accompanied by dancing girls and even rowers of his official barge were women.'

Later, Kripa Ram was removed and Moti Ram was appointed for the second time as governor, but soon he was sacked. Then Sher Singh was appointed as governor. He was not successful and was followed by Mihan Singh. As per Sufi, it is during his rule that Hugel, Vigne and Henderson visited the Valley. Vigne and Hugel mention his love of wine, and many a time he was so drunk that they found it difficult to meet him.

G.T. Vigne, who was in Kashmir in 1835 writes, 'The entire suppression was one of a few measures that Sher Singh, the present Maharaja of the Punjab, could claim any credit for during his tyrannical viceroyalty in Kashmir.'

Baron Schonberg, who visited Kashmir during the later part of the Sikh rule, says 'I have been in many lands, but nowhere did the condition of people present a more saddening spectacle than in Kashmir.'

J.P. Ferguson in his book *Kashmir* describes the miserable conditions of Kashmiris under the Sikh rule. He says, 'Sikhs were conquerors who owed their power to their military capacity and were interested only in reaping the advantages of their conquest. A policy of settled government or administration with the welfare of the people as the main object was something foreign to their outlook. They looked on Kashmiris with contempt and if one was killed by a Sikh, the compensation allowed to his family was four rupees if a Hindu and two rupees if a Muslim.'

Sufi also quotes French naturalist Victor Jaquemont[113] as saying, 'A few thousand stupid and brutal Sikhs with swords at their sides or pistols on their belts drove this ingenious and numerous, but timid people like a flock of sheep. Cashmere surpasses all imaginable poverty.'

However, the brutalities committed by the Sikhs are best described by William Moorcroft and his associate George Trebeck[114] in their book *Travels in Kashmir*. Moorcroft visited Kashmir from 1819 to 1825.

When Moorcroft was leaving for Bukhara, he could see the tragic suffering of the people and he says, 'The number of Kashmiris who were to accompany us over mountains proved to be no exaggeration and their appearance, half-naked and miserably emaciated, presented a ghastly picture of poverty and starvation. Relentless Sikhs levied a picca a head for permission to pass the post, had we not interfered.'

Moorcroft wrote, 'They look upon Kashmiris a little better than cattle. The murder of a native by a Sikh is punished by a fine from sixteen to twenty rupees, of which four rupees are paid to the family of the deceased, if a Hindu and two rupees if he was a Musalman.'

Describing his journey to Bukhara, Moorcroft says further about the Kashmiris who were accompanying him saying, 'Some people accompanying us were seized by Sikhs as unpaid porters and were not only driven along the road by a cord tying them together by the arm, but their legs were bound with ropes at night to prevent their escape. Thus, the Sikh rule in Kashmir was one of the darkest episodes.'

R.K. Parmu, an eminent scholar who made an in-depth study of the Sikh rule and produced a comprehensive book titled *A History of Sikh Rule in Kashmir*, has given details of various kinds of atrocities that the Sikh governors committed against the general run of Kashmiris, particularly the Muslims, who formed an overwhelming majority of the population. Unfortunately the nature also inflicted miseries through many spells of famine.

Parmu wrote, 'The Kashmiri masses suffered all the stresses and strains of political subjugation. They were left high and dry during the most gruelling famines which the malevolent nature caused from time to time, additionally.'

Parmu doesn't, however, forget to explain to his readers that even under these trying circumstances, Kashmiris maintained the secular character of their social relations and suffered miseries of life with fortitude, which has perhaps few parallels in history. One reason why Muslims suffered more is that it is this community that provided to the system the weavers of shawls and producers of other handicrafts.

Almost all the Sikh governors exhibited their zeal for expanding their own culture in Kashmir. While the Jamia Masjid and other mosques were closed and azan was prohibited, they built numerous gurduwaras and a large number of Sikh preachers entered Kashmir. But, essentially that situation didn't disturb Kashmiris as they were, as a class, tolerant.

The only pain and misery they felt was through the cruelty that the Sikh governors inflicted upon Kashmiris, particularly Muslims. The greatest tragedy was that there was no court of appeal.

Parmu, however, remained consistent in his opinion that atrocities were committed on Kashmiris, particularly Muslims, during the Sikh rule. He says in this connection that, 'It was government, not administration, particularly during Ranjit Singh's regime that was responsible for causing atrocities on the people... His greater concern lay in receiving regularly the stipulated remittances than in affording even marginal satisfaction to the producers of this wealth.'

Parmu describes further, 'The cumulative effect of famines, starvation, deaths and extreme administrative harassments led many agriculturists, shawl-weavers, artisans, labourers and noblemen quit the country and they settled in near or distant places according to their resources, physical and material. Their plight, troubles and tribulations consequent on their exodus can be better imagined than described.'

Parmu goes on to describe the exodus and says, 'However, new Kashmiri colonies grew up in Bhadarwah, Kistawar, Jammu, Reasi, Punch, Rajouri, and Mirpur in the neighbouring hill states; in Simla, Bilaspur, Chamba, Mandi, Rampur and Nurpur in the Punjab hills and in Lahore, Armitsar, Sialkot, Hoshiarpur and Gujranwala in the undivided Punjab.'

In my opinion, it was a tragic that Ranjit Singh was unable to fulfil his desire to visit Kashmir and the communication between him and the respective governors was very weak. This seems to have aggravated the miseries suffered by Kashmiris. What buttresses my opinion is the fact that the Sikh governors were sacked, one after another, during the entire period of Sikh rule. In addition to this, the respective governors had created their own lobbies in the Lahore durbar, who would invariably report as if everything was going on well in Kashmir.

My assessment is also that the atrocities committed by the respective governors in Kashmir may not have occurred at the instance of Raja Ranjit Singh at all. This assessment receives support from Baron Von Hugel, who writes in his book *Kashmir under Maharaja Ranjit Singh*, 'The administrative record of these governors is full of failings and deeds of corruption except one Mian Singh whom the Kashmiris still remember as one of the best governors sent by the Lahore durbar.'

About the instructions from Ranjit Singh to his administrators, Parmu also quotes from *Umdat-ut-Tawarikh-III* by Lala Sohan Lal Suri (1961, p. 180): 'Whoever of my officers is appointed in Kashmir, before occupying himself with anything, he must make the people happy and earn their good wishes. For Kashmiris are worshippers of one Universal Almighty, and their prayers shall bring the Maharaja and his Kingdom prosperity and felicity.'

27

SHEIKH GHULAM MOHIUDDIN: KASHMIR'S GREAT FRIEND

Sheikh Ghulam Mohiuddin is an important character in Kashmir's history, and Kashmiris, irrespective of religious beliefs, remember him as a great friend.

Sheikh Mohiuddin was born to a cobbler in Hoshiarpur, Jalandhar (Punjab), and after some education, became a munshi with a prominent Hoshiarpur citizen and was later employed by Shiv Dayal, the son of Diwan Moti Ram.

In 1823, Azim Khan, the ruler of Kabul, organized a strong attack on the Sikhs. Ranjit Singh was not in a position to fight and thought negotiation was a better option. By then, Sheikh Mohiuddin's reputation had spread. Ranjit Singh decided to send him as a negotiator. Sheikh Mohiuddin succeeded in this task. In 1827, he became deputy administrator to Diwan Kirpa Ram and then Sher Singh, who ruled Kashmir.

In 1839, he was made administrator of Jalandhar as he had proved his dedication and sincerity to the Lahore durbar.

By then, Sher Singh realized that certain Sikh governors had gone wrong with the administration of Kashmir and Kashmiris were disgusted. Sheikh Mohiuddin's appointment could provide them some solace.

In his book *A Complete History of Kashmir: The Ancient Hindu*

Kings, The Muslim Kings, The Khalsa Kings,[115] Mohammad-ud-Din Fouq mentions that Sheikh Mohiuddin took over the reins of Kashmir's administration in 1841 and ruled for two years and seven months.

Sheikh Mohiuddin was extremely loyal to the Lahore durbar, but handed justice to the people of Kashmir. He respected the religious sentiments of Kashmiris and this attitude won him their respect and affection.

He paid obeisance to Sheikh Ghulam Ahmad Tarabali, who enjoyed considerable clout among Kashmiri Muslims as a learned and saintly person.

On his request, Sheikh Mohiuddin reopened the Shahi Masjid (Jama Masjid), which had been closed under the Sikh rule for more than twenty years. This was a powerful gesture of reconciliation with Kashmiri Muslims.

He also ordered the cleaning and repair of Lachme canal, which irrigated the lawns of the mosque and repaired the Chashma Shahi in 1842. He set up an international trade market on both banks of the famous canal, Nala Mar. Sheikh Mohiuddin had a passion to serve people and soon realized that what went wrong should be corrected.

The price of paddy had been unjustly fixed at one-and-a-half khirwar (two-and-a-half maunds) per rupee. He raised the price and satisfied farmers. He made Hindus and Muslims till lands that were left fallow. This led to an increase in paddy production.

Sheikh Mohiuddin was an able and enlightened governor and the people of the Valley could have maintained the progress. However, instability at the Lahore court with increasing British interference and intrigue at the frontiers thwarted his efforts. The rising power of Gulab Singh in Jammu, however, dominated his actions till his death in 1846.

It was unfortunate that after Ranjit Singh's death in 1839, the Lahore durbar began the intrigue that weakened the administration, badly affecting Kashmir again.

Around this time, rajas such as Zabardast Khan took advantage of the weak Lahore administration and rebelled against Sheikh Mohiuddin.

The conspiracy hatched by the British and Gulab Singh culminated in the signing of the Treaty of Amritsar on 16 March 1846. This further weakened Sheikh Mohiuddin's grip on the administration. By then, he had grown old and fallen ill.

His death is indicated by Mohammad Din Fauq as 1262 Hijri, which corresponds to 1845–46. Shodhganga[116] (a portal hosted by the UGC) reported how Ghulam Mohiuddin's last days were a period of stress and strain. He was confined to bed and died suddenly on 24 March 1846, shocked by the news of the Treaty of Amritsar, declaring Gulab Singh as the ruler of Kashmir. Out of his large family consisting of two sons, brothers and many cousins and nephews, only his eldest son, Sheikh Imam-ud-Din, was by his deathbed. Considering the multitudes of people who had gathered to pay their homage, his funeral service was performed at the extensive Idgah ground. But he was burried in the Dargah of Sheikh Hamza Makhdoom, on the south-western slope of Hari Parbat hillock, as a mark of gratitude to the man who gave much to Muslims since 1841.

The information in the UGC-hosted portal is based on *Wajiz-ut-Tawareekh* by Nabh Shah, Jammu & Kashmir Government Research Department, Srinagar, and *Tawareekh-e-Kashmir* by Khalil Mirjanpuri, Jammu & Kashmir Government Research Department, Srinagar.

Mohammad-ud-Din Fauq in his book writes that a plaque was placed at his grave with the following couplet:

Sheikh Afzal Ghulam Mohiuddin
Was matchless in generosity;
He bade goodbye to the world
And went to other world
The divine revelation said the date is
'The holy Prophet was kind to him

There is much confusion about the period of his reign and chronology of dates. If he took over in 1841 and ruled for two years and seven months, then logically his rule had to end in 1843. But he is said to have ruled till his last breath on 24 March 1846.

This confusion is removed, to some extent, by the following detail contained in *Kashmir: Distortions and Reality,*[117] which is as follows: 'The valley of Kashmir had been under Sikh rule of Lahore, consequent to signing of the Treaty of Lahore (9 March 1846) between Sikh kingdom in Lahore and Gulab Singh and the Treaty of Amritsar (16 March 1846) between Gulab Singh and the British. Gulab Singh was recognized as an independent ruler of all territories already in his possession along with the Valley of Kashmir, which till then formed a separate province. Kashmir valley was then controlled by Sheikh Imam-ud-Din as governor appointed by the Lahore durbar.

'He was secretly instructed by Prime Minister Lal Singh, who had personal enmity with Gulab Singh, not to hand over the possession of the Valley to Gulab Singh. Therefore, Gulab Singh's army faced stiff resistance when it reached Kashmir to occupy it as per terms of the Treaty of Amritsar. Lakhpat, one of the top generals of Gulab Singh, lost his life during this unexpected encounter. Thus, Gulab Singh had to resort to superior and effective force to get Kashmir despite his claim to it. On behalf of the Lahore durbar, one Nathu Shah was controlling Gilgit. He transferred his allegiance to Gulab Singh, who now became the master of Gilgit as well. By 1850, Gulab Singh turned de facto and de jure master of Jammu, including Poonch, Rajauri and Bhimber, Kashmir Valley, Ladakh, Baltistan and Dardistan including Gilgit. The states of Hunza, Nagar and Ishkuman adjoining Sinkiang were added to the state by his son, Maharaja Ranbir Singh.'

28
FIGHT AGAINST THE DOGRA ARISTOCRACY

The Kashmiris have fought for their freedom relentlessly for 360 years and their struggle culminated in August 1947.

They fought the Mughals, Afghans, Sikhs and Dogras. They did not spare the Mughals although the Mughals were comparatively mild-mannered. The Kashmiris fought against the Afghans consistently and tried to keep the outside world informed on how they (Afghans) committed atrocities and plundered their (Kashmiris') land. They fought against the Sikh rule, which had no parallel in human history as for the brutalities against Kashmiris were concerned. In the last phase of slavery, Kashmiris fought against the autocratic, undemocratic and unjust Dogra rule with valour. The difference in the style of their struggle was visible as the period of subjugation suffered by Kashmiris in different phases and under different circumstances kept changing. For example, the struggle against the Mughals was far different from that against the Afghans. The Mughals tried to be just rulers, but the Kashmiris never forgot that they had captured Kashmir by deceit and not by victory on the battlefield. The Mughals had also crushed Kashmir's martial spirit.

The Kashmiris considered the Afghans, who were great tyrants and plunderers, as sub-humans. They refused to cooperate with the administration under the Afghans.

It was tragic that the Kashmiris had themselves invited the Sikhs to rule over them. There are some historians who rated the Sikhs better than the Afghans, but an unbiased recording of events reveal that the Sikhs were rapacious and took great delight in committing atrocities against native Muslims. The Sikh approach to administration was barbaric.

The Dogras came to rule Kashmiris through the infamous Treaty of Amritsar, 1846. The Kashmiris felt humiliated as their homeland had been sold for just Rs 75 lakh by the British to Gulab Singh. This kind of treaty was decidedly unknown in the world and Kashmiris felt deeply hurt.

Captain Knight, in his book *Diary of a Pedestrian in Kashmir and Tibet*, denounced this infamous treaty: 'For seventy-five lacs of rupees, the unfortunate Kashmiris were handed over to the tender mercies of the most thorough ruffian that ever was created—a villain from a kingdom down to half penny.'

Robert Thorp, in his book *Kashmir: Misgovernment*, condemned this treaty, saying, 'Kashmir's legendary beauty messed awkwardly with the destitution, illiteracy and infirmity of the vast majority of its people. Ever since March 1846, when the British "sold" it for seventy-five lakh of rupees to the Dogra warlord Gulab Singh, predominantly Muslim Kashmir together with the principality of Jammu and the frontier districts including Buddhist Ladakh experienced unmitigated autocratic rule.'

This was never accepted by the civilized world as a treaty. Signed by the British on the one hand and Gulab Singh of Jammu on the other, it was more like a sale deed.

Mahatma Gandhi described it on 6 August 1947 as the worst form of a sale document, while Jawaharlal Nehru called it a document for slaving people against their will. Sheikh Mohammad Abdullah, who had launched a movement against the infamous document, rejected it as a sale deed against people who were not party to it. Maulana Masoodi, who appeared before the court of Indu Bhushan, described it as a deed of auction.

Sardar Budh Singh, a prominent Sikh leader and a senior leader of the National Conference, popularly known as Mahatma Budh Singh, had described the Treaty as an ignominious document.

The British earned infamy and disgrace all over the world for being party to this obnoxious conspiracy against the people who had no means to protest.

Sir Muhammad Iqbal (a Kashmiri by origin) denounced the treaty in the following verses:

O, morning breeze! If you happen to pass by Geneva!
Say a word to United Nations again,
The peasants, the land, the waters, the gardens, all sold out,
Say! They sold a nation, and how cheap they sold it out!

Kashmiri is used to be in slavery,
He carves out an idol from the stone of a grave,
His conscience doesn't carry splendid thoughts,
He doesn't recognize what ego is,
He is not known even to his own self,
It is he who weaves a silken gown for the wealthy trader,
He himself covers his body with rags;
He doesn't look forward, anymore,
He has lost the zest to change his fate
Oh, God! Bestow upon him the spirit of consciousness,
So that he breaks his chains of slavery!

The iron fist of suppression and cruelty made them
into a miserable lot,
Like a scissor, it clipped their wings.
O, God, break into pieces the tyrannical hand of the usurper,
Who trampled the spirit of freedom of Kashmiris!

A learned scholar and writer, G.N. Khayal believes that Iqbal's denunciation of the treaty deeply influenced the Sheikh, who had started an organized movement against the Dogra rule in 1931.

The relentless war that the Kashmiris fought against their subjugation by foreigners was not documented properly till Maulana Mohammad Sayeed Masoodi, the then general secretary of the Jammu & Kashmir National Conference, deposed as an accused before Indu Bhushan, sessions judge in Srinagar on 14 October 1946.

Masoodi was accused of inciting a crowd at Hazratbal on 5 July 1946 in response to a call by the party and he had elaborated before the crowd the background of why the people of Kashmir were asking the Dogra maharaja to quit Kashmir and install a responsible government. This, according to the prosecution, amounted to treason.

Masoodi along with many others, were arrested on the same day he made the speech and was produced before the magistrate on 14 October 1946.

The opening words of Masoodi's statement startled the magistrate as the accused said in his deposition that he would support the prosecution and not try to defend himself. The deposition was expressed in a lucid style as to how Kashmiris had been fighting for freedom from their subjugation for 360 years. He explained how they fought the Mughals, Afghans, Sikhs and Dogras with the same zeal and zest. The crux of the deposition was that the prosecution correctly lodged a case of treason against him and the CID reporter had played down certain portions of his speech. Masoodi admitted his speech could have provoked sentiments; it had been meant for that!

The statement explained that the genesis of the accused's crime was not in his speech of 6 October 1946, but in 1557 when Kashmiris started their darkest period of slavery and then suffered a long period of deprivation under the Mughals, which had deepened under the Afghan rule. Then, they went through the most tyrannical and brutal rule under the Sikhs when they were treated like animals. The accused explained how the subjugation under the Dogras was the continuation of suppression of their basic rights. The accused explained that their land had been sold to Gulab Singh by the British for Rs 75 lakh and it was a depressing situation for a nation that they got sold. This had crushed their spirits, leaving no trace of hope for realizing their genuine human aspirations.

He told the magistrate that he should decide the case lodged by the prosecution only after hearing from him the story of Kashmir's subjugation. Masoodi told the court he had the compulsion of relating the whole story, otherwise his speech would be misunderstood. He referred to how the Sikhs conspired and the Treaty of Amritsar was signed. Kashmiris were helpless and none knew if Rs 75 lakh was enough to barter the future of a nation!

Masoodi explained that the Mughals never allowed the Kashmiris to find a place even at the lower echelons of administration, and during floods and famines they would extend some relief that looked like distributing alms. The Afghans were devoid of any human values and they were in a great hurry to direct their greed all around. The Sikhs were rapacious and wanted to collect as much money in a short time. Masoodi explained that Kashmir had become the richest province in terms of revenue receipts of the Sikh kingdom in a short time. The Dogras looked a little better than the Sikhs. Otherwise, Kashmiris suffered indignation and humiliation at the hands of their rulers the same way as they had suffered earlier. The entire period of subjugation brought nothing but humiliation to Kashmiris.

He mentioned before the magistrate that the prosecution had not recorded the passion with which he had urged the people to revolt against the Dogras, to make them quit Kashmir and break the infamous Treaty of Amritsar.

The comprehensive statement made by Masoodi in court (both the written text with his verbal elaboration) was later published in a book and G.M. Sadiq, a member of the working committee of the National Conference, wrote an impressive foreword to it. This book is of great value to those who want to know the miseries that the Kashmiris have suffered.

After hearing Masoodi, the magistrate ordered his imprisonment for a year with a fine of Rs 200. In view of his stature, he was, however, provided a special class in the jail.

29

J&K CONSTITUENT ASSEMBLY

The accession of Jammu and Kashmir with the Union of India under the deed of accession signed by Hari Singh had been made subject to a plebiscite in the state by the Governor General of India, Lord Mountbatten, who recorded, 'Consistently with their policy that when the issue of accession had been subject of dispute, the question of accession should be decided in accordance with the wishes of the people of the state. It is my government's wish that as soon as law and order have been restored in Kashmir and its soil cleared of the raider, the question of the state's accession should be settled by a reference to the people.'

The expression 'reference to the people' certainly meant plebiscite. As Alastair Lamb said in his book *Kashmir: A Disputed Legacy*,[118] 'Jawaharlal Nehru had explored something like this line of reasoning when in his broadcast on All India Radio of 2 November 1947, he confirmed that "we have declared that the fate of Kashmir is ultimately to be decided by the people, that pledge we have given and we will not and can't back out".'

Ajit Bhattacharjea in his book *The Wounded Valley*[119] tells us an interesting story of how Mountbatten made this more difficult by proposing to Jinnah a plebiscite under the UN at a meeting in Lahore called by Pakistan on 1 November 1947. He says, 'Nehru did not go to the meeting but Mountbatten proceeded to Lahore on his own and laid the foundation of a commitment that India would regret.'

Bhattacharjea refers to H.V. Hodson, who gave details of the Lahore meeting in his book *The Great Divide: Britain-India-Pakistan.*[120] He writes, 'On 1 November 1947, Louis Mountbatten left for Pakistan to begin talks between the Governor-General of India and Governor-General of Pakistan over the issue of Kashmir. The talks lasted for three-and-a-half hours, where Mountbatten offered to Jinnah that India would hold a plebiscite in the state of Jammu and Kashmir, provided that Pakistan withdrew its military support for the Azad Kashmir forces and their allies.'

Again in this connection, Bhattacharjea says, 'The next step involving the UN came a month after Indian troops had been ordered to fly to Srinagar. Mountbatten, continuing his role as a neutral middleman, managed to get Nehru to confer with Liaquat Ali Khan.'

Bhattacharjea is of the definite opinion that by this time, differences between Nehru and Mountbatten had sharpened. He quotes Mountbatten defending his position in a letter to Nehru, which included this para: 'When I first suggested bringing UNO with the dispute, it was in order to achieve the object I have quoted above to stop the fighting and to stop it as soon as possible. Surely, the main object should be to bring UNO here at the earliest possible moment to come out and deal with the business and help to stop the fighting within a matter of days, can we do nothing to hasten this object?'

But, no amount of argument would convince Nehru on the correctness of the course of action that Mountbatten had adopted. Around this time, Mountbatten was constantly in touch with Clement Richard Attlee.

Bhattacharjea has referred to a paragraph of a cable saying that in a tone of unaccustomed mortification, Mountbatten had told Attlee, 'Any prestige that I may have previously had with my Government has of course been largely lost by my insisting that they should make a reference to the UNO with the assurance that they would get a square deal there.'

While the differences between Nehru and Mountbatten continued and both of whom were vigorously in touch with Attlee, the intervention of Attlee seems to have influenced Nehru finally to agree to make a reference of the issue to the Security Council. India's application to the Security Council was dispatched on 1 January 1948.

In fact, India could not have expected Mountbatten to respond to the Kashmir situation in the same manner in which Nehru did.

Mountbatten's mind must have been working in the same frame as the decision-makers in Britain. He had received proper briefing on the matter from the quarters that should have mattered to him.

Bhattacharjea described a briefing Mountbatten had received from his press secretary, Alan Campbell Johnson, who had returned from a visit to London where he met those connected with the subcontinent and influencing its affairs. Among them was the Commonwealth Secretary Philip Noel-Baker, who later strongly criticized India at the Security Council.

Bhattacharjea says, 'Reporting to Mountbatten, Campbell Johnson said that Noel-Baker suggested that it was through international agencies that British help and influence both in India and elsewhere might be most effectively brought to bear.'

It shows in ample measure that Mountbatten was giving advice to Nehru in the light of his understanding of the British government's perception on the entire issue.

So, there was no positive response to India urging the Security Council to take notice of the urgency involved in the matter and act accordingly. The Security Council took its time and months after, a commission landed in Kashmir and while the focus shifted to the UN organizing a plebiscite in Kashmir, the council didn't take notice of India's urgent appeal to declare Pakistan an aggressor.

In the meantime, Nehru thought there was clear evidence that the Anglo-American dispensation in respect of the Kashmir issue was having an obvious tilt towards Pakistan.

As H.V. Hodson says, 'The Government of India requested the Security Council to call upon Pakistan to put an end immediately to the giving of such assistance, which is an act of aggression against India. If Pakistan doesn't do so, the Govt. of India may be compelled, in self-defence, to enter Pakistan territory, in order to take military action against the invaders. The matter is, therefore, one of extreme urgency and calls for immediate action by the Security Council for avoiding a breach of international peace.'

Nehru was not satisfied with the outcome of India's complaint before the Security Council, and through his personal monitoring of the proceedings at the UN, he came to believe the Anglo-American bloc had neither understanding nor any sympathy with the cause for which India was fighting.

Bhattacharjea describes the goings on at the UN, which left Nehru flabbergasted. He says, 'Although London was the prime mover in India's discomfiture at the UN, Nehru saw Washington as also keen to support Pakistan for its own strategic objectives. As early as 17 January 1948, he cabled Gopalaswami Ayyangar, who was leading India's delegation to the UN, that diplomatic reports suggested that if Pakistan was willing to cooperate with the US in providing military facilities against the Soviet Union, Washington might support it on Kashmir.'

Bhattacharjea felt that the subsequent developments showed that Nehru was correct in his assessment of the players at the UN. He says, 'This came true when Pakistan became a member of both the CENTO and SEATO–Anglo-American military pacts. But, Nehru managed to combine awareness of realpolitik with continuing naiveté. His letter to his sister, Vijayalakshmi Pandit, on 16 February indicates the process of learning in its simplest terms.'

The letter to Vijaya Lakshmi indicated quite a lot on how Nehru's mind was working on the issue before the UN at that moment.

'The USA and the UK have played a dirty role, the UK probably being the main factor behind the scenes. I have expressed myself strongly to Attlee about it and I propose to make it perfectly clear to the UK government what we think about it. The time for soft and meaningless talk has passed.'

Bhattacharjea says further, 'Nehru then called Attlee in chilling tones that Noel-Baker had told Abdullah that India's charges that Pakistan had given assistance and encouragement to the raiders were untrue and that he was satisfied that the Pakistan government was blameless.'

Nehru had further to say to Attlee, 'You will forgive me, if I say frankly that the attitude revealed by this conversation cannot but prejudice continuance of friendly relations between India and the UK.'

It was on 1 January 1949 that the UNCIP adopted a resolution, which brought a ceasefire into effect between India and Pakistan.

Over a period of time, India lost interest in the UN debates and its resolutions and it adopted its own way to move forward.

The Sheikh was also disillusioned with the UN for a different set of reasons. He analyzed the position in his book *Aatish-e-Chinar*[121] as follows: 'Since I was the member of Indian delegation led by Ayyangar, I had witnessed the scene very closely. Among other things, I saw a situation of big powers playing a chess game of politics, keeping their strategic interests in view. It was America, Russia, Britain and France playing the game as it suited their strategic interests. A great country like China was not represented while a small island under Chiang Kai-shek was accepted as a representative. In effect, the representative of Taiwan was just dancing to the tune of America. America and Britain toed the same line almost on all matters. America, however, respected the UK's opinion on the Indian subcontinent as they knew that Britain had ruled over India for nearly 200 years.'

The Sheikh had noted with discomfiture the interference of British delegate Noel-Baker, who also raised questions while the Sheikh was giving his own version of the situation. The Sheikh had then retorted that it was the Britishers who were responsible for all problems of the subcontinent, including the partition of India. This retort was spontaneous and it, in part, marked a break from the set pattern of speeches at the UN. Observers had noted that Noel-Baker had decided to keep his mouth shut thereafter, and the Sheikh continued and completed his intervention. It was noted by all that the Sheikh had done an adequate rebuttal of the opposite camp. The Sheikh records in his autobiography, 'After I finished, the Russian delegate Jacob Malik was the first to congratulate me and he firmly shook my hand.'

'The members of Indian delegation had deeply appreciated a factual rebuttal of the Opposition camp. After hearing me, Noel-Baker expressed desire to Ayyangar for a meeting with me. I accepted the invitation and he made me wait for some time when I went to see him. While I wanted to leave, Noel-Baker came and we started talking and it was a hard talk and he tried to convince me that raiders had attacked Kashmir on their own and Pakistan was not involved at all. I told Noel-Baker clearly that he was holding a wrong brief and the meeting ended in acrimony.'

Nehru had subsequently brought this episode to the notice of Attlee and Cripps.

The Sheikh writes further in the autobiography, 'I had gone to the

UN with high hopes that the real story on what had happened would be heard properly and it would also be possible to move forward. But, while I was there, I had come to the conclusion that it was a waste of time to explain the position at a forum where discussions had never led to successful conclusions.'

He also records an incident while he was in the plane returning to India, saying, 'Ayyangar was sitting next to my seat and he handed over a piece of paper to me on which he had recorded that in his view, the best solution, perhaps, was to allow Kashmir to be independent as its borders are vast and touching many countries in the neighbourhood, etc. I could then understand that Ayyangar and myself, by and large, happened to be on the same line on this issue.'

After some time, the Sheikh had to go to the UN again and during that visit, among others, he happened to meet Choudhary Mohammad Ali and Mohmmad-u-Din Taseer. He says, 'We discussed Kashmir issue for hours together and I told these gentlemen that whatever had happened was because of Pakistan's leadership. Both of them had many things to say against their own leadership and they finally asked me as to what needed to be done in future. I frankly told them that it was wastage of time to look for solution to others and I am returning to India with a feeling that we can sort out our differences best ourselves. Both of them had agreed with me at that time. Since we were talking in a very cordial atmosphere, I proposed that they could consider keeping Kashmir as a buffer between the two countries. At this, Mohammad Ali thought Sardar Patel would not agree to this proposal and I left the discussion at that. However, to my satisfaction, both leaders had accepted that Pakistan leadership had not handled the issue properly.'

The Sheikh returned from the UN as an utterly disgusted person as he thought that he could sort out matters with the Union of India keeping his commitment with the people of Jammu & Kashmir in view. In particular, he thought of building a well-defined relationship with the Union of India to achieve the goals he had enunciated in the famous manifesto widely known as 'New Kashmir'. Since he knew full well that Nehru had rightly come to the conclusion that the Anglo-American bloc would not allow a solution of Kashmir issue that would also satisfy India, he (the Sheikh) thought that he could definitely sort out matters with the Union of India. So, he thought of seeking the institution of the Jammu & Kashmir Constituent Assembly as the first milestone towards the goal of achieving the maximum possible autonomy within the Union of India to safeguard the best interests of the people of the state.

When he broached the subject, there was a kind of commotion in Delhi and even Nehru was not initially agreeable. Among other things, Nehru thought that the idea of creating a Constituent Assembly for Jammu & Kashmir would cause a lot of opposition in the country besides, creating difficulties at the UN where India was now a regular partner in a dispute with Pakistan. The initial effort to move forward on this question became difficult as Nehru was conscious of the fact that if the Constituent Assembly was instituted, then nobody could stop the Sheikh from ensuring a complete internal autonomy for the state. But, there were two situations that made it possible for the Sheikh to proceed further in this connection. One was that Nehru was deeply disillusioned with the UN and the other factor was that the Sheikh had decided to fight a decisive battle with the Union of India. The Sheikh decided to explain the position to National Conference cadres, who were, fortunately, solidly behind him. The people of Kashmir had also become aware that the Security Council had conducted prolonged debates on Kashmir and nothing seemed to be materialising into a situation of settlement between the two countries. They were conscious of the fact that the Security Council's debates on Kashmir constituted a situation of debates for the sake of debates and would not produce any acceptable results.

The Sheikh summoned the General Council of the Jammu & Kashmir National Conference in Srinagar on 27 October 1950 and passed a resolution urging the people of Jammu & Kashmir, the real masters of their fate, to institute a Constituent Assembly in the state on the basis of adult franchise and elect their representatives to carve out their own destiny.

This resolution created a great political awakening in the state and the Union of India also took notice of the fact that in view of the intensity of the feelings in Kashmir on this issue, steps should be taken to move forward on this question.

In *The Truth About the Article 370*,[122] Arvind Lavakare explains the position in this regard: 'A large number of Indian states were represented in the Indian Constituent Assembly and though it was initially envisaged that the states would have separate constitutions for their internal administration, the idea of a separate Constitution for each state was forsaken as a "legacy from the ruler's polity which could have no place in a democratic set-up. Thus, by November 1949, the Rulers and Raj Pramukhs had issued proclamations making the Constitution of India operative in their states".

About Jammu & Kashmir, Lavakare says, 'Jammu & Kashmir chose to act differently. It insisted that as provided by clause 7 of the Instrument of Accession, which said, "Nothing in this Instrument shall be deemed to be a commitment in any way as to acceptance of any future constitution of India or to fetter my (ruler's) discretion to enter into arrangement with the Governments of India under any such future Constitution, it could act differently".

The Sheikh launched an unprecedented movement for the institution of the Constituent Assembly in the state to safeguard the interests of the people of Jammu & Kashmir for all times to come. Since he succeeded in sensitizing the minds of the National Conference cadres on this crucial issue, the Union leadership accepted the compulsion created by the prevailing circumstances and, grudgingly though, accepted the proposal.

The state's four representatives, nominated earlier to the Indian Constituent Assembly in June 1949 by the Yuvraj of Jammu & Kashmir on the advice of the council of ministers of the state's interim government led by the Sheikh, had made it clear to the Union of India that all matters beyond the Instrument of Accession would be sorted out only by the Jammu & Kashmir Constituent Assembly. Thus, the Union of India made the institution of the Constituent Assembly in Jammu & Kashmir possible through the proclamation of 1 May 1951 issued by the Yuvraj of Kashmir, heir to the Maharaja of Kashmir who, excepting the subjects of defence, external affairs and communications, retained his complete residuary sovereignty even after he signed the Instrument of Accession.

It was a unique achievement for the Sheikh, who was at that moment at the crest of his popularity.

The National Conference then organized the elections to the Constituent Assembly of Jammu & Kashmir and Bakshi Ghulam

Mohammad was made in charge of the elections. The state was divided into 100 constituent assemblies out of which twenty-five were reserved for Pakistan-held Kashmir. Thus, seventy-five seats were open for contest.

While certain parochial elements raised a hue and cry against the institution of the Jammu & Kashmir Constituent Assembly and there was some disagreement among the Congress leaders also, Nehru was by then clear that its institution was a compulsion produced by the circumstances.

The Praja Parishad had no hope of winning the elections, as it was, by and large, a slogan-mongering organization fanning communal passions, but having no record of service to the people in Jammu. It, therefore, raised objection to the very idea of the Constituent Assembly and boycotted the elections. But, in some Hindu-majority areas of Jammu, the Praja Parishad put up some candidates who could compete. Unfortunately, some candidates from the Praja Parishad got rejected on technical grounds, which gave a pretext to the Praja Parishad to boycott the polls. This organization declared that elections wouldn't be held honestly. The fact, however, remained that the candidates put up by the National Conference were those who had good record of service and had participated in the struggle against the autocratic rule.

An impression has, however, persisted as to how the National Conference bagged a 100 per cent result in the Constituent Assembly.

About the complaints of rigging and unconstitutional and illegal means adopted by the National Conference in Jammu province, the Sheikh admitted in his autobiography that since Bakshi Ghulam Mohammad sometimes exhibited a kind of culture that showed that he had no taste for adhering to rules and regulations, there must have been an element of truth in the complaints. But, then, the Sheikh emphasized that the Praja Parishad could have taken recourse to making a proper complaint about such incidents, which it didn't do.

Since many people have raised a question of how all the seats were won by the National Conference, I want to explain the matter in a little more detail on my understanding of this important episode of Kashmir history. We must appreciate that when the elections to the Constituent Assembly were held, the National Conference's graph of popularity was at its zenith. All the people who had been given tickets by it to contest the elections happened to be accredited leaders of the particular areas and they were involved for years in the struggle for a responsible government, under the leadership of the Sheikh. Almost all of them had been to jail during the freedom struggle at one point of time or the other. So, the talk of the election process being unfair was totally wrong.

As the Sheikh records in his autobiography, 'The Constituent Assembly got constituted and it held its first session on 31 October 1951 and the enthusiasm of the people on that occasion was undescribable. The people of Kashmir had become conscious of the fact that their period of subjugation was over and it was now the time that their aspirations would be fulfilled. The crowds had gathered in colourful attire and greeted the procession in which I had been taken to the assembly hall at Darbargarh, Srinagar. I was greeted in the hall with a thunderous applause and incessant cheers.'

Maulana Masoodi presided over the first session of the Jammu & Kashmir Constituent Assembly and then the House adopted the rules of business and procedure for the assembly and adjourned for the day.

The Constituent Assembly held its next session on 1 November 1951 where G.M. Sadiq was elected as its first president.

That very session determined the powers of the president of the Assembly, appointment and powers of office-bearers, etc. The Constituent Assembly next met on 5 November 1951 to discuss a crucial agenda before it.

The Sheikh made his first comprehensive speech on his vision for the future of Jammu & Kashmir. He declared that it was the day of their destiny for all times to come. He, therefore, invited the attention of the House to the 'New Kashmir' manifesto, which had enunciated the contours of urges and aspirations of the people of the state. He, therefore, told the House that it should be conscious of the goals that had been set already in the said manifesto, the first principle of which was that: 'The source of all sovereignty resides fundamentally in the nation... sovereignty is one and indivisible, inalienable and imprescriptible. It belongs to the nation.'

The Sheikh further made his vision quite clear in the following words: 'You are no doubt aware of the scope of our present constitutional ties with India. We are proud to have our bonds with India, the goodwill of whose people and government is available to us in unstinted and abundant measure. The Constitution of India has provided for a federal Union and in the distribution of sovereign powers has treated us differently from other constitutional units with the exception of the items grouped under defence, foreign affairs and communications in the Instrument of Accession; we have complete freedom to frame our Constitution in the manner we like. In order to live and prosper as good partners in a common endeavour for the advancement of our peoples, I would advise that, while safeguarding our autonomy to the fullest extent so as to enable us to have the liberty to build our country according to the best traditions and genius of our people, we may also by suitable constitutional arrangements with the Union establish our right to seek and compel federal co-operation and assistance in this great task, as well as our fullest co-operation and assistance to the Union.'

While the Jammu & Kashmir Constituent Assembly was set to take epoch-making decisions, the atmosphere in Jammu got vitiated through the propaganda on communal and parochial lines by the Praja Parishad, which received encouragement, including financial support, from the maharaja.

We must, therefore, take notice of the fact that while the maharaja was in Jammu, he exhibited a bitter behaviour.

Bhattacharjea in his book describes the atmosphere like this, 'The situation did not improve after accession. On 5 and 6 November, two convoys carrying 5,000 Muslims from Jammu city to the Pakistan border were ambushed by Hindu and Sikh refugees from Pakistan, with heavy causalities. The Indian troops guarding the second convoy beat off the main attack. On 7 November, Nehru expressed his frustration to his secretary, Dwarkanath Kachru, who was liaising for him in Kashmir.

He quotes Nehru as saying, 'We are all agreed here that the maharaja's attitude has been bad and is bound to lead to trouble. The attempt to evacuate Muslims from Jammu was an amazingly stupid thing to do… I am quite clear that the maharaja is played out and has no understanding of the situation. Nevertheless in the present legal context, he can create difficulties. These should be avoided.'

Bhattacharjea says further, 'Abdullah had no doubt that the Jammu killings were organized by the maharaja, his bigoted wife and Mahajan. In this hate intrigue, Maharani Tara Devi played an important role. She was under the influence of a mysterious guru Sant Dev (this name has also been mentioned, in a different context, by Karan Singh) described by some people as the "Rasputin of Kashmir".

While this was happening through the agonizing incidents of communal frenzy, Mahatma Gandhi at a prayer meeting expressed the hope and said, 'My prayer is that Kashmir would become a beacon of light in this benighted subcontinent.'

Surely, Kashmir showed the element of its Kashmiriyat by maintaining perfect communal harmony and peace so much so that Gandhi could feel fully satisfied and said in a prayer meeting, 'Only Kashmir is a ray of hope in the time when the subcontinent is in darkness.'

Quoting the Sheikh's autobiography, Bhattacharjea described a later event, that is, the most unfortunate assassination of Mahatma Gandhi on 30 January 1948. 'The Maharaja openly sided with the RSS and dispersed the condolence rally organized by the National Conference. RSS volunteers distributed sweets in Jammu. According to eyewitnesses, trays full of sweets arrived at the palace gate.'

Anyway, the Constituent Assembly went along with its business and adopted several resolutions before it; it set up the Basic Principles Committee, discussed threadbare the abolition of landed estates, Chakdari and big landholdings, termination of the system of autocracy in the state and also the election of Karan Singh as Sadre-Riyasat, that is, as a constitutional head of the state for five years. This designation had been suggested by Maulana Azad, who had also proposed a life-term for Karan Singh as Sadre-Riyasat, which was declined by the Sheikh.

As for accession, the Sheikh told the House that the state had three options before it. 1. Accession to India. 2. Accession to Pakistan. 3. To remain independent.

On this occasion, the Sheikh made a very interesting analysis of this problem and said, 'The third course open to us has still to be discussed. We have to consider the alternative of making ourselves an Eastern Switzerland, of keeping aloof from both states, but having friendly relations with them. This might seem attractive in that it would appear to pave the way out of the present deadlock. To us as a tourist country, it could also have certain obvious advantages. But, in considering independence, we must not ignore practical considerations. Firstly, it is not easy to protect sovereignty and independence in a small country, which has not sufficient strength to defend our long and difficult frontiers bordering so many countries. Secondly, we must have the goodwill of our neighbours. Can we find powerful guarantors among them to pull together away in assuring us protection from aggression? I would like to remind you that from 15 August to 22 October 1947, our state was independent and the result was that our weakness was exploited by the neighbour with whom we had a valid standstill agreement. What is the guarantee that in future, too we may not be victims of a similar aggression?'

Interestingly, the Sheikh stuck to the letter and spirit of this speech until he had agreed with Nehru on a formula that became broadly known as the Delhi Agreement. The reflection of the spirit of this speech can be seen in what he spoke on the Delhi Agreement in the Constituent Assembly on 24 July 1952.

These were enormously difficult times and the Constituent Assembly was required to take crucial decisions that were on its hands.

He describes in his autobiography, 'The task before the Constituent Assembly was not an easy one. The Union supported the institution of the J&K Constituent Assembly rather grudgingly. The Union was watching our discussions and the activities with suspicion and had numerous reservations. The Union also felt that there were so many matters that had to be sorted out. It was a matter of regret that our decisions in consonance with keeping our pledge to the people of Jammu & Kashmir such as abolition of landed estates, etc., were not to the Union's liking as it had continued to be conservative on the efficacy of revolutionary measures of not paying any compensation to the landlords and jagirdars.'

The Sheikh had explained that the fact remained that the Constituent Assembly went ahead with the revolutionary decisions like abolition of landed estates with the provision that no compensation would be paid to the landlords, in spite of the Union's reservations. This was also possible because the Supreme Court's jurisdiction had not been extended to the state by then.

30
THE DELHI AGREEMENT OF 1952

Since the Constituent Assembly had taken some epoch-making decisions, it had provoked quite a lot of thinking and some unease in the minds of the Union leaders, they wanted us to sort out matters before the Constituent Assembly proceeded further. In certain areas, the decisions taken by the Constituent Assembly needed further consideration by the Union particularly when the bulk of business related to the Constitution of India had been completed and it was thought that amendments might be needed in respect of certain decisions already taken by the Jammu & Kashmir Constituent Assembly.

The Sheikh and his party appreciated the fact that there was the need for thorough discussion between the Jammu & Kashmir leadership and the Union of India. It was a very difficult situation for both sides, but the Government of India had started feeling a kind of unease on the proceedings that were taking place in the Jammu & Kashmir Constituent Assembly. On the other hand, there was so much of business pending before the Constituent Assembly as the Basic Principles Committee had not yet submitted its final report.

The Sheikh was prepared to sort out matters with the Union and Mirza Mohammad Afzal Beg was detailed to Delhi to have initial discussions on the state's constitutional relationship with the Union of India.

While Beg started having initial discussions, the Sheikh explained to the House that at that moment, the basis of Jammu & Kashmir's relationship with India was the Instrument of Accession. It was limited to defence, external affairs and communications.

The Sheikh explained that the arrangement involved a division of sovereignty which happened to be the normal feature of the federation and therefore, beyond the powers transferred by it to the dominion, the state enjoyed complete residuary sovereignty. It had, therefore, become important to decide on the position of Jammu & Kashmir while framing the Constitution of India. At this time, it was agreed between the two governments that in view of the special problems arising in respect of the state and the fact that Government of India had assured its people that they would themselves finally determine their political future, some special position had to be accorded to Jammu & Kashmir while framing the Constitution of India.

Later, representatives were nominated from Jammu & Kashmir to the Constituent Assembly of India. These were the Sheikh, Mirza Mohammad Afzal Beg, Maulana Mohammad Syeed Masoodi and Pandit Moti Ram Beigra. On the one hand, the Jammu & Kashmir Constituent Assembly was seriously deliberating crucial matters for the future of the state, while on the other hand, the Union was drifting away with all kind of suspicions about the nature of the discussions that were being conducted in the Constituent Assembly. Then, the communal forces—the Praja Parishad, Hindu Mahasabha, the Rashtriya Swayamsevak Sangh (RSS) and others—had raised an organized movement against the very existence of the Constituent Assembly and its proceedings.

The representatives of Jammu & Kashmir had reiterated their views that the state's association with India should be based on the terms of the Instrument of Accession. It was also made clear that while the accession of Jammu & Kashmir with India was complete in fact and in law to the extent of the subjects enumerated in this instrument, the autonomy of the state with regard to all other subjects outside the ambit of the Instrument should be preserved.

Taking into account the special circumstances in which the state was placed, a special constitutional arrangement was evolved and provided in the Article 370 of the Constitution, which defined the position of Jammu & Kashmir state as follows:

'Notwithstanding anything in this Constitution.

(a) The provision of Article 238 shall not apply in relation to the State of Jammu and Kashmir;

(b) The power of Parliament to make laws for the said State shall be limited to:

   (i) Those matters in the Union list and the Concurrent list which, in consultation with the Government of the State, are declared by the president to correspond to matters specified in the Instrument of Accession governing the accession of the State to the Dominion of India as the matters with respect to which the Dominion Legislature may make laws for that State; and

   (ii) Such other matters in the said lists as, with the concurrence of the Government of the state, the President may by order specify.

   Explanation: For the purpose of this Article, the Government of the State means the person for the time being recognized by the President as the Maharaja of Jammu and Kashmir acting on the advice of the Council of Ministers for the time being in office under the Maharaja's proclamation dated, the fifth day of March, 1948.

(c) The provisions of Article 1 of this article shall apply in relation to that State:

(d) Such of the other provisions of this Constitution shall apply in relation to that State subject to such exceptions and modifications as the President may by order specify. Provided that no such order which relates to the matters specified in the Instrument of Accession of the State referred to in paragraph (i) of sub-clause (b) shall be issued except in consultation with the Government of the State: Provided further that no such order which relates to matters other than those referred to the last preceding proviso shall be issued except with the concurrence of the Government.

The Sheikh in his autobiography *Aatish-e-Chinar* further explains an important feature of the constitutional set-up in the following words: 'That the matters specified in the Instrument of Accession shall apply in relation to the Jammu and Kashmir State in consultation with the Govt. of the Jammu and Kashmir State and all other matters which do not fall within the terms of the Instrument of Accession shall not apply in relation to our state except with the final concurrence of the Jammu and Kashmir Constituent Assembly.'

The Sheikh had told the Constituent Assembly that the Constitution of India had clearly envisaged the convening of a Constituent Assembly for Jammu & Kashmir, which would be finally competent to determine the ultimate position of the state in respect of the sphere of its accession, which would be incorporated in the shape of permanent provision of the Constitution.

Meanwhile, the Jammu & Kashmir Constituent Assembly in its session of 7 November 1951 appointed a 17-member Basic Principles Committee with the Sheikh as the chairman, including Mirza Afzal Beg, Girdarilal Dogra, D.P. Dhar, Syed Mir Qasim and others as members.

The Basic Principles Committee gave its interim report on 10 June 1952 in which it made a very crucial recommendation as follows:

'The committee strongly feels that consistent with the democratic aspirations of the people of the State, the office of Head of the State should be based upon the elective principle and not upon the principle of heredity. This would afford opportunities to all citizens to rise to the highest point of authority and position with the support and confidence of the people.'

The report of the Basic Principles Committee was adopted on 12 June 1952.

By the time the Jammu & Kashmir Constituent Assembly met for its most crucial session on 11 August 1952, it had gained the comfort level of taking decisions on four important subjects.

1. Drafting a Constitution on the basis of the aspirations of the people
2. Abolition of landed estates and Jagirdari system
3. Termination of the autocratic rule in the state
4. Decision on the finality of the accession

As for the finality of the accession with India, all members had been provided the opportunity to express the opinion on this important issue and the Sheikh had made his ideas quite clear in his two speeches of historic importance before the Constituent Assembly—the one on 5 November 1951 and the other on 11 August 1952. Since many issues had cropped up in the discussions, particularly on the question of finality of the accession and, on the other hand, the gulf that had occurred on many crucial issues between the approach of the Union leaders and the leadership of the National Conference, therefore, there was an urgent need for understanding and reconciliation. Hence, the discussions were organized and the two sides were represented by the following.

While Nehru, Maulana Azad, Gopala Swami Ayyanger and Sir Girja Shankar Bajpai represented the Centre, Jammu & Kashmir was represented by the Sheikh, Bakshi Ghulam Mohammad and Mirza Afzal Beg. These discussions were prolonged and the atmosphere remained charged, but finally, both sides came to an agreement which came to be known as the Delhi Agreement.

It was during these debates that Nehru whispered into the Sheikh's ear: 'Sheikh Saheb, you have to remain with me all the time.' The Sheikh whispered back, 'If I didn't, then what?' Nehru replied in the whisper again, 'Then, we shall get you along in golden chains.' The Sheikh had smilingly warned him, 'Please don't do that, you might then lose Kashmir.' The Sheikh gives details of this whisper in his autobiography *Aatish-e-Chinar* in the chapter 'Aiyeen Saaz Assembly (The Constituent Assembly)'.

While the Delhi Agreement had been accepted by the Sheikh with a sense of achievement as the agreement enshrined protection of the rights and aspirations of the people of Kashmir, the Union continued with a set of suspicions. This diversion of opinions is reflected in the two speeches of historic importance, the one that was made by Nehru in the Lok Sabha on 24 July 1952 and the other made by the Sheikh on 11 August 1952 in the Jammu & Kashmir Constituent Assembly. While Nehru's speech was broadly an expression of rhetoric and sentiment along with his commitment to Kashmir, the Sheikh spoke on the Delhi Agreement decisively as an achievement for the people of the state. However, the Sheikh had made it clear that further discussions would be held in a cordial atmosphere on the differences on certain issues within the Delhi Agreement.

The provisions in the Delhi Agreement as provided by the Parliament

Secretariat to me on 12 October 1995 are as follows:

The prime minister made a statement in the Lok Sabha on 24 July 1952. The statement was the outcome of the talks which government of India had with the leading members of the Jammu and Kashmir government. At the time to define the state's relationship with the Union. The statement is loosely referred to as 'Delhi Agreement', although no formal agreement as such was made. A similar statement was made by the Sheikh Mohammad Abdullah in Jammu and Kashmir State Constituent Assembly in August, 1952.

The initial portion of the statement contains an account of the geographical and historical position of Jammu and Kashmir state. The following salient points emerge from the statement.

1. The accession was complete. The facts that the subjects to which Jammu and Kashmir state had acceded were limited or less than those applying to other states produced the misunderstanding as if the accession was partial. That was not so. Accession was complete. In fact, all the erstwhile princely states acceded only in regard to the three subjects, namely Foreign Affairs, Defence and Communications, to begin with.

2. The three subjects foreign affairs, defence and communications were each a category of subjects, not a small subject.

3. Article 370 was of a transitional nature. It enabled the president to add other subjects.

4. Government of India had no desire to make the relationship as static, unchanging or finalized. The position was dynamic and changing.

5. The Jammu and Kashmir Constituent Assembly with enviable speed put through land reforms. It was not correct to say that they expropriated landlords. They put a ceiling roughly at 23 acres plus orchards which were not touched and which were very important for Kashmir. Considering the average holding of 2 acres of land in Kashmir, the ceiling was fairly generous.

6. Jammu and Kashmir state is a constituent part or unit of the Indian Republic, a part of the territory of India.

7. Full citizenship applied there. But, in addition, for the permanent

residents, certain privileges regarding acquisition of land, the services, state scholarship, etc., had been safeguarded.

8. Fundamental Rights: While it was generally agreed that there should be fundamental rights and these fundamental rights should apply to the state, the Jammu and Kashmir's land legislation was to be preserved. The state government should have the authority to deal with continuing tensions, infiltration, sabotage, espionage, etc., the constant tension of an enemy trying to come in to create trouble.

9. The Supreme Court should have original jurisdiction in respect of disputes mentioned in Article 131 of the Constitution, and in regard to fundamental rights which applied to Kashmir. The state government wished to consider further the point that the Supreme Court should be the final court of the appeal in all civil and criminal matters as laid in the constitution.

10. The head of the state should be the person recognized by the president on the recommendation of the legislature of the state. The Jammu and Kashmir Constituent Assembly's inaugural address mentioned as one of their policies for election, by democratic process, of the head of state. He would hold office during the pleasure of the president.

11. The Sheikh had publicly stated that the national flag was the supreme flag and had the same status and position in Jammu and Kashmir State as in the rest of the country. The state flag was in no sense a rival to it but for historical and sentimental reasons connected with the struggle for freedom in Kashmir, they wanted this state symbol to continue.

12. Financial arrangements between the state and the Government of India were to be considered further. The position was dynamic and changing one. These arrangements had to be gradually worked out.

13. Emergency powers: Article 352 would apply with the rider that in regard to internal disturbances, it would apply at the request, or with the concurrence, of the Government of the State.

14. These are the principal things that have been discussed and on which satisfactory decisions were reached. There was nothing final about this and gradually, we could fill in other details later.

In his epoch-making speech on the Delhi Agreement on 11 August 1952, the Sheikh had a kind of relief in his mind after certain crucial decisions like the abolition of landed estates entailing comprehensive agrarian reforms without any compensation to landlords and other crucial decisions like the abolition of autocracy in the state and election of Karan Singh as Sadre-Riyasat for five years, etc. had already been taken. The Sheikh had also felt that the crucial question of not paying any compensation to jagirdars was particularly possible as the jurisdiction of the Supreme Court had not been extended to the state till then. He had, therefore, some reservations on the extension of the jurisdiction of the Supreme Court of India to Jammu & Kashmir and the discussions were on.

The Sheikh had further explained to the Constituent Assembly that there were areas in which the two sides had differences of opinion, but he had assured the House with confidence that these would be resolved.

It is so tragic that while the Sheikh was clinching the issues in the Constituent Assembly and proceeding to give a final shape to the constitutional relationship with the Union of India, the small minds within the Sheikh's own party and within the Union of India had started hatching a conspiracy against him. One doesn't understand why he was suspected of toying with the idea of an independent Kashmir, when he had made his mind clear all these years that his first preference was for an independent Kashmir. But, simultaneously, he had made it clear that it was not possible to be independent under the circumstances that prevailed at that moment. In his speech on 11 August 1952, he had not drifted away from the letter and spirit of his speech of 5 November 1951. It seems that the future conspirators had made up their mind to go ahead with the conspiracy, ignoring his two speeches of historic importance made before the Constituent Assembly.

Ajit Bhattacharjea in his book *The Wounded Valley* lamented the misgivings about the Sheikh, particularly, the ones relating to the national flag and head of state as he felt the Union flag to which we continue our allegiance as a part of the Union of India will occupy supreme and distinct place in the state. As for the head of state, the Delhi Agreement laid down specifically that such a person would hold office during the pleasure of the president.

Bhattacharjea deeply grieved about the approach of communalists, saying, 'But, the Delhi Agreement soon came under attack joined by the Jana Sangh elsewhere in the country; the Praja Parishad launched a massive campaign in Jammu, where the police found themselves opposing demonstrators carrying the national flag and President Rajendra Prasad's portrait before them. The National Conference government was portrayed as the enemy of nationalism, a sentiment conveyed by a rhythmic chant that soon spread widely. *Ek desh mein do vidhan; ek desh main do nishan; Ek desh mein do pradhan; nahin chalenge, nahi chalenge* (Two constitutions, two flags, two heads of state in one country will not be tolerated).'

It was so tragic that the communalists created an atmosphere in which the Delhi Agreement was not appreciated in its proper perspective and finally the Sheikh was not only dismissed undemocratically and unconstitutionally but also arrested. That obnoxious decision of the Union of India not only created havoc all around, triggering large-scale killings in the Kashmir Valley, but also caused a deep wound in the psyche of Kashmiris never, perhaps, to heal in the course of time.

While I was describing how small minds played havoc with the system and tried their utmost to divide the society on communal and sectarian lines in Jammu, there were also people who raised their powerful voices and played their glorious role for the cause of humanity at different epochs of time. The names of this galaxy of leaders that come to my mind readily are Baba Jitto, who, as per Narender Sehgal's book, *A State In Turbulence: Jammu & Kashmir*, was born in Aghar near Katra (Jammu) in 1433 and had died fighting feudalism in June 1458. Some centuries later, the spirit of Baba Jitto's struggle was followed by the people like Mahatma Budh Singh, Comrade Danwantri, Bhagat Chaju Ram, Moti Ram Baigra, Krishan Dev Sethi, Girdari Lal Dogra, Om Prakash Saraf, R.P. Saraf, and others.

By early 1960s, these leaders were joined by a group of young leaders like Ved Bhasin, Amrit Malhotra, Balrajpuri, Rangil Singh and others and they together organized a fight against the parochial and communal elements and held the torch of secularism and togetherness of mankind aloft in their hands. The present-day Jammu can really feel proud of these people who represented this element of character in the people of Jammu. At present, the Congress party in Jammu and some other non-RSS–BJP–Shiv Sena groupings have among them men and women who envision a future of togetherness in the J&K state.

As for the Sheikh's arrest and its aftermath, many people were wiser after the event. Syed Mir Qasim had once told me that the group of leaders, including him, led by Bakshi Ghulam Mohammad and G.M. Sadiq, were wrong by not siding with the Sheikh in 1953. He was explaining the point to me that the Union of India could not succeed in removing the Sheikh from the scene but there were people among the ranks of the Kashmiri leaders who fell into the trap created by the small minds at the national level. Syed Mir Qasim took the position that he was, of course, not in the forefront meaning thereby that Bakshi Ghulam Mohammad, G.M. Sadiq, D.P Dhar and the then Sadre-Riyasat were the main people in the conspiracy. Syed Mir Qasim in his autobiography *Dastan-e-Hayat*[123] leaves it to future historians to assess Bakshi Ghulam Mohammad's character in toppling the Sheikh's government, but he says that he found Bakshi Ghulam Mohammad was dead-set to take up the leadership around that time. He seemed nearly inclined to agree that Bakshi Ghulam Mohammad did what he did for his greed for capturing power. He takes shelter behind Prem Nath Bazaz, who had said in his book *The History of Struggle for Freedom in Kashmir*,[124] that Bakshi Ghulam Mohammad was having parleys secretly with Praja Parishad leaders in Delhi where a conspiracy was being hatched to topple the government. Syed Mir Qasim was, however, puzzled over the development as it was during those critical days that Bakshi had started saying that his love for and devotion to the Sheikh was the sixth element of his faith (one more than five tenets of a Muslim's faith in his religion).

Krishen Dev Sethi, who remained steadfast in his struggle for the toiling classes, regrets the Sheikh's dismissal and arrest and says in his book *Yad-e-Rafta*[125] that there are many people who now try to save themselves from their responsibility of the 1953 episode and give reasons to show that they were in agreement with the Sheikh from the very beginning. He also refers to Syed Mir Qasim, who had said in his autobiography *Dastan-e-Hayat* emphatically that he had no knowledge of the conspiracy that was hatched against the Sheikh.

Sethi doesn't accept that argument and holds Syed Mir Qasim also responsible. Sethi has been forthright in his book on many things. He writes in *Yade-e-Rafta*, 'Bakshi Ghulam Mohammad was from the very beginning in league with the communal forces, particularly with the Praja Parishad and soon after becoming Prime Minister of the State, he developed very sweet and cordial relations with all the communalists, particularly, the Praja Parishad.'

Sethi adds, 'In a public meeting organized at Museum Ground, Jammu, Bakshi described Prem Nath Dogra like his father and he addressed a large public meeting at Goda Slathiyan (Jammu) organized by the Praja Parishad and sang praises for that rabidly communal organization.'

Coming back to Nehru's famous whisper, it is so tragic that he implemented what he had said, though grudgingly, by agreeing with the Cabinet that was unitedly demanding action against the Sheikh. The communal forces, inside and outside Parliament, had raised a hue and cry against the Sheikh and also on Nehru's Kashmir policy, under the cover of their fake brand of patriotism. The die-hards cared two hoots for the federal character of the Constitution of India in relation to Kashmir.

Alas, the small minds didn't comprehend the price India would pay for that gigantic misjudgement. These small minds also didn't share Nehru's vision and idea of India as a vibrant democracy, secular and pluralistic society, with a deep sense of unity in diversity!

There are still some people who say that Nehru had not approved the dismissal of the Sheikh much less his arrest. To such people, I would like to quote just one authority, Y.D. Gundevia, who said in his book *The Testament of Sheikh Mohammad Abdullah*[126]: 'When I asked Sheikh Abdullah this question, not long ago, his answer was simple. "The reactionary elements," he said, "had ample access to Delhi. Sardar Patel and several others had no faith in me—and that is putting it very mildly. I would say Nehru first resisted this campaign of vilification against me but ultimately, he succumbed". This explains a lot.

Ansar Harvani, who was a seasoned parliamentarian, had considerable access to Nehru, once told me as to what really happened in the Cabinet meeting when it was decided to dismiss Abdullah. He explained, 'Nehru had very grudgingly agreed with the action proposed by a totally hostile Cabinet. It was a situation that Nehru was voted out by his own Cabinet on this issue. Nehru had, however, warned that the proposed action would create havoc in Kashmir.'

I believe Nehru was proved correct in his warning. A revolt did occur in Kashmir in the aftermath of the events of 9 August 1953 and hundreds were killed mercilessly by the forces.

It is really unfortunate that in spite of being party to the Delhi Agreement, which came as a situation of agreement on various issues between the Jammu & Kashmir state and the Union of India, the latter persisted with its consistent effort to dilute the autonomy that happened to be the crux of the Delhi Agreement.

Even the then Sadre-Riyasat, Karan Singh, who has been described by the Sheikh in his autobiography *Aatish-e-Chinar* as one of the main actors of the conspiracy of 1953, later lamented the Union of India's blunder of diluting the autonomy of the state.

In an interview to *The Week* magazine (reported by *The Indian Express* on 22 December 1996) Karan Singh said, 'The Centre's only consistent policy has been to erode JK's autonomy.'

It is so tragic a situation in the constitutional relationship between J&K and the Union of India that while Kashmir stood steadfast with secular India, the Union didn't!

31
THE ARMED MILITANCY AND ITS AFTERMATH

It is not easy to say if the recent turmoil in Kashmir spanning over twenty-seven years has represented a movement of resistance or an aberration in Kashmir's history.

Undoubtedly, Kashmiris of all denominations have always lived together peacefully and in perfect harmony despite social upheavals disturbing inter-communal equilibrium at times. But, those small upheavals were definitely an aberration.

A different situation arose when armed militancy started in late 1988. It was visibly sponsored by the neighbouring country. It carried, in some measure, communal undertones, but it needs to be largely ascribed to political factors that ignited the fire. The most important question often raised was, though the militancy was a sponsored situation, how did the Kashmiri youth get attracted to it and willingly agree to receive training in arms in Pakistan-held Kashmir?

The most plausible argument accepted was the rigging in J&K Legislative Assembly polls of 1987 that led to a huge unrest among the youth. The Muslim United Front (MUF) had many followers in some segments of Kashmir that could give it a noticeable position in the Legislative Assembly. They could have won at least 10 to 12 seats. It would have initiated a forward movement on the graph of a democratic and harmonious relationship of the J&K state with the Union of India. Unfortunately, New Delhi's power elite, backed by intelligence agencies and Dr Farooq Abdullah (he represented a powerful position in the political arena of Kashmir), became restive and decided to retain power, so to say, at any cost. New Delhi not only fell in line, but also actively supported the stance of the National Conference. It would have been a priceless opportunity to allow the MUF to gain access to political dispensation in the state, which was legitimately its right.

Rajiv Gandhi and Dr Abdullah came closer before the elections and Dr Abdullah decided to hold power. I had advised the managers in the system that an alliance could be better formed after the elections. I had reminded Dr Abdullah that he could afford to create the same situation as he had succeeded to do in June 1983 when he fought elections to the J&K Legislative Assembly and also for a byelection to Baramulla parliamentary constituency successfully. But he was swayed into a pre-poll coalition that manipulated the elections. Dr Abdullah had got unnecessarily demoralized after his unlawful dismissal as chief minister in 1984.

It was unfortunate that Dr Abdullah had admitted before a gathering in Jammu sometime in October/November 1986, when he was warming up to Rajiv Gandhi, that he would never repeat his bad behaviour towards the governor (Jagmohan Malhotra) or to others.

Soon after the results of 1987 elections, the atmosphere got surcharged and the MUF and its supporters raised an alarm. The MUF was not allowed to win as that was perceived to be a threat to the Union of India. The short-sighted politicians started learning a lesson that a bigger unacceptable situation than the MUF was taking shape, soon after the government was formed in 1987.

Dr Abdullah had once remarked, perhaps, in a lighter vein, 'We have to retain power at any cost as we have to serve the people. I am not going to sit in the Opposition.'

It was evident that some of his colleagues had become impatient for power and wrongly advised him. Dr Abdullah's mother, Begam Akbar Jahan, realized things were going in the wrong direction, but could not alter the course of events. The newly formed government had to face the anger of the masses and within a couple of months youths started exhibiting their militant attitudes in some areas of the Kashmir Valley. Pakistan must have been waiting for such an opportunity to occur.

In October-November 1988, people in some areas of the Valley started taking notice of youths carrying weapons. Information also trickled in that a sizeable number of young men had crossed borders for training in arms.

After a number of selective killings, a fear psychosis gripped the Valley by March-April 1989.

In the 1987 elections, some candidates and their election agents were roughed up and thrashed openly. Many were put behind bars. It affected people such as Peer Mohammad Yousuf Shah of Soibugh, Budgam—now widely known as Syed Salahuddin, chairman of the United Jihad Council (UJC)—who was fighting the election to the J&K Assembly from Amira Kadal constituency and should have won.

He was browbeaten and his polling agents jailed. Around this time, the Jammu Kashmir Liberation Front (JKLF) seized the opportunity and tried to make best use of the atmosphere.

None can, however, take the position finally and decisively that the rigging in 1987 elections was the sole reason for causing unrest in the minds of the youths. There were so many episodes of mistrust that the Union of India had created with the people of Kashmir since it had acceded to India. The rigging in the elections of 1987 only became a turning point for youth to show its anger against the Union of India.

The JKLF had been founded by Amanullah Khan way back in May 1977 with association by Mohammad Maqbool Bhat (who was subsequently executed in the Tihar Jail on 11 February 1984). They set up a Kashmiri nationalist organization and wanted to set up branches at many places in Europe to explain the Kashmir problem. It gained recognition in Pakistan-held Kashmir. It also gained attention in Kashmir through Mohammad Yasin Malik, Ashfaq Majeed Wani, Abdul Hameed Sheikh, Javaid Ahmad Mir and their associates.

Many of them had worked as polling agents in the 1987 elections. Since these youth leaders had participated in the polls and experienced rigging in many assembly segments, they served as catalysts for a violent movement organized across the border by government agencies in Pakistan-held Kashmir and also by non-state actors. Thus in 1987, armed militancy was launched in Kashmir.

In the aftermath of the 1987 elections, the JKLF took clear shape in Kashmir. It is also the year when Amanullah Khan returned from England to Pakistan.

Amanullah Khan had never been in the good books of the Pakistan establishment. But, around 1987, he became a star to the Pakistani Army and the ISI. So, the JKLF became an effective instrument of armed operations by youths in Kashmir. The alienated youths came handy to Pakistan and full patronage was available to JKLF cadres whose slogan for independence became a hit by 1989. By 1990, the JKLF's popularity came full circle. Armed militancy along with processions in the Valley became the order of the day and the state's administration crumbled down.

An atmosphere of selective assassinations made the armed youth master of the situation. Some CRPF personnel and a prominent worker of the National Conference, Mohammad Yousuf Halwai, were killed on 7 August 1989, followed by the killing of Tika Lal Taploo, a Kashmiri Pandit leader on 14 September 1989, and Neel Kanth Ganjoo (a retired session judge) was killed on 4 November 1989. These incidents gripped the Valley and created an atmosphere of fear and suspicion. The mainstream parties became almost a redundant factor in the social life of Kashmir.

When the youths raised the slogan for independence under the banner of the JKLF, they attracted the masses. Pent-up feelings were released and their acceptability graph rose. Pakistan was waiting for such an unrest to occur in Kashmir and turned it into a big opportunity to gain political mileage before the international community. It was a situation of full-fledged armed militancy sponsored and supported by Pakistan. Many training camps were set up in Pakistan-held Kashmir and as per credible information, the task of organizing armed militancy in Kashmir was given to Pakistan's trusted intelligence agency, the ISI.

In-between came a situation that gave tremendous strength to the JKLF. Rubaiya Sayeed, the 23-year-old daughter of Mufti Mohammad Sayeed, who was then the home minister of India, was abducted by JKLF militants on 8 December 1989. The JKLF approached a leading daily published from Jammu, the *Kashmir Times*, on phone the same day claiming responsibility for her abduction. They demanded the release of their members—Ghulam Nabi Bhat, Noor Mohammad Kalwal,

Mohammad Altaf and Mushtaq Ahmad Zargar—to ensure the release of Rubaiya. The state government put in a sizeable effort to get her released. But, the family involved a friend, Moti Lal Bhat, the then judge of Allahabad High Court, to open direct negotiations with the militants.

The Union government was not convinced that Farooq Abdullah's government was doing enough for her release. While the state government argued its case and tried to convince the Union, Rubaiya Sayeed would remain safe and they would succeed in getting her released, the Union government became restive and two senior Union ministers—Inder Kumar Gujral and Arif Mohammad Khan—flew to Srinagar on 13 December 1989 to meet Dr Abdullah. They insisted that the four militants be released immediately. Dr Abdullah strongly argued the state administration was already under strain and if such an action was taken, the law and order situation would go out of hand. He assured the ministers that Rubaiya's release would be ensured. The ministers were not convinced and declared that in case he didn't agree, his government would be dismissed!

The state government ordered the release of the four militants, which led to a celebration in downtown Srinagar, particularly in Rajouri Kadal area, where the released militants and the crowd that gathered there fired shots in the air, showing their strength. This was a death knell to the already weakened state administration. Then, the Union government committed the grave mistake of appointing Jagmohan Malhotra as the governor on 19 January 1990, which led Dr Abdullah to resign as the chief minister on the same day.

Then followed the Gaw Kadal massacre and killings on a large scale throughout the Kashmir Valley as the security forces were pitted against extremely agitated people. Senior politicians such as Harkrishan Singh Surjeet, Chandrashekhar and others at the national level tried to dissuade the then prime minister and home minister from appointing Jagmohan as the governor for the second time. I also led a delegation to dissuade Mufti Mohammad Sayeed from appointing Jagmohan Malhotra as the governor.

Jagmohan soon imposed governor's rule in the state on 20 January 1990. Chaos ensued and the entire Kashmir Valley turned into a valley of death and destruction. Governor Jagmohan soon realized that he had accepted an impossible job and got extremely nervous.

The killing of five members of the Indian Air Force in Rawalpora, Srinagar bus stand on 25 January 1990 had added a new dimension to the armed strife. It was largely alleged by the security agencies and observers at the national level that the JKLF had led the group that killed the IAF personnel.

By this time, the JKLF had become more powerful. But then, the ideological strain had occurred imperceptibly at various levels, both among the populace and the militant ranks, which caused great strife and unease for the general run of the people.

While the militancy in Kashmir gained an unprecedented momentum, the killings of innocent people continued. Since the administration had crumbled down totally, it was possible for the militant outfits to assassinate senior religious and political leader Mirwaiz Maulvi Mohammad Farooq on 21 May 1990 and that deepened the crisis. The JKLF had categorically denied having any hand in his assassination. The Union of India itself became nervous and realized its mistake and Jagmohan was compelled to resign on 25 May 1990.

Even though Jagmohan was removed, the strife on the ground continued as there was no policy shift visible from the Union of India that could have sown the seeds of a long-term reconciliation between the people of Kashmir and the Union of India on the one hand and between India and Pakistan on the other.

The assassination of a very prominent political leader and a scholar of Islam, Maulana Mohammad Syeed Masoodi, at his residence in Ganderbal on 13 December 1990 by unknown militants carried a quiet message all around that the militants could go to any extent in establishing their authority on the ground. The maulana was eighty-seven and a cancer patient.

The killing of H.N. Wanchoo, a prominent trade union leader, on 5 December 1992 sent shockwaves throughout India and the people of Kashmir denounced it unequivocally.

Much later, prominent political leader Abdul Gani Lone was assassinated on 21 May 2002 while he had joined a congregation organized to commemorate the assassination of Maulvi Farooq at Eidgah grounds,

Srinagar. That killing was widely lamented and it was characterized, nationally and internationally to be a message that there was no room for moderate and democratic thinking on issues.

India's security agencies suspected that while all this was happening in Kashmir, Pakistan had become jittery by full-throated slogans for independence. India's security agencies and well-informed sources confirmed that the ISI helped to set up other groups that worked overtly and covertly, as the circumstances suggested, for Kashmir's accession with Pakistan. Many credible observers at the national level also perceived that the JKLF's popularity did not suit Pakistan anymore, as it wanted nothing short of Kashmir's accession with it. They thought it was most opportune time for them to complete what they called the unfinished agenda of 1947.

What followed was incessant bombings, killings and a bloody situation of death and destruction. Thousands got killed in the crossfire between the armed forces and countless independent armed groups such as Lashkar-e-Taiba, Hizbul Mujahideen, Jammu and Kashmir Students Liberation Front (JKSLF), Hizbullah, Al-Umer, Muslim Janbaz Force, Allah Tigers, Albaraq, Jamiat ul-Mujahideen, Harkat-ul-Mujahideen, Muslim Mujahideen, Hizbul Moomineen, Jaish-e-Muhammad, etc. A Srinagar daily reported that there were eighty such armed groups operating in Kashmir.

Observers at the national level assessed that almost all outfits except the JKLF promoted the concept of Kashmir's accession to Pakistan. Many of these organizations also tried to weave the concept of Islam into the texture of armed militancy.

In his concise *History of Kashmir Movement*,[127] researcher Shabnam Qayoom lamented that even before the so-called freedom fighters had gained sizeable momentum, the militants of many shades took up the causes that could, at best, be postponed and they earned a bad name, not only in India, but also at the international level and they were dubbed as 'terrorists'. They imposed closure of cinema halls, ban on alcohol, asked women to wear veil, abducted Rubaiya Sayeed and other women and killed people like H.L. Khera, a central government officer on 10 April 1990 and Musheer-ul-Haq (vice chancellor of Kashmir University) and his private secretary Abdul Gani Zargar on 11 April 1990 and committed numerous acts of atrocities against their own people, most of whom were totally innocent. As Shabnam elaborates, it is a long story of how people of Kashmir suffered enormous cruelties in the crossfire between the security forces and the armed militants.

The abductions, particularly of women, had caused a wave of resentment against the Kashmiri militants.

My daughter Naheed Soz was abducted on 27 February 1991 from outside her residence at Chanapora, Srinagar, when she was returning from work. She remained in captivity of the Ikhwan-ul-Muslimeen for nine days and there are graphic details of her confinement in the book *Khatoon-e-Kashmir*[128] written by Shoukeen Kashmiri. It is actually a book on a female militant leader, Farida Behanji who has described the abduction in detail and asserted that she had asked her own sister to be with Naheed during the captivity. Behnaji further justified the abduction of Rubaiya Sayeed, Naheed and Khem Lata Wakhloo as according to her everything was right in a situation of war and asserted that all these women were shown respect and were treated properly.

However, the release of Naheed needs a little explanation about how things worked at that point of time between India and Pakistan. Soon after my wife phoned me in Delhi about the abduction, I rushed to Parliament and told the then MoS Home, Subodh Kant Sahai, not to make any statement in Parliament until I had brought this episode to the notice of the then Prime Minister Chandrashekhar.

Chandrashekhar was a different kind of a man in the chair. When he heard me in the afternoon on that day, he phoned Abdul Sattar, the high commissioner of Pakistan, in my presence and told him to visit him at his residence immediately. I had told the PM that my worry was that certain elements in Pakistan had taken the course of eulogizing the militants. Among other things, he told me I had done the right thing in asking Subodh not to make any statement in Parliament.

While he asked me to stay in touch, I left his South Avenue residence with the satisfaction that the prime minister would handle the case well. The next day, the PM asked me to meet him immediately. I found the PM in a relaxed mood and he apprised me of what had happened in-between. First of all, the PM enquired whether I had brought this matter to the notice of Rajiv Gandhi, who was on a tour to Iran. He said that Rajiv had talked to him and the PM had assured him that everything possible would be done. I then confirmed to the PM that Rajiv had also enquired from me about the episode. Then the PM narrated an interesting story. He said that Sattar had contacted then Pakistani Prime Minister Nawaz Sharif in Beijing and asked him to talk to him (the PM). With a smile, the PM said that when he talked to Sharif he was assured that whatever was possible would be done and he confirmed that he had spoken to Maulana Kausar Niazi, the then federal minister of information, who had let the people concerned know that it was an un-Islamic act and Naheed should be released. Since I enjoyed his confidence, he told me, rather pleasantly, that his call to Beijing had been intercepted and the then chief of RAW had met him that very morning. The PM had told the officer that he was happy to know that India's communication system was in good shape and complimented the RAW for having done its duty.

While I have narrated the above episode, I must record my gratefulness to the people of Kashmir, particularly the media, which had sympathized with our family and urged the militants to release Naheed.

There was another abduction that attracted attention from all over the subcontinent. Khem Lata Wakhloo, former minister in the state government, was abducted on 4 September 1991 along with her husband, and the couple remained in captivity for forty-five days and suffered a great deal in isolation from the family. Eventually the couple returned home safe and sound and what I came to know subsequently, directly from Khem Lata Wakhloo, was that during all the days in captivity, she and her husband kept telling the militants that the course they had adopted for a political cause was not correct and she felt the captors didn't mind the polite words of advice.

The new situation characterized a qualitative shift in Pakistan's policy towards Kashmir. The idea of Pakistan as an Islamic state and its right to 'complete its unfinished agenda' was explained to Kashmiris through trained armed militants. While Hizbul Mujahideen sustained its strength and the JKLF survived as an idea representing the aspirations of Kashmiris for independence, all other militant organizations almost vanished from the scene.

After so many years of armed militancy in Kashmir and some parts of Jammu, the militancy had come down considerably and people had, by and large, realized that no political problem can be resolved through gun culture and extremism. People had got fed up with armed militancy soon after it gained peak in 1991-93, as many fake militants had also joined the ranks who worked against their own people and made their lives miserable. This expression was adopted by the press in Kashmir to describe a category among militants who didn't appear in public eye to be fighting for a cause, but they had their own agenda of making hay while the sun of militancy was shining.

As early as November 1991, a widely circulated weekly *Afkar-e-Milli* (Delhi) carried an article by Masood Hussain, who analyzed the details of how fake militants, who existed in almost every militant organization, committed crimes against innocent people. Around 1993–94, there were around eighty armed militant outfits. Hussain gave graphic details of how some fake militants had made life of the people miserable and warned them that there would be widespread anger and the people of Kashmir would rise against the fake militants. Masood was correct and there were demonstrations against fake militants who committed undescribable crimes.

Khawaja Sanaullah, editor and founder of *Aftab Srinagar*, who had otherwise carried statements by militant organizations from time to time became distraught with the excesses committed by some fake militants and narrated details of the unacceptable high-handedness of the so-called mujahideen in his book *Ahad Nama-ai-Kashmir*.

In this connection Shabnam Qayoom narrated a story on how two Australian journalists met him in early 1992 and told him that the freedom fighters had lost the cause by bringing in issues like imposing veil for women, closing cinema halls and liquor shops, etc. The journalists told Shabnam that the international community had already lost interest in Kashmir and they had started calling the freedom fighters as terrorists.

Elaborating the story further, Shabnam Qayoom narrated another interesting story of his visit to Pakistan where he called on Prime

Minister Nawaz Sharif in Islamabad in June 1992. As per Shabnam, Sharif lamented the fact that freedom fighters had themselves spoiled the very cause they were espousing by such nefarious activities. Sharif was also angry because these activities had discredited Pakistan before the international community.

Shabnam is not one-sided on his analysis of turmoil in Kashmir. He has given details of the atrocities committed by the armed forces in Kashmir, particularly the suffering of women. His book *Kashmir Mein Khawateen Ki Behurmati*[128] is replete with details of rapes and molestations like the widely-publicized Kunan-Poshpora incident to other such events.

It is for a long time that people of Kashmir have raised their voice against human right violations committed by the armed forces, who admitted many times that innocent killings had taken place and apologized for it. In some cases, punishments were also awarded. But largely, police and paramilitary forces said in situations of sponsored armed militancy, innocent people got involved and sometimes got killed.

There are families throughout Kashmir with details of atrocities committed by the armed forces, from time to time and many cases were lodged against them. There are numerous cases still pending in courts. Then, there are families whose dear ones disappeared and could never be traced. Laws like the AFSPA and Disturbed Areas Act were responsible for civilian killings by the armed forces. These laws gave immunity to forces of not being accountable for any of their actions in the field.

While the Disturbed Areas Act was suspended later, the AFSPA continued. Many sections of the AFPSA make it a draconian law. Since there is no effective mechanism to control the misuse of this law, certain sections among the forces committed grave errors of judgment on many occasions and almost the entire population in Kashmir became angry with them.

Following are a few examples of how this law was misused by the forces:

The infamous Machil fake encounter on 29–30 April 2010 in which three innocent youths were taken into custody at Nadihal Baramulla and then they were taken to Machil (a distant place in Kupwara district) and killed in cold blood. This inhuman act created a commotion in Kashmir.

A widespread public outcry compelled the army to institute an inquiry, which established the guilt of the forces who had committed the crime in expectation of rewards. That unfortunate incident roused intense feelings of anger and led thousands of youths to indulge in stone pelting that again attracted disproportionate response from the forces killing 120 youngsters.

Tufail Mattoo, a seventeen-year-old boy, died of a teargas shell while returning from a tuition class. The entire Kashmir rose in revolt and joined the mourning. The devastated family is still fighting for justice in court. The army subsequently accepted the crime and apologized. It also claimed that punishments would be awarded. However, punishments were not made public.

Much earlier, there were many incidents of killings of innocent people by the armed forces and the people of Kashmir felt convinced on the complicity of the forces in such incidents.

The Chattisinghpora massacre on 20 March 2000 caused another wound in the psyche of Kashmiris. While Hizbul Mujahideen and other militant organizations denied their involvement in this heinous crime against Sikhs, the state and central governments remained silent and held militant outfits responsible, without giving any solid proof.

The Pathribal and Brakpura killings towards the end of March 2000, in the wake of Chattisinghpora massacre, attracted attention at the international level. The families, who suffered, raised an alarm and people joined in support. They described these killings as cold-blooded murders. Subsequently, the CBI confirmed before the Supreme Court on 19 March 2012 that the encounter at Pathirbal in which seven people were killed by the army was a fake encounter.

The Supreme Court asked the army to institute a credible inquiry on its own and to ensure public confidence in the rule of law and dispensation of justice.

Meanwhile, the state government instituted a high-level judicial inquiry led by Justice S.R. Pandian, a retired judge of the Supreme Court. This commission went into the killings at Brakpora and concluded its report in five months. Justice Pandian established the fact that the act of firing on innocent people at Brakpora was unwarranted and unjustified and seven officials of SOG Anantnag, Camp Brakpora, were directly responsible for this massacre.

The unwarranted and unjustified use of force against common people, mostly youth with the support of the AFSPA and other laws, has caused widespread anger among the people.

That is why the killing of Burhan Wani, a Hizbul Mujahideen commander, on 8 July 2016 proved to be the straw that broke the camel's back. That killing led to unprecedented shutdown for more than four months when all businesses, enterprises, transport, educational institutions, that is, all economic, social and political activities in Kashmir came to a standstill. More than 150 persons, mostly teenagers got killed and more than 3,000 boys and girls got eye injuries due to pellets fired by the armed forces. Many of them were even blinded. Undoubtedly anger of the Kashmiris especially the youth reached its height.

India should realize that Kashmir is a political dispute that must be resolved politically. Intelligence agencies should not be allowed to deal with political concerns. Even army generals have said that bullets cannot resolve the crisis and the politicians must play their role. But then, the security agencies had also seen the reason to help the process of a dialogue with the people who mattered on the ground. It was thought that a workable process of dialogue could be initiated with the then Hizbul Mujahideen commander Abdul Majid Dar and the Government of India nominee Kamal Panday, the then home secretary. Pandey met Hizbul Mujahideen commanders Riyaz Rasool, Masood, Farooq Riyaz and Zaffar. The People's Political Front chief and Hizbul Mujahideen nominated mediator Fazal-Haq Qureshi and his two associates, Musadiq Aadil and G.M. Naikoo, were chosen to help in the process of dialogue. This led to an offer of ceasefire made by Dar, which was welcomed by the then prime minister and home minister. The dialogue process with Hizbul Mujahideen was sustained for some time, although there was strain within the Hizbul ranks because of divergent opinions on the whole subject.

Later, Home Secretary Padmanabhan held talks with Dar and his commanders. However, the talks couldn't go beyond the first found. Dar was shot dead by unknown gunmen at Sopore on 23 March 2003. The rest is history of how Hizbul Mujahideen shaped on ground.

While the militancy had got reduced considerably and it appeared largely to be a phenomenon of the past, a political solution of the problem should have been found to reduce the tensions. Alongside promotion of a dialogue process with Pakistan, there should have been a decisive dialogue with the people of Kashmir.

The Atal Bihari Vajpayee government at the Centre and thereafter the Manmohan Singh government tried to organize a process of dialogue with Pakistan, but so far no tangible results could be obtained. Many a luminary took recourse to track-II diplomacy, but nothing materialized into a situation that could be characterized as a turning point in the ties between the two countries.

I also tried to organize a dialogue and my efforts bore some fruit when Mirwaiz Umer Farooq led a delegation of Hurriyat comprising Abdul Gani Bhat, Molvi Abbas Ansari, Agha Hassan and Bilal Lone to meet Prime Minister Manmohan Singh at his residence on 5 September 2005.

The agencies were deadly opposed to a scheduled meeting like this with the Hurriyat leadership. They did not succeed as the PM had made up his mind. Finally, the then national security adviser, M.K. Narayanan, persuaded the principal secretary to the PM, Kutty Nair, to fix a meeting during the day in South Block. But I insisted that the meeting should take place at his residence (7 Race Course Road) and it had to be open-ended. The PM agreed and the two-and-a-half hour meeting finally took place on 5 September 2005.

The prime minister was much impressed with the discussions held with the Hurriyat. Sources close to him had confirmed that Bhat had made good contribution in the discussions and he later had briefed the media properly.

Unfortunately, the process could not proceed further, essentially because the security agencies were not comfortable with it. On the eve of the meeting, the PM had been told by some senior officers in the PMO that the Hurriyat would itself give a written request for a meeting with the PM. But, I had convinced the prime minister that such a thing was not possible and it amounted to showing the Hurriyat leadership in poor light, which would not be in the national interest. I had advised the prime minister that unless respect was shown to the separatist leadership, no meaningful dialogue would be possible. It goes to the credit of Prime Minister Singh he agreed with me and a meeting with the Hurriyat was set up properly.

There is another interesting incident connected with the dialogue. The top bosses of the intelligence sought help of a senior civil servant with Kashmir connection, who flew to Srinagar on the eve of the dialogue, to seek a written request from Mirwaiz Umer Farooq for scheduling a meeting with the prime minister, but such a thing didn't happen.

The Union of India must take serious notice of what former home minister P. Chidambaram had to say. He has openly voiced the need for revoking the draconian AFSPA in public interest. During his time as Union minister, he had also placed before the Cabinet things that were going wrong in Kashmir and the process had to be reversed. Chidambaram had emphasized that the political problem needs to be resolved politically. Instead of appreciating his timely advice, some of his colleagues, including the then defence minister, had misunderstood his advocacy for a policy shift in Kashmir.

He is much more misunderstood by the present dispensation at the Centre. The ruling party members and others don't hesitate to give him lessons on 'nationalism'.

Hazratbal Shrine, Srinagar.

The shrine of Shah-e-Hamdan or Khanqah-e-Moalla
on the bank of the Jhelum River. It is one of the oldest
Muslim shrines in Kashmir.

Famous shrine of Hazrat Sheikh Nooruddin at Charar-e-Sharief.

Martand Sun Temple dedicated to the Hindu Sun God.
Martand is another Sanskrit name for the Sun God.

Jamia Masjid, Srinagar.

The famous and popular Kheer Bhawani temple dedicated to
Goddess Kheer Bhawani.

The shrine of Baba Zain-ud-Din Wali Ashmuqam.

The Ram Temple also known as the Dhar Temple at Safa Kadal, Srinagar.

Watercolour painting: Masood Hussain

A view of Budshah's tomb at Shehr-e-Khaas, the largest and
the most densely populated area of Srinagar.

Shalimar Bagh, Srinagar, is the largest Mughal garden in the Kashmir Valley built by Mughal Emperor Jahangir in 1619 for his wife Empress Nur Jahan.

Nishat Bagh is a terraced Mughal garden built on the eastern side of Dal Lake. It is the second largest Mughal garden in the Kashmir Valley.

32
THE PANDIT EXODUS

I went on a visit to the Rupa Bhawani temples on 9 September 2015 in Safa Kadal (Srinagar), Manigam and Waskura (Ganderbal) and was satisfied that despite the violent strife in the Valley and the disturbance all around, the spirit of togetherness and communal harmony survived.

I met many Muslims and Kashmiri Pandits who helped me have a better understanding of the exodus of the Kashmiri Pandits from the Valley.

It was heartening to know how Muslims maintained and protected the temples and remained steadfast on the age-old tradition of togetherness and harmony. These years of turmoil have been trying, but people have showed resilience and courage of conviction.

I also felt pleasantly surprised how Pandit families of around more than 20,000 people continued to stay back in Kashmir and many of them continued to reside in predominantly Muslim localities.

I had set a difficult task for myself to get to know the real cause of the exodus of Pandits as I had felt enormously dismayed on the exodus as that situation had really impaired the spirit of Kashmiriyat. I started first questioning people who held extreme views on the subject. There were those who held Governor Jagmohan responsible for the exodus. Some people said Pandits left on their own because of the frightening situation in the Valley. Such people naturally emphasized how sponsored armed militancy destroyed peace and ruined communal harmony. A few said Kashmiri Muslims did nothing to prevent the Pandit exodus, although many felt the majority community was itself scared and it was impossible for them to stop the exodus.

Nothing seemed to be under control and there was chaos everywhere in the 1990s.

Numerous sources offered credible evidence to assert that the mass exodus had occurred because Governor Jagmohan, who had been appointed on 19 January 1990 for the second time, thought it prudent to organize the exodus for two reasons: one, that way alone Pandits would feel safe and secure and further sectarian killings would be stopped; second, he would be able to deal with the situation better where stringent laws to curb militancy were already in force and these laws could not be used freely on a mixed population. Many believed this approach was not ethically sound and he had faltered. Some people suspected that he had been sent to Kashmir to teach the Muslims a lesson. In fact, Jagmohan's dispensation was greatly flawed because of his perception on things, particularly, for the fact that he treated the crisis in Kashmir, broadly as a law and order situation created by members of the majority community. It was the design of the dispensation from the time he was appointed in January 1990 till he was removed in May the same year. He had thought that his strong methods would work and he would be able to restore peace within a short time. Even after his removal, a situation of chaos remained on the ground which got deepened by the day and more lethal laws like the AFSPA (enacted on 6 July 1990) had to be imposed.

These acts, particularly the AFSPA gave a lot of power to the armed forces to open fire, set fire to houses, make arrests and take any action against those who might render assistance to militants.

Sanaullah Bhat, editor of the daily *Aftab*, narrated the details about this chaos in his book *Ahad Nama-e-Kashmir*[129] and asserted that laws like the AFSPA had deepened the crises in Kashmir. Bhat also accused Jagmohan of having let loose a reign of terror by organizing a siege of Srinagar.

The governor imposed curfew which did not work on the ground and almost the entire population of Srinagar gathered in mosques and raised slogans for independence. Next day, the curfew was violated in the entire valley and forces opened fire at a number of places. A massacre took place at Gawkadal on 21 January 1990, where fifty-two people were killed (the official figure was thirty-five). Bhat held Jagmohan responsible and blamed Mufti Muhammad Sayeed for his appointment. He thought Mufti Muhammad Sayeed did it to take revenge against Dr Abdullah and criticized Mufti Muhammad Sayeed for his shortsightedness. Bhat also thought it was one of the biggest mistakes Mufti Muhammad Sayeed had committed in his life.

Shabnam Qayoom wrote extensively on why and how the Pandit exodus occurred at the behest of Jagmohan. Qayoom had received a number of letters from leaders of the Pandit community, who described the exodus as a very unfortunate experience and held Jagmohan responsible for it. Many such letters appeared in newspapers like *Alsafa*, *Roshni* and *Srinagar Times*. One such letter was written by K.L. Kaul from Nagrota camp in Jammu. Many Pandits wrote a joint letter to the editor of *Roshni* signed by eleven Pandit leaders who described the exodus as an organized event holding Jagmohan responsible. I had also received such letters from the Pandits.

Many prominent Pandit leaders wrote to me directly and described the exodus of Pandits as a tragic situation and they supported my opposition to Panun Kashmir, who demanded a separate homeland for Kashmiri Pandits.

Intellectuals who wrote to me on Kashmir's critical situation included K.L. Dhar (a direct descendant of Birbal Dhar, a great name in Kashmir history) and B. Kaul (son of J.L. Kaul, an eminent scholar and one-time principal of Sri Pratap College, Srinagar).

S.L. Pandit, a renowned scholar and former head of English Department, Kashmir University in an emotional letter applauded the common heritage of Kashmiris. He hoped the two communities would always remain together. These and many other letters throw light not only on the untold miseries the Pandits suffered but also on the need to promote understanding for a unique togetherness which is the essence of Kashmiriyat.

The categorical assertions on the then governor's role in the Pandit exodus did not dissuade me from seeking certain other opinions on the subject.

I met Omkar Nath Pajnoo at Safa Kadal, Srinagar, where he looks after the birthplace of Rupa Bhavani (1620), a saintly figure and poetess, belonging to a Pandit family, who had built many temples. Pajnoo has lived all these years in this locality considered by many as the vulnerable part of downtown Srinagar. He said the times were difficult, but he continued to go to the nearby temple and thence to the Rupa Bhavani shrine. He added he never felt threatened even though the locality (Khankahi Sokhta–Safa–Kadal) happens to be a predominantly Muslim mohalla. Pajnoo believed like many others the Pandit exodus was an organized episode, but he would not say at whose behest the exodus had occurred.

Next, I met Sanjay Tikoo, a non-migrant Pandit leader. He had first-hand knowledge on what transpired between a delegation of Pandit leaders who met Jagmoham around the last week of January 1990. He said Jagmohan had emphasized he would not be able to provide security to Pandits at different places and, therefore, they would have to move to some designated place where they could be provided security and that the government would select a secure place. All discussion veered around this proposal. As per Tikoo, when the delegation left the Raj Bhawan its members, Hira Lal Chatta and Hriday Nath Jattu felt Jagmohan had refused them security and asked Pandits to leave Kashmir immediately. Tikoo believed Jattu and Chatta exaggerated Jagmohan's attitude. They had contacted every Pandit family and urged them to leave. But Tikoo confirmed, undoubtedly Jagmohan looked nervous and extremely scared and he couldn't inspire confidence among members of the Pandit delegation who met him. The alarm that Jattu and Chatta created further scared the Pandits and exodus occurred. He also said certain families confirmed transport was provided on a particular night but Tikoo had no information as to who provided it. He said the exodus occurred around 20–21 January 1990 and another exodus occurred in the second week of March 1990.

Khem Lata Wakhloo, a former minister and a senior Congress leader, who suffered along with her husband great odds during their 45-day captivity at the hands of militants, narrated the ordeal later in a book. She told me recently that in 1990, a policeman had knocked on their door in Gagribal (Srinagar) one evening saying if they wanted to leave Kashmir. He added that they would be provided transport, but if they wanted to stay back that would be their own choice. She and her family decided not to leave. They had no knowledge on who had sent the policeman to their residence.

Dina Nath Raina described the exodus in his book *Kashmir: Distortions and Reality*[130] as gruesome chronology of selective assassinations within the Pandit community at the hands of militants, which had decidedly created scare among this minuscule minority.

But the fact remains that the exodus was an orchestrated event and somebody in authority had put in a sizable effort in executing it.

There is evidence that the transport was provided in a planned manner to Pandit families in particular localities and the police department was fully involved in organizing the exodus.

There is overwhelming evidence that Jagmohan was squarely responsible for organizing the exodus of Pandits, which some people allegedly described as his effort to organize the safe passage of Pandits to Jammu and elsewhere.

A couple of Jagmohan's associates shared with me the fact that Jagmohan had a great unease in his mind regarding the mistreatment of Pandits in Kashmir and he would often describe, in confidence, the condition in his mind as an inspiration from Guru Teg Bahadur, whom he held in highest esteem.

Jagmohan's article 'Kashmir in Sikh History' published in the *Hindustan Times* on 24 December 1995 creates a clear impression that he was following the spirit of Guru Teg Bahadur's concern for Kashmir.

There is no doubt that Jagmohan had a sectarian angle on Kashmir and, unfortunately, this condition remained on his mind all the time. In his article 'Breaking Kashmir Impasse', *Times of India* dated 6 August 1992, Praful Bidwai said, 'The bulk of Kashmiris have been seriously alienated from India after the brutal turning point of January, 1990. The policy of encouraging the Pandits to leave the Valley widely attributed to Mr Jagmohan and fundamentalist attacks upon them embittered inter-community relations and led to painful migration.'

Among a host of letters from Kashmiri Pandit leaders who had become refugees in Jammu, a comprehensive letter written by K.L. Kaul from Nagrota camp appeared in newspapers in Srinagar in which he had held the communal elements, particularly Jagmohan, responsible for the Pandit exodus, which he had also described as a very unfortunate event in the history of Kashmir.

A senior Kashmir police officer Israr Khan, who retired very recently, has given clinching evidence of J&K Police Department having been pressed into service by the Raj Bhawan to organize the Pandit exodus in the early months of 1990. *Kashmir Life*, published from Srinagar, in its issue of 22 to 28 October 2017 carried a comprehensive interview with Israr Khan who said on record that in April 1990 when he was sub-divisional police officer (SDPO) at Kothibagh Police Station, Srinagar (the hub of police activity those days), he was summoned to the Raj Bhawan where Jagmohan's principal secretary and SSP Srinagar Allah Baksh asked Khan to ensure the smooth transit of buses carrying the Pandits to Jammu and render all assistance to them. Jagmohan himself directed him, '*Loading shoding mein madad karna aur koi attack shatak nahi hone deyna* (Help the people move their belongings and see that they are not attacked).'

33

KASHMIR–THE WAY FORWARD

After almost thirty years of armed militancy, which caused an unprecedented turmoil of death and destruction in Kashmir, the people had reasonably thought that the cult of seeking a solution to political problems through violence would yield space for arguments exchanged democratically. Alas! That hope did not sustain as a new kind of strife has surfaced. The ongoing unrest in Kashmir, caused by the killing of Hizbul Mujahideen commander Burhan Wani and its after-effects, have been discussed in a previous chapter.

The unrest in Kashmir after his killing has taken an entirely different proportion—wider in implication and more popular in essence.

Now, Kashmir is in a mode of revolt. The deep simmering unrest suggests an acceptable political settlement of the Kashmir issue has to be found. As M.K. Narayanan,[131] security adviser to former Prime Minister Manmohan Singh, said recently, 'It is necessary to recognize that in marked contrast to earlier periods of trouble in Kashmir, the present movement is almost entirely homegrown.'

The unrest is led by angry youth, the majority of them teenagers, and nothing is left in the hands of elder politicians.

Though the international community agrees that the basic party to the dispute happens to be the people of Kashmir, it would be pragmatic to see an agreement between India and Pakistan that will be acceptable to Kashmiris. This is what an average Kashmiri would also like to think.

Practically, it means to extricate Kashmiris from the tormenting dispute and move forward to what can be described as an 'achievable goal'.

At this critical moment in Kashmir's history, it is necessary to go into the genesis of why Kashmir could not get into a settled situation for a long time since 1947.

One must learn in the historical perspective as to how and why Kashmir acceded to India. The legality of Kashmir's accession to the Union of India through the deed of accession signed by Maharaja Hari Singh is only an aspect of the relationship that has been in dispute from the beginning. Many Kashmiris blamed their leader the Sheikh for the relationship with India, which has not worked well, primarily because India did not honour its commitments to the people of Kashmir.

The Sheikh and his colleagues decided to convert the Muslim Conference into the Jammu & Kashmir National Conference in 1938, as a common platform for all sections of society in the state. He remained keenly involved with the people of Jammu & Kashmir, whose emancipation he had made his first concern. On the eve of the conversion of the Muslim Conference into the National Conference, there were voices from Jammu and elsewhere also asking for an end to the autocratic rule of the maharaja and its replacement by the establishment of a responsible government in the state.

The Sheikh had invited the people of the state to the concept of a 'New Kashmir' and a blueprint thereof had been carefully drafted with the help of learned persons, and this concept drew good attention from the Indian leadership, mainly represented by the Indian National Congress. While the Congress leadership established a close relationship with the Sheikh, and leaders such as Mahatma Gandhi, Jawaharlal Nehru and Maulana Abul Kalam Azad got attracted to his movement for the establishment of a responsible form of government in the state, the Muslim League and its accredited leader, Mohammad Ali Jinnah, had taken no serious notice of the Sheikh. It had also ignored another political movement in India, the All India States Peoples' Conference, which had close ties with the Congress.

As the Muslim League's influence swayed the subcontinent and

Jinnah assumed the status of the sole leader of Muslims in India, the Sheikh became a popular leader in Jammu & Kashmir. Still, he had realized the necessity of developing some understanding with Jinnah. He held a meeting with him in Delhi sometime around 1940 when Bakshi Ghulam Mohammad also accompanied him. But the Sheikh did not buy the two-nation theory, although Jinnah shared his personal experience to convince him. The Sheikh had explained that Jammu & Kashmir had a unique position on the map of India and various communities wanted to have a common political cause and the National Conference had been accepted as a common platform representing the aspirations of the people of the state.

Jinnah visited Kashmir for the second time on 10 May 1944 and the Sheikh offered due courtesies, but they did not unite. The Sheikh organized a large public meeting in honour of Jinnah at Pratap Park, Srinagar. Unmindful of the repercussions, Jinnah appealed to Muslims to join the Muslim Conference, an affiliate of the Muslim League, but that appeal didn't work on the ground. It was known to all that the Muslim Conference had a limited existence in Kashmir. The Sheikh retained his popularity with the masses.

In his book *Indira Gandhi, the 'Emergency', and Indian Democracy*,[132] economist P.N. Dhar (who was in Kashmir at that time) describes the situation vividly, 'The summer of 1944 was full of political excitement in Kashmir. It turned out to be one of those times when the fate of a country is decided. Jinnah arrived in June and was given a welcome reception by Sheikh Mohammad Abdullah and the National Conference. He was received as a distinguished visitor and was not expected to interfere in the political affairs of the state. But, unlike the neutral posture of his previous visit, this time Jinnah spent his entire six weeks mobilizing the support of Kashmir Muslims in favour of the dormant Muslim Conference. His success elsewhere in the country had made Jinnah grossly underestimate the Sheikh's standing among Kashmiri Muslims. The Sheikh accepted Jinnah's challenge and launched a counteroffensive against him. He roused Kashmiris to a pitch that compelled Jinnah to abandon his visit. Jinnah left Kashmir as a disappointed man.'

After Jinnah's departure, the National Conference concentrated its attention on preparing the manifesto for a 'New Kashmir'. It became a revolutionary document and answered the needs of the common people of not only in Jammu & Kashmir, but also for the entire country.

The manifesto reflected shades of communism. The Sheikh explained that even though the National Conference was influenced by Russian and French revolutions, it accommodated salient ideas of these movements without adopting any particular ideology. Many people in the Muslim League as well as the Congress criticized the National Conference without bothering to study the situation closely.

The National Conference held its annual session on 3 August 1945 in Sopore, where the party adopted its historic and revolutionary manifesto of 'New Kashmir' in the presence of Nehru and other leaders.

The National Conference also adopted a resolution on the people's right to self-determination and gave a clear idea of liberating the peasantry and labour classes from the tyrannies of exploitative autocratic rule.

On 9 May 1946, the Sheikh launched the 'Quit Kashmir Movement' for the establishment of a responsible and popular form of government in the state.

Meanwhile, bigger developments were taking shape at the national and international levels. Winston Churchill's rule in Britain came to an end and the Labour Party came to power with Clement Attlee as the prime minister. Soon, the British government sent a Cabinet mission to India with Lord Frederick Pethick-Lawrence as its chairman and Stafford Cripps and A.V. Alexander as its members. It was being discussed as to which of the dominions the states' rulers would join when India became free.

It was said that the rulers would decide which way to go. Nehru and the Congress party opposed that plan and stressed that the people should decide their future. Jinnah and the Muslim League supported the idea of the rulers being allowed to decide. Many learned observers thought that Jinnah had set his eyes on princely states such as Hyderabad and Junagadh and had not appreciated, in full measure, the basis on which the British had decided to partition India. The Sheikh went to Delhi to meet Gandhi and said that sovereignty vested with the people, who alone should decide their future. Gandhi assured him that while he was correct, he should discuss with other leaders to come to a conclusion.

Meanwhile, the Cabinet mission arrived in Srinagar on 19 April 1946 and the Sheikh sent a telegram to the mission from Lahore and explained to it the background of Jammu & Kashmir's subjugation through the Treaty of Amritsar and then made a strong plea that after independence, the people of the state should decide their future.

Around this time, Bakshi Ghulam Mohammad and G.M. Sadiq were already in Lahore, explaining before the political leadership the concept of the Quit Kashmir Movement and the future of Kashmir.

Congress party president Acharya Kriplani was against the Quit Kashmir Movement and tried to influence Patel and Gandhi, but Nehru remained strong and steadfast, and Gandhi lent support to Nehru.

It was so tragic that Jinnah and the Muslim League didn't take notice of the cruelties and injustice that the people of Kashmir had suffered under the Dorgra autocratic rule and instead Jinnah supported the maharaja and Prime Minister Ram Chandra Kak's high-handedness and declared that the Quit Kashmir Movement was run by 'hooligans' under the influence of external forces. However, Pakistani media supported the Quit Kashmir Movement.

Popular Urdu daily *Inquilab*, published from Lahore, not only supported the movement, but also denounced the Muslim League as a backward organization. Other newspapers such as *Zamindar* supported the movement, representing the aspirations of the people of Kashmir. Many intellectuals and widely respected personalities such as Agha Shorish Kashmiri, Faiz Ahmad Faiz and Hafeez Jalandari also gave full support to the movement.

In his book *Kashmir*,[133] Sofi Mohiuddin speaks of prominent Kashmiri leader Amanullah Khan lamenting the role of the Muslim League and said that instead of supporting the Sheikh for spearheading the Quit Kashmir Movement, it declared the sponsors of the movement as a group of hooligans. The Congress leadership, however, gave full support to the Sheikh.

While the Sheikh was lodged at Bhaderwah jail along with some of his colleagues, reports reached them that Gandhi and Kriplani had visited Kashmir. Gandhi's visit created a wave of affection and understanding.

Gandhi refused to accept any courtesies offered by the maharaja and stayed at Seth Kishori Lal's house in Baghat Barzulla, Srinagar.

However, Gandhi accepted the request to go to the palace and meet the maharaja for a while, but he expressed his unhappiness on the treatment of the people by the maharaja. There is a famous story that when the maharani offered a glass of milk to Gandhi, he refused to take it, saying he would not take the milk from the raja whose praja is not happy with him. A large number of people met Gandhi and he publicly described the Treaty of Amritsar as a 'commercial document'.

He went around Srinagar and going through the narrow lanes of the city, he reached the house of the Sheikh and sat with Begum Akbar Jahan and other members of the family and sympathized with them.

When the independence of India was announced and Pakistan became a reality, an unfortunate and tragic atmosphere of bloodshed gripped some areas of the subcontinent, especially the Punjab. The maharaja's administration was already nervous. It removed Ram Chandra Kak and appointed the maharaja's uncle, General Janak Singh, as the prime minister of Kashmir.

The maharaja, who was already under pressure, shifted the Sheikh to Badami Bagh, Srinagar, before releasing him on 27 September 1947.

On 3 October 1947, a grand public meeting was held at Hazuri Bagh, Srinagar, where senior freedom fighter Saduddin Shawl presented a welcome address to the Sheikh on behalf of the people. The Sheikh told the gathering that he did not know why he was arrested and then released. He said when he went to jail, the country was one and now it was divided into two dominions and he would suggest a course for the future that suited the aspirations of the people of the state.

He made it clear that though Nehru was his friend and he respected Gandhi enormously, the question of accession would be decided after careful consideration and he and his party would adopt the course that protected the people's rights. However, he made it clear that he and his party would never accept the two-nation theory, which had already brought disaster to the subcontinent.

While things were moving fast, the Sheikh wanted to open a dialogue with Pakistan to understand on what terms Kashmir could accede to it and whether Pakistan would concede internal autonomy to Kashmir. Bakshi Ghulam Mohammad, G.M. Sadiq and Chaudhary Mohmmad Shafi were already in Pakistan to approach the prime minister of Pakistan (and, if possible, Jinnah), and discuss the crucial matter with them. These leaders had struggled to sort out matters with Prime Minister Liaquat Ali Khan.

The most credible evidence of how Pakistan, particularly, Liaquat Ali Khan, treated the emissaries of the Sheikh is recorded by no less a person than Sirdar Shaukat Hayat Khan, who was one of the closest colleagues of Jinnah, in his book *The Nation that Lost Its Soul*.[134] He says, 'Sheikh Abdullah sent Bakshi Ghulam Mohammad to meet Liaquat Ali Khan in Lahore. Unfortunately, Bakshi's visit was mishandled. He sat cooling his heels in Lahore for several days before Liaquat condescended to meet him. This made a poor impression on Bakshi. Sheikh Abdullah went to Delhi to meet Pandit Nehru, who with the Congress welcomed him in sharp contrast to the treatment Bakshi got in Lahore.'

In the second week of October 1947, G.M. Sadiq, the Sheikh's emissary, had gone again to Lahore to assess the possibility of whether Pakistan would accommodate Kashmir's aspirations regarding internal autonomy in case the state acceded to Pakistan. He met the same fate as Bakshi Ghulam Mohammad and returned to Kashmir barely a day before the state was attacked by raiders on 22 October 1947.

In the meantime, the Sheikh left for Delhi on 24 October to have discussions with the Congress leadership. He had, however, kept Pakistan informed that he would subsequently visit it for discussions.

Meanwhile, news trickled in that raiders had attacked Kashmir on 22 October and they had already reached Muzaffarabad.

At this critical juncture, the Sheikh gave a clarion call to cadres of the National Conference to ensure perfect communal harmony in Srinagar and elsewhere and told them to remain vigilant.

He had also told prominent leaders of the National Conference that they should organize a resistance movement against the reported attack by raiders.

The Standstill Agreement offered by the maharaja was accepted by Pakistan, but not India. Under the agreement, Pakistan unfurled its flag at the post office of Srinagar.

Jammu & Kashmir Prime Minister Janak Singh got the flag down. The Pakistani authorities reacted by stopping supplies of salt and other necessities to Kashmir. The state witnessed a great crisis as all supplies came to the Valley through the road that passed via Pakistan.

While Kashmir faced an extreme shortage of essentials and there was uncertainty around that time, the raiders having attacked Kashmir on 22 October 1947 were reportedly proceeding forward from Muzaffarabad. The maharaja's army was in disarray and the state's administration had crumbled down completely.

On 25 October, Maharaja Hari Singh left for Jammu with the maharani and others along with properties that could be carried with a long convoy of vehicles.

While Jammu was witnessing a large-scale communal frenzy in which the Muslims suffered enormously, the maharaja wrote to the Indian government for military support against the Deed of Accession carried by V.P. Menon with him to Delhi on 26 October.

The maharaja had addressed the letter to Lord Mountbatten and explained his difficulty and wanted military support to fight the raiders. He explained he wanted to maintain his independence and have good relations with both dominions, but because India did not sign the Standstill Agreement while Pakistan had done it, a difficulty arose for him. He wrote further how circumstances compelled him to send the request for military help along with a letter of accession limited to three subjects—defence, foreign affairs and communications—for approval by the Indian government.

Mountbatten decided to accept the request for accession, subject to the condition that when normalcy prevailed, the Deed of Accession would be subjected to a plebiscite. The maharaja was informed of this approval on 27 October and the Indian army was rushed to the state the same day. The army arrived at Srinagar airport on 27 October and immediately got into action against the raiders at Shalteng near Srinagar.

There is no doubt that the Pakistan-sponsored raid on Kashmir altered the very political situation in which the Sheikh could have visited Pakistan to have parleys on the question of Kashmir's accession to Pakistan. The Sheikh had written a letter to Pakistani Prime Minister Liaquat Ali Khan on this line of thinking.

There is another story of authentic evidence to show that while Jinnah may not have been kept informed on the attack on Kashmir by the raiders, Liaqat Ali Khan was fully associated with the developments, and knowledgeable sources have since confirmed the fact that the raid had been organized with his approval. No less a person than K.H. Khurshid, Jinnah's trusted aide and private secretary for a long time before he became the president of Pakistan-held Kashmir, gives us an exclusive peep into the circumstances in which the raid on Kashmir had been organized.

In an interview to a Lahore-based Urdu magazine *Atish Fishaan*[135] Khurshid said, 'In the rise and fall of nations, certain personalities grow to a stature where the whole movement for freedom gets associated with them. It can be said without any hesitation that the entire freedom movement in Kashmir had got associated with the person of Sheikh Mohammad Abdullah. It is from the very beginning that Sheikh Abdullah considered the struggle in Jammu & Kashmir away from the Congress party and the Muslim League. When he associated himself with the socialistic ideas of the Congress, he was not clear as to what was going to happen to India in future. But he was clear on one thing that while the Congress was fighting for independence and the Muslim League was fighting for the creation of Pakistan, Kashmir was fighting a distinctly different movement. It was fighting for freedom from the autocratic rule of the maharaja. Since he thought that if India was granted freedom, the maharaja would continue to rule over Kashmir and, therefore, he started the famous 'Quit Kashmir Movement' in 1946. When the Cabinet mission visited India, it became clear that Sheikh Abdullah was right in fighting his own battle around that time as in my opinion, he gave his deep thought to the question of future of Kashmir. So, while he was in jail, India was divided into two dominions. After his release, he addressed a public meeting in Srinagar on 3 October 1947. I was then in Srinagar and attended that public meeting and I remember some sentences of his speech.'

As per Khurshid, the Sheikh had, among other things, said, 'When

I went to jail, India was one country, and when I came out of the jail, India has got divided into two dominions. Now, we have to think about our future differently. I will take a course of action that suits the future of Kashmiris and they feel contented and lead a life of dignity consistent with their aspirations. Pakistan is our neighbour, our rivers flow to that side; our roads connect us to that country; so many of our fellow Kashmiris have received education there; we can't brush these facts aside. So, I will visit Delhi and thereafter, I will go to Karachi. We shall have to assess on what terms we can consider to accede to Pakistan.'

In this connection, Khurshid said, 'I feel convinced that if Kashmir had not been raided on 22 October 1947, the history of Kashmir would be different. I know it personally that Qaid-e-Azam had said that Pakistan would not be party to any disruption in Kashmir.'

Khurshid goes on to add, 'On my return to Pakistan, I went straight to Liaquat Ali Khan and asked him that Qaid-e-Azam was sure that Pakistan would not be a party of any disruption in Kashmir, so why Kashmir was attacked and I insisted for an answer, but Liaquat Ali Khan never spoke a word. I felt satisfied that the raid in Kashmir had been organized without any knowledge to the Qaid-e-Azam. I came to know later that Khan Abdul Qayoom Khan of north-west province was instrumental in organizing the raid in Kashmir.'

In her book *Kashmir of Sheikh Mohammad Abdullah*,[136] C. Bilquees Taseer offers proof of the fact that the raid had been organized with the approval of Liaquat Ali Khan, who had presided a meeting in this connection attended by prominent personalities like Nawab Mamdot, Ghulam Mohammad (finance minister), Choudhray Mohammad Ali, Inspector General Qurban Ali, Mushtaq Ahmad Gurmani, Major General Iskander Mirza (later president of Pakistan), Abdul Qayoom Khan (president of Azad Kashmir), Sirdar Shaukat Hayyat Khan, Abdul Rahim ICS, Major General Akbar Khan, Brigadier Sher Khan, Khursheed Anwar, Colonel Shahid Hamid, Air Commodore Janjua and General Mohammad Zaman Kiyani of the Azad Hind Fauj and many other civil servants.

Mian Amiruddin and Mohammad Din Taseer, two of the most prominent public figures of Pakistan, had visited Kashmir during those turbulent times on behalf of the Pakistan authorities to resolve matters regarding Kashmir's future. What happened later is best described by Mian Amiruddin in his book *Yaad-e-Ayyam.*[137]

Amiruddin confirms the fact that the raid organized by Pakistan had altered the situation of the possibility of Kashmir's accession to Pakistan. He says in the book, 'It was decided that Sheikh Mohammad Abdullah would visit Pakistan on 25 October 1947 for discussions on the future of Kashmir, but three senior leaders—Liaquat Ali Khan, Sir Choudhary Zaffarullah and Choudhary Mohammad Ali organized the raid on Kashmir under Col. Khursheed Anwar of the Muslim National Guard, without consulting the Qaid-e-Azam.'

It will be interesting to dwell a little more on other opinions on the consequences of the raid on Kashmir from Pakistan.

Kuldip Nayar, in his book *Beyond the Lines—An Autobiography*[138] throws considerable light not only on the adverse consequences of the raid on Kashmir from Pakistan but also on Sardar Patel's consistent view that Kashmir should be part of Pakistan. Nayar writes, 'My impression is that had Pakistan been patient it would have got Kashmir automatically. India could not have conquered it, nor could a Hindu Maharaja have ignored the composition of the population, which was predominantly Muslim. Instead, an impatient Pakistan sent tribesmen along with regular troops to Kashmir within days of Independence.'

Nayar goes on to say, 'While it is true that Nehru was keen on Kashmir's accession to India, Patel was opposed to it. Even when New Delhi received the maharaja's request to accede to India, Patel had said, "We should not get mixed up with Kashmir, we already have too much on our plate".'

Patel remained consistent on his perception that while Pakistan shouldn't talk of Hyderabad, Kashmir should go to Pakistan.

Chaudhri Mohammad Ali (later prime minister of Pakistan) who happened to be financial adviser, War and Supply in the government of India in 1946 had later joined as a member to the steering committee, as representative of Pakistan. This committee was responsible to the Partition Council, headed by Mountbatten, for the immense tasks involved in Partition. From the Indian side, H.M. Patel was a member of the committee.

Chaudhri Mohammad Ali gives us an interesting detail on Patel's perception on Kashmir in his book *The Emergence of Pakistan*.[139] Hewrites, 'While attending a meeting of the Partition Council, Sardar Patel, although a bitter enemy of Pakistan was a greater realist than Nehru. In one of the discussions between the two Prime Ministers at which H.M. Patel and I were also present, Liaquat Ali Khan dwelt at length on the inconsistency of the Indian stand with regard to Junagadh and Kashmir. If Junagadh, despite its Muslim ruler's accession to Pakistan, belonged to India because of its Hindu majority, how could Kashmir, with its Muslim majority, be a part of India simply by virtue of its Hindu ruler having signed a conditional instrument of accession to India? If the instrument of accession signed by the Muslim ruler of Junagadh was of no validity, the instrument of accession signed by the Hindu ruler of Kashmir was also invalid. If the will of the people was to prevail in Junagadh, it must prevail in Kashmir as well. India could not claim both Junagadh and Kashmir.'

Chaudhri Mohammad Ali writes, 'When Liaquat Ali Khan made these incontrovertible points, Patel could not contain himself and burst out, "Why do you compare Junagadh with Kashmir? Talk of Hyderabad and Kashmir and we could reach an agreement".'

Chaudhri comments further, 'Patel's view at this time and even later was that India's effort to retain Muslim majority areas against the will of the people was a source not of strength but of weakness of India. He felt that if India and Pakistan agree to let Kashmir go to Pakistan and Hyderabad to India, the problems of Kashmir and Hyderabad could be solved peacefully and to the mutual advantage of India and Pakistan.'

Sirdar Shaukat Hayat Khan in his book, *The Nation That Lost Its Soul* relates a very interesting story on how Patel consistently followed his line of thinking on Kashmir. After the Redcliff Award, many problems were to be sorted out and Hayat Khan was actively involved in various activities on behalf of Pakistan.

He says, 'Later, during the attack on Kashmir, Mountbatten came to Lahore. At a dinner attended by Liaquat Ali Khan, Governor Mudie and the four Ministers of West Punjab, Lord Mountbatten conveyed the message from Patel, the strongman of India, asking Liaquat Ali to abide by the rules over the future of Indian states previously agreed upon between the Congress and the Muslim League that those states whose subjects made up of a majority of a community and the state was contiguous and adjoining a Dominion would accede to the adjoining country.'

Hayat Khan explains further, 'Patel had said that Pakistan could take Kashmir and let go Hyderabad Deccan which had a majority Hindu population and was nowhere near Pakistan by sea or land.'

Hayat Khan goes on to say, 'After delivering this message, Lord Mountbatten went to sleep in the Lahore Government House. I being overall in-charge of the Kashmir operations went to Liaquat Ali Khan. I suggested to him that as the Indian army had entered Kashmir in force and we would be unable to annex Kashmir with tribal mujahids or even with our inadequate armed forces, we should make haste to accept Patel's proposal.'

Hayat Khan says further, 'Nawabzada (Liaquat Ali Khan) turned round to me and said, "Sirdar Saheb, have I gone mad to give up Hyderabad which is much larger than the Punjab for the sake of the rocks of Kashmir?" I was stunned by the Prime Minister's reaction and ignorance of our geography and his lack of wisdom. I thought he was living in a fool's paradise and did not understand the importance of Kashmir to Pakistan while hoping to get Hyderabad, which at best, was only quixotic wishful thinking. It was not connected with Pakistan anywhere. As a protest, I resigned from the position I was holding in Kashmir Operations.'

Chaudhri Mohammad Ali and Sirdar Shaukat Hayat Khan are not the only people who felt sorry on Liaquat Ali Khan's attitude to Patel's pragmatic approach to the Kashmir question.

A.G. Noorani, an accredited scholar having considerable knowledge on the Kashmir issue, has quoted the then president of Pakistan lamenting Liaquat Ali Khan's attitude to Patel's proposals. In his article, 'A Tale of Two States'[140] Noorani tells us, 'A quarter century later, on 27 November 1972, the President of Pakistan Zulfikar Ali Bhutto, told a tribal Jirga at Landikotal that India's first Home Minister and Minister for the States, Sardar Patel had at one stage, offered Kashmir to Pakistan in exchange for Junagadh and Hyderabad. But, he added, Pakistan 'unfortunately' didn't accept this offer with the result that it not only lost all the three native states but East Pakistan as well.'

On the other side of the spectrum of hot debates on Kashmir both in India and Pakistan, Kashmir was experiencing a kind of commotion in the wake of the raid.

In the tormenting situation of the raid, both Muslims and Kashmiri Pandits were involved in the 'people's resistance movement' with lathis and wooden guns. This was only to galvanize the people against what was described widely as 'attack on Kashmir's sovereignty'.

In this connection, Noorani, doesn't seem to be correct in his assessment that the Quit Kashmir Movement, was ill-timed and said, 'Neither the Muslim League nor the Congress was impressed by Abdullah's impetuous Quit Kashmir Movement in 1946.'

K.H. Khurshid's analysis shows that not only was the Quit Kashmir Movement timely, but the Sheikh fought it effectively towards the right conclusion.

Once a semblance of administration got organized in Srinagar, the Sheikh decided to invite Nehru to Kashmir to repeat his pledge to the people of Kashmir on the question of holding a plebiscite in the state to decide the question of accession of the state finally.

Nehru responded positively. Accompanied by Rafi Ahmad Kidwai and Indira Gandhi, he paid a visit to Kashmir on 13 November 1947. He first went straight to Baramulla and on return addressed a huge meeting of historic importance at the square around Amira Kadal, which came to be known as Lal Chowk after that crucial meeting. Nehru assured the people that the accession of the state would be subjected to a plebiscite and even if the verdict would be against India, it will be accepted.

But, as the days passed, the Sheikh got disturbed by the agitation of the Praja Parishad. Hindu organizations such as the Hindu Mahasabha, the Jana Sangh, the RSS and other similar groups vociferously declared opposition to Article 370 under which autonomy to the state was guaranteed.

The Sheikh was particularly perturbed by the agitation of the Praja Parishad in Jammu which, according to him, was supported and financed by the maharaja. He wrote to Nehru about this and the latter took up the matter with Patel. Patel was never happy with the Sheikh and his politics and he supported the Praja Parishad. This atmosphere meant a great discouragement to the Sheikh, who had lent his moral support to the accession only because he thought the only Muslim majority state in India would remain secure with secular India. As events later unfolded, the so-called nationalists and patriots, represented by the communal organizations, continued to oppose the Sheikh and his policies. It was a situation that he never expected.

By 1952, he became alienated with the Union of India and thought Nehru had become weak on his commitment to the people of Kashmir, who had rejected the two-nation theory and opted for secular India. The Sheikh lamented that Nehru showed signs of succumbing to the pressure of communal forces, who pretended to be nationalists and patriots.

He had expected Nehru would continue to treat Kashmir as Gandhi's beacon of light for a secular India. I feel that while Nehru retained his interest in Kashmir, his commitment for safeguarding its special status got somewhat impaired because die-hard Hindu organizations created quite a lot of difficulty for him, and his vision of building a strong, modern, democratic and truly secular country was not shared by communal outfits.

There was another factor responsible for Nehru showing signs of fatigue on his commitment to Kashmir's autonomy and it was that the home ministry was not really working in tandem with him. The onslaught of the Praja Parishad in Jammu was so intense that the Jana Sangh not only jumped on the bandwagon, but also started a vigorous campaign of vilification against the Sheikh and presented him as someone antagonistic to the nation. Vociferous leaders of the Jana Sangh such as Balraj Madhok regularly maligned the Sheikh and criticized Nehru for supporting him. The Hindu Mahasabha and its leader Shyama Prasad Mukherjee also maligned the Sheikh and criticized Nehru and his policy towards Kashmir. While Patel was known as a person not sympathetic to the Sheikh, his sympathy with the maharaja and the Praja Parishad was fairly known.

One reason why the Praja Parishad, the Jana Sangh, the Hindu Mahasabha and the RSS had started a vigorous campaign against the Sheikh was a thoroughly parochial and sectarian idea that revolutionary reforms envisaged in the 'New Kashmir' manifesto such as abolition of landed estates, the institution of the board for cancellation of debts, etc., were meant to benefit only Muslims. Undoubtedly, the land reforms were revolutionary and other pro-people measures had no parallel in the subcontinent, but it was not true that these were meant for Muslims alone. These Hindu organizations never cared to accept the reforms had benefited the entire labour and peasantry (largely Hindus) in Jammu province also.

Gandhi was a bridge of understanding between Nehru and Patel. On his assassination, Nehru lost a big support. He felt lonely and gradually lost his vigour to combat communal forces inside and outside Parliament. Patel did not support him on many occasions. Azad's support wasn't something powerful to help Nehru fight his enemies. Surprisingly, Nehru had imagined the Sheikh would gradually appreciate his difficulties.

While Nehru's speech in Parliament on the Delhi Agreement (on 24 July 1952) constituted a weak defence of the agreement and the agreement was not put on records, the Sheikh presented the same agreement to the Jammu & Kashmir Constituent Assembly and spoke on it on 11 August 1952 as his lifetime achievement.

Alas! The builder of modern India, the visionary who looked to India's future as a federal, secular, progressive and vibrant democracy, got weakened in his support to the Sheikh on the question of autonomy envisaged in the Delhi Agreement.

The Sheikh had earlier lamented the fact that leaders such as Sardar Patel and Rajendra Prasad had not supported Nehru on the question of special status to Jammu & Kashmir. He took particular notice of Patel's antagonistic stand on many issues he raised with Nehru. He records in his autobiography *Aatish-e-Chinar* that once a senior officer of the Intelligence Bureau (IB), B.N. Mullik, was sent to Srinagar in the middle of 1949 to report the factual situation in Kashmir. Mullik met, Mohyuddin Kara, Bakshi Ghulam Mohammad, G.M. Sadiq, D.P. Dhar, Maulana Masoodi and others. He sent a report to his office in Delhi and Nehru felt happy and sent copies of the report to all embassies. When Patel came to know of it, he summoned Mullik and admonished him for sending the report directly to Nehru. Mullik got nervous and immediately told Patel that he had only sent the report to the senior officer of the IB.

In his book *Kashmir-My Years with Nehru*,[141] Mullik notes, 'Sardar spoke against Sheikh Mohammad Abdullah and said he differed with Nehru on his assessment of him and considered the Sheikh as dangerous and staunchly anti-Hindu. Mullik got the hint and his later reports to Delhi got accordingly changed. The Sardar made Mullik chief of the Intelligence Service superseding thirty officers and the rest is history.'

The Sheikh says further, 'What colour Mullik gave to the reporting about him (the Sheikh) and his activities later, during that fateful time, was, essentially, what was expected of him by the Home Ministry.'

But it was clear that the Sheikh would not accept any dilution of autonomy granted to the state. When he found things drifting and relation with the Union getting awry, he publicly showed his disgust.

The Sheikh's dismissal and arrest on 9 August 1953, apart from causing a revolt in the state, caused a deep wound in the psyche of Kashmiris. It meant while Kashmir remained steadfast with secular India, the Union didn't!

Writing in his book *Maverick Unchanged, Unrepentant*,[142] prominent jurist Ram Jethmalani expresses a strong feeling that the institution of the Constituent Assembly for Jammu & Kashmir had settled the political issue once and for all saying, 'Commentators and sympathizers of the Kashmir problem would do well to remember that the Constitution of India was not foisted upon the state and that it applies only in those parts that have been voluntarily accepted by the people of Jammu & Kashmir. The state is primarily governed by its own Constitution, unlike any other state in India, Kashmir has voluntarily become part of a free progressive, secular republic. That is Azadi.'

While Jethmalani expresses these thoughts in his book, he feels that jingoistic elements have spoiled the constitutional relationship with Kashmir. I know it at personal level that Jethmalani has his own set of grievances with Pakistan, but he has continued to be of the view that neighbourhood can't be changed and India has to find ways to have cordial relations with Pakistan.

Jethmalani further writes, 'The Kashmir problem is not insurmountable and could have been solved long ago, but the political will and adroitness to do so has been lacking. If the president of Pakistan is ready for negotiation, the prime minister of India has to be willing. If parties like the BJP advocate immediate cessation of diplomatic relations, the people of India should and will dismiss it as a political bankruptcy and electoral insanity.'

Perhaps, Jethmalani wrote these lines after General Pervez Musharraf's famous formula for peace between the two countries had not found favour with the Atal Bihari Vajpayee government.

On the sidelines of a seminar on Kashmir initiated by former Pakistan foreign minister Khurshid Mahmud Kasuri on 11 April 2017, Jethmalani told me in presence of Kasuri, Mani Shankar Aiyar and O.P. Shah that soon after Musharraf championed his formula for peace and lasting friendship between India and Pakistan, Jethmalani had told Musharraf that he agreed with him and he would not change even a comma of the formula. On this occasion, Jethmalani lamented that when he had raised the issue with the then Prime Minister Atal Behari Vajpayee and shared his mind with him, Vajpayee hadn't revealed his mind. Jethmalani presumes that while Vajpayee was clear in his mind, his real difficulty was created by his party.

The Way Forward

I have lived through the years of turmoil in Kashmir, always considering myself to be part of the life of Kashmiris. I had got elected to the Lok Sabha in a by-election in June 1983 and since then I invested time to understand the life and times of Kashmiris.

Over a period of time, I became conscious that I should have some credible knowledge of Kashmir's history and the contours of the current turmoil and how to move forward. I did invest time to understand the situation.

I have expressed my thoughts on various aspects of Kashmir's history, and now I am in a position to imagine how best we could move forward.

As is known to the people of the subcontinent as also to the world at large, India and Pakistan have never come to an agreement on Kashmir. It has also remained a live situation as an item on the agenda of the

United Nations. Strangely enough, all the three basic stakeholders to the dispute—India, Pakistan and the people of Kashmir—have, by now, become absolutely disillusioned with the UN for a different set of reasons.

In my opinion, it is futile to look to the UN for any workable help for the resolution of the dispute as the powers holding the authority of veto have all along responded to the situations keeping their own strategic interests in view. It is why the whole world, seemingly in one voice, offers one simple advice, 'Let India and Pakistan sort out the dispute bilaterally.'

My primary concern has been to suggest a way out for the Union of India which, as per my perception, has gone wrong by impairing the constitutional relationship between Kashmir and the Union of India established on the basis of the Instrument of Accession, the institution of the Jammu & Kashmir Constituent Assembly and the Delhi Agreement of 1952.

Keeping the present scenario in view, I have conceptualized an outline on what is the way forward to reach a settlement on this dispute. My quest for a possible solution has led me to suggest the following.

1. In my opinion, the primary responsibility goes to the Government of India, which must take steps to help the people of Kashmir to move out of the tormenting cycle of violence. The initial steps could be to show a gesture of compassion for creating a situation of relief in the minds of Kashmiris, who have suffered immense miseries from the very day the central government started dragging its feet from its commitments to willingly accept the decisions of the Jammu & Kashmir Constituent Assembly and the provisions of autonomy guaranteed under the Delhi Agreement of 1952.

Apart from the commitments of the Indian government at various points of time, the clear commitment made by the then prime minister of India, P.V. Narasimha Rao should serve as a guiding principle to take measures to resolve the dispute.

When the crisis caused by the armed militancy in Kashmir had touched its peak in 1995, Prime Minister Narasimha Rao had felt the compulsion of making a decisive statement on Kashmir while he was on a tour abroad in Burkina Faso, Africa. He made a categorical commitment in the following statement: 'From a long distance away from home, I am addressing an appeal through this statement to the people of Jammu and Kashmir, at a time which could well turn their destiny once again in glorious manner, so as to make that lovely land a peer to paradise—jannatnishaan, as it has been called for centuries.' The statement further clarified that it would be a situation 'short of azadi and sky was the limit for it'.

Keeping the situation explained herein-above, the first step in this direction could be to initiate a dialogue with the primary stakeholder, the people of Kashmir. And, if the Union of India has to talk to the people of Kashmir, it will have to decide the grouping with which it will initiate the dialogue. In my opinion, it is the political conglomerate called the Hurriyat. Then, the ball will certainly move to what is broadly known as the 'mainstream'. Under the present circumstances, it is possible that ultimately the Hurriyat and the mainstream might have to move to a broader political consensus on an 'achievable goal'.

2. The Government of India should have realized much earlier that it was wrong for it to dilute the autonomy that was enshrined in Article 370 of the Constitution of India and the Delhi Agreement of 1952 between Nehru and the Sheikh. History offers lessons and anybody who does not learn from mistakes is bound to repeat them. The Union of India suffered for its short-sightedness. Nehru had realized that India's policy had gone wrong in Kashmir and it was the greatest blunder committed by the Government of India to have dismissed and arrested the Sheikh unconstitutionally. Nehru had regretted the action, but the Union of India itself hadn't learnt the lesson as it repeated its mistake by incorporating a clause in the Indira-Abdullah Accord of 1975 aimed at examining all the central laws promulgated in Jammu & Kashmir since 1953, but never showed its nerve to implement the same. The Centre committed mistakes subsequently also by taking recourse to issuing orders unlawfully like the presidential order of 1954. It repeated another blunder by dismissing the Farooq Abdullah government unconstitutionally on 2 July 1984.

It committed yet another grave mistake by appointing Jagmohan Malhotra as the governor of Jammu & Kashmir for the second time on 19 January 1990, against the protest by the Farooq Abdullah government. It is widely believed that Jagmohan was squarely held responsible by the people of Kashmir for creating a chaotic situation of death and destruction in the state and also organizing the exodus of Kashmiri Pandits. So, it is the Union of India that caused unrest in the minds of the people of Kashmir and deepened it over a period of time by committing mistakes one after the other. The Union of India has to adopt a mechanism to assess properly as to what has gone wrong and how it can be corrected.

3. The Government of India should implement a policy shift in Kashmir. The basic tenet of that would be the realization that no amount of repression in Kashmir, be it through bullets or pellets, can solve the problem. The anger in the minds of the people of Kashmir, particularly in the minds of the youth, has to be addressed. The policy shift will also envisage that the army, the paramilitary forces and the Jammu & Kashmir Police have to design a policy to win back people for a dignified and peaceful normal life. I am convinced that the vast majority in India feels that Kashmir can't be treated as a law and order problem. If that is so, then, let me say what the present-day military leadership should do in the days to come.

The leadership of the army should realize that instead of providing more supplies of arms to control the mobs, it would be better to reach out to the people of Kashmir and address the unrest there. General (retd) D.S. Hooda had, perhaps, this very situation on his mind when he suggested in his article 'In Valley, No Magic Bullet'[143] that there was a need to kill terrorism in Kashmir rather than terrorists. He had also cautioned that along with the tangibles like number of violent incidents, soldiers killed, terrorists killed there was a need to pay attention to equally important non-tangibles. His article explained the fact that it was of utmost importance to reach the minds of the youth through a path away from bullets and pellets.

At this point, I feel an urge in me to caution all the jingoistic elements in the system to take notice of what great political philosopher Edmund Burke had told the British Parliament during his strong plea for Britain's proper response to American condition on 22 March 1775, 'First, permit me sir, to observe, that the use of force alone is but temporary. It may subdue for a moment; but it doesn't remove the necessity of subduing again; and a nation is not governed, which is perpetually to be conquered!'

4. The Government of India should realize that the people of Kashmir have suffered enormously in the period of turmoil, spanning nearly three decades. A couple of years ago, the government itself admitted that more than 45,000 people have been killed in the crossfire in Kashmir during the past three decades. The people put that figure to be more than 70,000. Among other sufferings, there are reports of disappearances. Human rights activists, Parvez Imroz and Khurram Parvez, have put the figure of the disappearances at more than 5,000. This and other areas of suffering of the people in the crossfire during a long period of turmoil must be probed by a commission of inquiry. This way, the Government of India would bring great relief to the people of Kashmir, and it will constitute a substantial move towards removing the deficit in trust between the Union of India and the people of Kashmir.

5. The current crisis might require the mainstream political class of the Indian state and the separatists represented by the Hurriyat to come to a common understanding for the settlement of the Kashmir dispute, so that the society moves to a 'possible goal'. This is easier said than done, but the compulsion of the present situation demands that ultimately wisdom prevails upon foolhardiness that is detrimental to the interests of the society that wants to move to a situation of hope and fulfillment.

6. While this approach gains momentum, the Union of India could help to organize an internal dialogue among the people in the three regions—Jammu, Kashmir and Ladakh—and within a region, among the people of sub-regions like Kargil and Ladakh regions or/and Chenab valley and Pir Panchal, so that democracy permeates into the entire area of political, social and economic development on the basis of equity and justice. There are areas of public concern on which Kashmir and Jammu vehemently differ with one another. A vigorous dialogue alone can remove differences in approach and the Union of India can play a big role in this. Let me emphasize this aspect of relations between Jammu and Kashmir regions. While Kashmiris have not, in the past, appreciated the urges of the people of Jammu in respect of settlement of various categories of refugees, Jammu has never come forward to realize the significance of the proposals like resettlement of Kashmiris having migrated to Pakistan at various points of time since 1947, back in

Kashmir. Interestingly, a Constitution Bench of the Supreme Court had ruled on 15 November 2001 that the resettlement resolution adopted by the Jammu & Kashmir Legislative Assembly had become a law way back in 1982 when the assembly had adopted it for the second time and the then governor had given assent to it as per rules.

7. The Union of India will have to consider that the presence of the army and paramilitary forces in Kashmir and elsewhere in the state is not needed in this magnitude. So, call it demilitarization or give it another name, something must happen in that direction so that a situation of peace and relief is caused in the minds of the suffering people.

8. The Armed Forces (Special Powers) Acts (AFPSA) is draconian and, to the best of my knowledge, has been misused in Kashmir. Even the army has accepted that the law has been misused on a number of occasions and has apologized. Its revocation will bring a great physical and psychological relief to the people of Kashmir. The army and paramilitary forces have enough powers already to deal with all cases of disturbances. The Indian Arms Act of 1959, Indian Penal Code (updated since 1860) and many other laws give enough powers and protection to the army and paramilitary forces, not to speak of acts such as the J&K Public Safety Act, which should also be revoked in due course of time or replaced by an acceptable law that aims at maintaining law and order in normal course. I am sure this gesture by the Government of India can cause a situation of relief in the minds of the people of Kashmir and pave the way for a meaningful dialogue with the leadership in Kashmir.

I wish the present leadership in the army and the paramilitary forces realize the fact that many vital organs of the Union of India like the Central Bureau of Investigation (CBI) have realized that laws such as the AFSPA had promoted unrest in Kashmir without yielding any advantage to the Indian government. It will be right to remind my readers at this point of time that it was the CBI that had gone to the Supreme Court on 19 March 2012 with the proof that the encounter at Pathirbal (March 2000) in which seven people were killed by the army was totally fake and the killings of innocent people were described by the CBI as cold-blooded murders. Subsequently, Justice (retd) S.R. Pandian's report to the Jammu & Kashmir government submitted on 27 October 2000, established the fact that three members of the Special Operation Group (SOG) and four jawans of the Central Reserve Police Force (CRPF) had opened fire in Barakpora on 3 April 2000, killing eight and injuring fifteen innocent people who were taking part in a peaceful procession seeking exhumation of bodies of five innocent persons killed at Pathribal, who had been dubbed as foreign militants. Lethal laws like the AFSPA have caused unrest in the minds of Kashmiris and led to further violence.

9. The people around control line and international border between India and Pakistan have suffered immense miseries, throughout the border in the J&K state. It is often that people around this line on the border have to move to the hinterland for long spells of time, due to shelling and crossfire. The migration causes havoc to the people. Migration from the border to the interior areas is not easy. It often entailed a great disturbance and added to the poverty of the resources of such people. Apart from this, the border shelling and crossfire meant loss of life and property. It is, therefore, necessary to provide relief to these people. This relief can come permanently when the dispute on Kashmir is resolved, finally. As of now, relief measures such as free education, employment of, at least, one member of the family, free rations for the period of migration, protection of cattle, etc. can be taken as and when required.

The Indian government should also think of providing insurance cover to the entire population on the border, say within the radius of five kilometres or more. It has to be done on humanitarian basis, besides respecting civil liberties, enshrined in the Constitution of India. Pakistan could take the same action on that side of the line of control.

10. Since our neighbourhood can't be changed and India and Pakistan can't live in perpetual animosity, the Union of India has to accept that it has to organize a dialogue on two axes—New Delhi-Srinagar/Jammu axis and New Delhi-Islamabad axis. I accept that proposition as a compulsion woven into the situation, that is, the Kashmir dispute.

While the expression 'Kashmir' represents the whole state, the fact remains that the people of Ladakh and Jammu didn't raise the issue regarding its accession to India. So, my reference to Kashmir as the main party to the dispute constitutes a compulsion rooted in history.

In this very text, I have sufficiently explained how the dispute on

Kashmir arose and who were the main actors responsible for it. Now, the problem on hand is to find a mechanism to move forward in search of a possible solution for the dispute.

While I have explained my outline on how to move forward, I want to take the position that Kashmir is not a complex problem but a simple proposition. It can be resolved if the leadership shows political sagacity and the resolve to find a solution. Essentially, the political will to grapple with the problem and find the solution has been lacking. It was certainly wrong for the Union of India to have had reservations on the decisions that the Jammu & Kashmir Constituent Assembly had charted for itself to sort out in due course of time. It was the Union of India itself that scuttled that process by dismissing and then arresting the Sheikh.

The speech that the Sheikh had delivered on 5 November 1951 in the Jammu & Kashmir Constituent Assembly and the spirit of which he retained in his mind while he spoke on the Delhi Agreement in the same Constituent Assembly on 11 August 1952 could have served as an inspiration for the decision-making elites in the Union of India, if the small minds and sycophants had not deliberately created confusion, which led to the dismissal of a person who was the chief architect of a workable constitutional relationship with India.

Against this background, the only option available to the Government of India is that it should realize the dimensions of the current crisis in Kashmir and respond to the situation. It should also take notice of the most important episodes of India's constitutional relationship with Kashmir.

It would serve a good purpose for the present leadership of India to understand that Nehru had come forward for a qualitative shift in India's policy in 1964. He had sufficiently explained to the nation that the Union of India had gone wrong in its relation with Kashmir. He had regretted the dismissal and arrest of the Sheikh and had finally succeeded in assuaging the feelings of the Sheikh for what had gone wrong in Kashmir in August 1953 and motivated the Sheikh to accept the crucial role of organizing a lasting peace and reconciliation with Pakistan through the settlement of the Kashmir problem and sent him to sort out matters with the then Pakistan President Ayub Khan. While the Sheikh was successfully negotiating with Pakistan, unfortunately Nehru died on 27 May 1964 and the process of the settlement with Pakistan got scuttled.

Now, cutting a long story short, one could see that the current unrest in Kashmir is a writing on the wall, and the stakeholders should respond to the situation and come forward for a possible solution. At a press conference in Srinagar on 30 August 2016, I had explained that the Delhi Agreement of 1952 could be incorporated into the texture of a formula for a lasting peace and an abiding friendship between India and Pakistan, which could be given any name.

The so-called Musharraf-Vajpayee-Manmohan formula envisaged same borders but free movement across the region—the erstwhile Jammu & Kashmir state, Gilgit-Baltistan, Pakistan-held Kashmir, Kashmir Valley, Jammu and Ladakh; autonomy on both sides; demilitarization, that is, phased withdrawal of troops from the region and a mechanism devised jointly so that the roadmap for a settlement is implemented smoothly.

As per credible sources, General Musharraf had convinced his top colleagues, both in the army and outside, that this was the only possible solution that would not yield a situation on ground as a defeat for one party and victory for the other. He had also convinced his colleagues that the resolutions of the UN on Kashmir had constituted a redundant situation as these meant a tight-jacket for Kashmiris whether they wanted to go with India or to Pakistan. Musharraf had explained that if Kashmiris were given a chance to exercise their free will, they would prefer to be independent. In fact, this assessment of Musharraf seems to be correct even today!

One word about the proposition for making borders irrelevant. When irrelevance of borders is offered within the so-called formula, an effective mechanism of safeguards would also be in shape so that the settlement of dispute won't cause any difficulty in respect of sovereignty and security of India and Pakistan. In fact, the settlement, through any formula meant for an abiding friendship between India and Pakistan, will certainly include a mechanism that will not cause any kind of negative impact as for security of the region is concerned.

If the leaderships of India and Pakistan are prepared to realize that the neighbourhood can't be altered and war won't now be a possibility, then the future of an abiding friendship and cordiality for peace and prosperity for the people of both countries has to be sought at all costs. Currently, the ties between India and Pakistan have taken a different course. But then, the neighbourhood remains.

When we refer to the Musharraf-Vajpayee-Manmohan- formula, we must appreciate the expression within a context. It was part of a non-paper that is still available in the records of the foreign ministries of both countries. The non-paper was getting finalized for a final discussion between the two leaders. There were many other areas on which a broader agreement had also been reached.

Former Pakistani foreign minister Khurshid Mahmud Kasuri and S.K. Lambha, former high commissioner of India to Pakistan, were privy to the discussions, testified in a recent meeting with me and others in New Delhi that the non-paper included many more areas than the famous four-point formula on which a broader consensus had been arrived at.

We must not forget that after the Lahore Declaration, there were serious attempts to promote an atmosphere of hope and optimism between India and Pakistan. Knowledgeable sources suggest that the idea of reconciliation between India and Pakistan was mooted by President Musharraf in his summit with Prime Minister Vajpayee in Agra on 14-16 July 2001. After the Kargil war, which didn't yield any advantage to Pakistan, Musharraf seems to have a calm reflection of what could be done for the future as for the Indo-Pak relations and the future of Kashmir dispute were concerned. Musharraf has realized that Pakistan would never gain anything through war with India.

In his book *Neither A Hawk Nor A Dove*,[144] Kasuri narrates an interesting story of how the churning of ideas, later woven into the texture of the Musharraf-Vajpayee-Manmohan formula, had taken place on several occasions after the Lahore Declaration signed by Prime Minister Vajpayee and his Pakistani counterpart Nawaz Sharif on 23 February 1999.

Such ideas had broadly been thrashed out during the Agra Summit (11-16 July 2001) between Vajpayee and Musharraf and in the meeting between Vajpayee and Musharraf in Islamabad (January 2004). There was a sustained effort to promote optimism for a lasting peace between India and Pakistan. Luckily for Musharraf, apart from his able foreign minister

Kasuri, many other knowledgeable persons like Tariq Aziz assisted him to promote optimism for a lasting friendship between India and Pakistan.

Musharraf's visit to New Delhi from 16 to 18 April 2005 further strengthened this process of promoting friendship. This atmosphere of optimism is lucidly described by Kasuri in his book. 'On 8 January 2007, when the peace process was going on very well and there was optimism, Prime Minister Manmohan Singh had remarked that he dreamt of a day, when one can have breakfast in Amritsar, lunch in Lahore and dinner in Kabul, while retaining our respective national identities.' The relevant point is that an idea never dies.

In June 2007, when I was a minister in the Cabinet, Prime Minister Manmohan Singh had invited me for a discussion on Kashmir. I found him unusually optimistic on Kashmir's solution. He shared with me that he would visit Islamabad next month to have a decisive dialogue with Musharraf—much to my relief. After two weeks when I attended a Cabinet meeting, perhaps in the second week of July 2007, I followed the PM to his chamber after the meeting and enquired as to what had happened to his visit to Islamabad. He told me that it was Musharraf who requested him for postponement of the crucial meeting and he would fix the date soon. That was unfortunate as that time never came till Musharraf was out of the system for a different role in public life!

It was unfortunate that Manmohan Singh could not fulfil his mission and his travel to Islamabad for the final and decisive meeting with Musharraf sometime later in July 2007 could not take place because Pakistan's internal security got vitiated by unfortunate events like Musharraf's avoidable dispute with the judiciary of Pakistan and the siege of Lal Masjid (3-11 July 2007) causing violence and unrest all around.

The governments of India and Pakistan should strive to settle the Kashmir dispute. The Musharraf-Vajpayee-Manmohan formula could then serve only as a background situation.

My dispassionate assessment is that a credible discussion and dialogue without any pre-conditions can be meaningfully initiated by the emissaries of the Union of India directly with the Hurriyat. The dialogue and discussion with other political parties and groups could then follow successfully.

I also have a feeling that the Union of India can convert the challenge in Kashmir into a situation of opportunity for itself if it initiates a purposeful dialogue in Kashmir and also consults the national Opposition, led by the Congress, transparently and effectively.

As has happened throughout the world, the parties to a particular dispute have always finally, come to the acceptable 'mean' through dialogue and discussion.

When the dialogue is initiated, the whole process will be permeated with the spirit of democracy and transparency. While the discussions open with Jammu and Ladakh, the option that is found suitable for Kashmir could also be available to those regions. If for any reason, these two regions don't find favour with what has been found suitable for Kashmir, these two regions will certainly have the freedom to adopt other possible options. It is always possible to ensure that the basic principles of equity and justice will not be impaired and these will be applied uniformly to the people of the entire state.

The two vital institutions of Indian democracy—the Union government and the Opposition—could also take a meaningful look at what had gone wrong in the Union of India's constitutional relationship with Kashmir. It is the dispassionate and credible knowledge of the past that can help the stakeholders concerned to move forward.

In his Independence Day speech delivered on 15 August 2017, Prime Minister Narendra Modi promised of winning the hearts and minds of the people of Kashmir through a cordial relationship and his talk of 'embracing' them has generated hope in Kashmir. By this remark, he accepted in full measure that the Kashmir dispute can't be resolved by force. It is, therefore, everybody's expectation that the Union of India will come forward for a visible and meaningful shift in its policy on Kashmir.

The hallmark of the Centre's shift in its policy on Kashmir could be done best by it by taking the crucial decision of initiating a decisive and purposeful dialogue with the leadership in Kashmir, particularly with the Hurriyat Conference, without losing any further time.

It is an unfortunate situation that the RSS ideology and narrative on Kashmir has always created a problem and this organization has never tried to be a part of the solution. Recently, it has added a serious dimension to the already tense situation of unrest in Kashmir by approaching the Supreme Court for the revocation of Article 35A of the Constitution of India. It is the same article that protects various rights of people of the state.

As Duga Das Basu, an authority on the Constitution of India in his book *Shorter Constitution India* (Eleventh Edition),[145] explains the effect of Article 35A saying, 'A most prominent feature of the Constitution of Jammu and Kashmir, as distinguished from the rest of India, is the provision for special treatment of the "permanent residents" of Jammu & Kashmir.'

A.G. Noorani, has rightly characterized the revocation of Article-35A as a threat to Kashmir's very existence, which Kashmiris can never accept, under any circumstances.

The Union of India could, therefore, be well-advised at this critical juncture to take a serious look at what went wrong in the past, as in many ways past is much more important than the present and the future can be organized well only on the basis of full knowledge on relevant events in the past.

Perhaps George Orwell[146] has said it best, 'He who controls the past controls the future.'

ACKNOWLEDGEMENTS

First and foremost, I express my deepest gratitude to my wife, Mumtazunnisa, for being a pillar of strength and support.

Next, I must deeply appreciate the dedication of my personal assistant Bilal Nazra who invested considerable time in preparing the manuscript. In fact, his patience is incomparable.

I must also place on record my deep gratitude to Masood Hussain, the renowned artist, who provided his rare paintings for this work. These invaluable paintings depict Kashmir's beauty, historical architecture, grand monuments and sacred places.

Sincere thanks to Aijaz Ahmad Banday of Kashmir University, who held prolonged discussions with me on the very interesting history of the Burzahom excavations that have opened new vistas for researchers to understand Kashmir's pre-historic past.

I am also thankful to Iqbal Ahmad, a knowledgeable numismatist with whom my discussions were always interesting and fruitful.

I am also indebted to Shafi Shauq, a scholar of Kashmir history who tried to awaken in me the interest in Thrikha Philosophy.

I sincerely acknowledge M. Asharaf Tak, chief editor, J&K Academy of Art, Culture and Languages for his help in completing this manuscript.

I also thank Abid Ahmad of the Academy.

Last, but not the least, I express my gratitude to Dibakar Ghosh of Rupa Publications for his interest in Kashmir's history and the current situation of strife and offering me good suggestions in the process of publishing this work.

NOTES AND REFERENCES

Chapter 1: Kashmir's Prehistoric Roots

1. Aijaz A. Bandey, *Prehistoric Kashmir* (Dilpreet Publishing House, New Delhi, 2009).
2. Khalid Bashir Ahmad, *Kashmir: Exposing the Myth Behind The Narrative* (Sage Publications, New Delhi, 2017).
3. Moti Lal Saqi, *Agur Naeb* (published with financial assistance from the Central Institute of Indian Languages, Ministry of HRD, 1998).
4. P.N.K. Bamzai, *A History of Kashmir, Political–Social–Cultural; From the Earliest Times to Present day* (Gulshan Books, Srinagar, 2016).
5. Iqbal Ahmad, a numismatist of considerable experience, is presently serving the Department of Archaeology, Government of J&K, Srinagar.
6. G.M.D Sufi, *Kashir: Being a History of Kashmir* (Capital Publishing House, New Delhi, 1996).
7. Balraj Puri, *5,000 Years of Kashmir* (Ajanta Publications, New Delhi, 1997).

Chapter 2: Herodotus Refers To Kashmir

8. M.A. Stein, *Ancient Geography of Kashmir* (Gulshan Books, Srinagar, 2005).
9. Herodotus was a Greek historian who was born in Halicarnassus (modern-day Bodrum, Turkey) and lived in the fifth century BC, and was a contemporary of Socrates.
    https://en.wikipedia.org/wiki/Herodotus
10. Scylax of Caryanda was a renowned Greek explorer of ancient time.

https://en.wikipedia.org/wiki/Scylax_of_Caryanda

11. Darius was the third king of the Persian Achaemenid Empire.
    https://en.wikipedia.org/wiki/Darius_I

12. Horace Hayman Wilson (Bengal Asiatic Society's Transaction of 1825).
    https://en.wikipedia.org/wiki/Horace_Hayman_Wilson

13. M. D. Anville, *Premier Geographe du Rio, etc.* (Paris, 1775) born in Paris on
    11 July 1697 was a geographer and cartographer. https://en.wikipedia.org/
    wiki/Jean_Baptiste_Bourguignon_d%27Anville

14. Johann Wilhelm Ritter (16 December 1776–23 January 1810, was a German
    chemist, physicist and philosopher. He was born in Samitz (Zamienice) near
    Haynau (Chojnow) in Silesia (then part of Prussia). He died in Munich.
    https://en.wikipedia.org/wiki/Johann_Wilhelm_Ritter

15. Christian Lassen (22 October 1800–8 May 1876) was a Norwegian–
    German orientalist.
    https://en.wikipedia.org/wiki/Christian_Lassen

16. Friedrich Wilhelm Heinrich Alexander von Humboldt was a Prussian
    geographer, naturalist, explorer and influential proponent of romantic
    philosophy. He was born on 14 September 1769 in Berlin. He was the
    younger brother of the Prussian minister, philosopher and linguist
    Wilhelm von Humboldt and died on 6 May 1859.
    https://en.wikipedia.org/wiki/Alexander_von_Humboldt

17. Hecataeus of Miletus (550–476 BC) was a Greek historian and geographer.
    https://en.wikipedia.org/wiki/Hecataeus_of_Miletus

18. Klaus Karttunen is a professor of South Asian studies at the University
    of Helsinki. He has written many books including *India in Early Greek
    Literature*, 1989.
    https://fi.wikipedia.org/wiki/Klaus_Karttunen

19. E.J. Brill and Luzac & Co., *The Encyclopedia of Islam* (A Dictionary of
    the Geography, Ethnography and Biography of the Muhammadan Peoples,
    1913–38).
    http://referenceworks.brillonline.com/browse/encyclopaedia-of-islam-1

Chapter 3: Ptolemy And The Valley Of Unmatched Beauty

20. Claudius Ptolemy (AD 100–170) was a Greco–Egyptian writer, known as a
    mathematician, astronomer, geographer and astrologer.
    https://en.wikipedia.org/wiki/Ptolemy

21. Sir Marc Aurel Stein was a Hungarian–British archaeologist, primarily
    known for his explorations and archaeological discoveries in Central Asia.
    He was also a professor at Indian universities.

https://en.wikipedia.org/wiki/Aurel_Stein

22. Chandrabhaga Beach is situated 3 km east of the Sun temple of Konark in the Puri district of Odisha.
https://en.wikipedia.org/wiki/Chandrabhaga_beach

23. Stephen Byzantium, also known as Stephanus Byzantinus of the sixth century AD, was the author of an important dictionary of geography entitled *Ethnica*. Of the dictionary itself only meagre fragments survive.
https://en.wikipedia.org/wiki/Stephanus_of_Byzantium

24. Panini known for his Sanskrit treatise on grammar was born in the fourth century BC in Gandhara. The detail of this reference is part of a dissertation entitled 'Religions of Ancient Kashmir, A Case Study of Buddhism' by Mohammad Ashraf Dar, Vikram University, Ujjain, Madhya Pradesh. It is an attempt to look into the growth of religions in ancient Kashmir.
https://en.wikipedia.org/wiki/P%C4%81%E1%B9%87ini

25   Al-Muqaddasi: Muammad ibn Amad Shams al-Dīn al-Muqaddasī or al-Maqdisī also translated as el-Mukaddasi (AD 945/946-991) was a medieval Arab geographer, author of *Asan al-taqāsim fimarifat al-aqālīm* (The Best Divisions in the Knowledge of the Regions).
https://en.wikipedia.org/wiki/Al-Muqaddasi

26. Al-Idrisi: Abu Abd Allah Muhammad al-Idrisi al-Qurtubi al-Hasani al-Sabti, or simply Al Idrisi (1100–65), was a Muslim geographer, cartographer and Egyptologist who lived in Palermo, Sicily, and served at the court of King Roger II.
https://en.wikipedia.org/wiki/Muhammad_al-Idrisi

27. Al-Masudi, Abu al-asan Alī ibn al-usayn ibn Alī al-Masūdī (AD 896–956) was an Arab historian and geographer. He is sometimes referred to as the Herodotus of the Arabs. Al-Masudi was one of the first to combine history and scientific geography in a large-scale work *The Meadows of Gold and Mines of Gems a World History*.
https://en.wikipedia.org/wiki/Al-Masudi

28. Please see detailed mention of Al-Beruni in a later chapter.
https://en.wikipedia.org/wiki/Al-Biruni

Chapter 4: How Far Did Fa-Hian Travel?

29. Samuel Beal (b. 27 November 1825) was an oriental scholar, and the first Englishman to translate direct from the Chinese the early records of Buddhism, thus throwing light upon Indian history.
https://en.wikipedia.org/wiki/Samuel_Beal

30. Alexander Cunningham (23 January 1814–28 November 1893) was a British army engineer with the Bengal Engineer Group who later took an interest in the history and archaeology of India. https://en.wikipedia.org/wiki/Alexander_Cunningham

Chapter 5: Hiuen Tsiang: The Most Credible Narrator

31. Alexander Cunningham, *Ancient Geography of India* (Tribner & Co. Publications, London, 1871).
32. The Seleucid Empire was the Persian kingdom of the Macedonian dynasty of the Seleucids, whose rule began with the collapse of Alexander's empire. https://www.ancient.eu/Seleucid_Empire/
33. M. Panthier, French orientalist, published a very interesting memoir on the doctrine of Tao, translated from the Chinese with a commentary extracted from the Tao-Te-King of Lao-Tseu (Google Books).
34. Samuel Beal, *Buddhist Records of the Western World* (Paragon Book Reprint Corporation, 1968). https://archive.org/details/siyukibuddhistre01hsuoft
35. Watters, Thomas, 1840-1901; Translated the work by Davids, T. W. Rhys (Thomas William Rhys), 1843–1922, ed; Bushell, Stephen W. (Stephen Wootton), 1844–1908, ed; Smith, Vincent Arthur, 1848–1920, On Yuan Chwang's Travels in India, AD 629–645 (Royal Asiatic Society, London, 1904). http://books.google.com/books?id=9NUMAAAAIAAJ&oe=UTF-8
36. Li is a Chinese unit of distance, equal to about 0.5 km (0.3 mile). https://en.wikipedia.org/wiki/Li_(unit)
37. Arhat is a saint of one of the highest ranks in Buddhism and Jainism. http://www.chinabuddhismencyclopedia.com/en/index.php/Arhat
38. Tushita is one of the heavens said to be reachable through meditation. https://en.wikipedia.org/wiki/Tushita
39. Anavatapta is the lake lying at the centre of the world, according to an ancient Buddhist cosmological view. The name Anavatapta means 'heat-free'; the waters of the lake were thought to be able to soothe the fires that torment beings. https://en.wikipedia.org/wiki/Anavatapta
40. Udyana is a country thickly populated by Buddhists (mentioned in the Policanon–Pali being a Prakrit language of the earliest extant Buddhist literature). https://en.wikipedia.org/wiki/Prakrit
41. Ananda is a Buddhist monk from Nalanda monastery. He served as an

attendant to Hiuen Tsiang (see Kavita Soni Shama, *The Tribune*, 3 May 2009).
https://en.wikipedia.org/wiki/Nalanda

42. Tathagata is an honorific title for Buddha.
https://en.wikipedia.org/wiki/Tathāgata

43. Sunil Chandra Ray, *Early History and Culture of Kashmir* (Munshiram Manoharlal Publishers, 1970).

44. Mohammad Yusuf Teng, *Sheeraza: Jammu, Kashmir and Ladakh*, Vol. 42, No. 6–9 (J&K Academy of Art, Culture and Languages, Srinagar).

Chapter 6: Al-Beruni's Kashmir

45. Hasan Askari Kazmi, *The Makers of Medieval Muslim Geography:* Al-Beruni (Renaissance, 1995, original from the University of Michigan).
https://books.google.co.in/books/about/The_Makers_of_Medieval_Muslim_Geography.html?id=5QCAAAAAMAAJ

Chapter 7: Kalhana's *Rajatarangini*: Comprehending Kashmir

46. Johann George Buhler was a scholar of ancient Indian languages and law. He was appointed as professor of oriental languages at the Elphinstone College, Bombay in 1863.
https://en.wikipedia.org/wiki/Georg_Bühler

47. An abridged edition of the *Rajatarangini* in Persian language was brought out by Haidar Malik Chadura during the reign of Jahangir.
www.shehjar.com/list/16/98/1.html

48. Gladwin Francis was a lexicographer and prolific translator of Persian literature into English. He was a founder member of the Asiatic Society of Bengal.
http://www.iranicaonline.org/articles/gladwin-francis

49. William Moorcroft was an English explorer employed by the East India Company. He travelled extensively throughout the Himalayas, Tibet and Central Asia.
https://en.wikipedia.org/wiki/William_Moorcroft_(explorer)

50. M. Anthony Troyer, a British captain with a talent for languages, published the first translation of *Rajatarangini* from Sanskrit into French, which Stein considers to be the book's first European translation.
https://www.abebooks.com/book-search/author/kalhana-troyer-m-a-nthony-translator/

51. General Alexander Cunningham took interest in the history and archaeology of India which led to his appointment in 1861 to the newly

created position of Archaeological Surveyor to the Government of India.
https://en.wikipedia.org/wiki/Alexander_Cunningham

52. Henry Thomas Colebrooke was an English orientalist and mathematician. He has been described as 'the first great Sanskrit scholar in Europe'. He was director of the Royal Asiatic Society in 1822.
https://en.wikipedia.org/wiki/Henry_Thomas_Colebrooke

53. A Kashmiri scholar of the late nineteenth century. Pandit Govind Kaul, who rendered most valuable assistance to Aurel Stein in translating *Rajatarangini*, is today almost a forgotten man.
www.koausa.org/Personality/GovindKaul.html

54. *Swarajya* Magazine, Kovai Media Pvt. Limited, RK Avenue, Bengaluru, in its issue dated April 26, 2015.

55. *Kashmir and Its People: Studies in the Evolution of Kashmiri Society* (APH Publishing House, J&K, 2004).

56. Kshemendra was a poet of the eleventh century, writing in Sanskrit. Born into an old, cultured and affluent family, both his education and literary output were broad and varied.
https://en.wikipedia.org/wiki/Kshemendra

57. Pir Hasan Shah Khoihami was a prominent historian of Kashmir.
www.worldcat.org/title/tarikh-i-hassan/oclc/69327348

58. Kalasa was a king of Kashmir between 1063 and 1089.
https://books.google.co.in/books?isbn=8173871248

59. Queen Suryamati was the wife of King Ananta (1028–63) predecessor of King Kalasa.
https://books.google.co.in/books?isbn=8177649957

60. Susala was the raja of Kashmir from 1112 to 1120.
kashmirsentinel.org/the-sacred-shrine-of-shiva-vijayeshvara-bijbehara-kashmir/

61. Akhtar Mohi-ud-Din, *A Fresh Approach to the History of Kashmir* (Book Bank Publishers, Srinagar, 1998).

62. R.S. Pandit, *Kalhana's Rajatarangini* (Sahitya Akademi, New Delhi, 1968).

Chapter 8: Spread Of Islam In Kashmir

63. G.M.D Sufi, *Islamic Culture in Kashmir* (Light & Life Publishers, 1979, original from the University of Michigan).

64. M.A. Stein, *Kalhana's Rajatarangini* (Gulshan Books, Srinagar, 2007).

65. Mohammad Ishaq Khan, *Kashmir's Transition to Islam: The Role of Muslim Rishis* (Manohar Publishers & Distributors, 1994).

66. Thomas Arnold W., *The Preaching of Islam* (London. 1913, pp. 154–93).

67. Tara Chand, *Influence of Islam on Indian Culture* (Indian Press, New Delhi 1936).
68. Muhammad Habib, *Sultan Mohmud of Ghaznin* (S. Chand Press, 1967)
69. A.B.M. Habibullah, *The Foundation of Muslim Rule in India* (Central Book Depot, New Delhi, 1961).
70. S. M. Ikram, Ab-i-Kawthar (Seventh Printing, Lahore, 1968).
71. I.H. Qureshi, *The Muslim Community of the Indo–Pak Subcontinent* (Renaissance Publishing House, New Delhi, 1996).
72. Khalid Ahmad Nizami, *Some Aspects of Religion and Politics in India During the Thirteenth Century* (Publications of the Department of History, Aligarh Muslim University, 1961).
73. Aziz Ahmad, *Studies in Islamic Culture in the Indian Environment* (Oxford University Press, New Delhi 1999).
74. Abdul Rakim, *Social History of the Muslims in Bengal* (Asiatic Society of Pakistan, East Pakistan, 1959).
75. Momtazur Rahman Tarafdar, *Husain Shahi Bengal: A Socio-Political Study* (Asiatic Society of Pakistan, Dacca, 1965).
76. Richard Maxwell Eaton, *Sufis of Bijapur, 1300–1700: Social Role of Sufis in Medieval India* (Princeton University Press, 2016). http://www.jstor.org/stable/j.ctt13x0qp2
77. Mohini Qasba Raina, *Kashur: The Kashmiri Speaking People* (Partridge Publishing, Singapore, 2013).
78. Ajit Bhattacharjea, *Kashmir: The Wounded Valley* (UBS Publishers and Distributors, 1994).
79. Dughlát Muhammad Haidar, *Tarikh-i-Rashidi* (S. Low, Marston and Company, New York, 1895).
80. Gaz is less than a metre. https://www.99acres.com › ... › Recent Threads on Residential in Dehradun

Chapter 10: Sultan Zain-ul-Abidin: The Budshah

81. Muhammad-ud-Din Fauq, *Tareekh-e-Budshahi* (Sheikh Muhammad Usman & Sons, Srinagar, 2015).
82. Sir Walter Lawrence, *The Valley of Kashmir* (Gulshan Books, Srinagar, 2011).
83. G.M.D. Sufi, *Kashir: Being a History of Kashmir* (Capital Publishing House, New Delhi, 1996).
84. N.K. Zutshi, *Sultan Zain-ul-Abidin of Kashmir: An Age of Enlightenment* (Gulshan Books, Srinagar, 2015).

Chapter 11: Marco Polo's Curious View

85. Clifford Collinson, *Exploration and Adventure* (George Allen and Unwin, London, 1934).
86. Saroja Sundararajan, *Kashmir Crisis: Unholy Anglo-Pak Nexus* (Kalaz Publications, New Delhi, 2010).
87. *Sheeraza*, a publication of J&K Academy of Art, Culture and Languages, Vol. 42, Srinagar.

Chapter 12: Francois Bernier's Vivid Account

88. Brigid Keenan, *Travels in Kashmir* (Oxford University Press, New Delhi, 1989).

Chapter 18: Lieutenant Robert Thorp's Truthful Accounts

89. F.M. Hassnain, *Kashmir Misgovernment* (Gulshan Publishers, Srinagar, 1980).
90. Arthur Brinkman, *The Wrongs of Kashmir* (WEIS Publications, London, 1868).
91. S.S. Charak, *Maharaja Ranbir Singh* (Jay Kay Book House, Jammu Tawi, 1985).

Chapter 19: Charles Ellison Bates And His Academic Pursuits

92. Francis Wilford (1761–1822) was an Indologist, orientalist, fellow member of the Asiatic Society of Bengal and a constant collaborator of its journal—*Asiatic Researches*—contributing a number of fanciful, sensational, controversial and highly unreliable articles on ancient Hindu geography, mythography and other subjects.
https://en.wikipedia.org/wiki/Francis_Wilford
93. Friedrich Wilhelm Heinrich Alexander von Humboldt (14 September 1769–6 May 1859) was a Prussian geographer, naturalist explorer, and influential proponent of Romantic philosophy and science.
https://en.wikipedia.org/wiki/Alexander_von_Humboldt
94. William Elmslie (1832–72), was a Scottish doctor and pioneer of medical mission work in Kashmir, who started first dispensary in Kashmir in 1865.
http://www.bu.edu/missiology/missionary-biography/e-f/elmslie-william-j-1832-1872-and-margaret-duncan-1852-1882/

Chapter 21: Arthur Neve And A Physician's Assessment

95.   Arthur Neve, *Thirty Years in Kashmir* (Edward Arnold, London, 1913).

Chapter 22: Sir Walter Lawrence And Kashmir

96.   Walter Lawrence, *The Valley of Kashmir* (Henry Frowde, Oxford University Press, London, 1895).
97.   William Hazlitt, *The Life of Napoleon Buonaparte* (Wiley and Putnam in 1847, book from the collections of the New York Public Library).
      www.walterscott.lib.ed.ac.uk/works/prose/napoleon.html
98.   Ghulam Nabi Aatish, *Lawrence Saheb Ka Gazetteer* (*Sheeraza*, J&K Academy of Art, Culture and Languages, Vol. 45).
99.   Mohammad Yousuf Teng, 'Lawrence of Kashmir: Kal Bhi Aur Aaj Bhi' (*Sheeraza*, J&K Academy of Art, Culture and Languages, Vol. 43).
100. Mohammad Yousuf Teng, 'Walter Lawrence and Kashmir Shinasi' (*Sheeraza*, J&K Academy of Art, Culture and Languages, Vol. 43).
101. Khushwant Singh was an Indian novelist, lawyer, journalist and politician. He was a Rajya Sabha MP too.
      https://en.wikipedia.org/wiki/Khushwant_Singh

Chapter 23: Major T.R. Swinburne's Holiday

102. Shaikh Abu al-Fazal ibn Mubarak also known as Abu'l-Fazl, Abu'l Fadl and Abu'l Fadl 'Allami (14 January 1551–12 August 1602) was the grand vizier of Emperor Akbar.
      https://en.wikipedia.org/wiki/Abu%27l-Fazl_ibn_Mubarak

Chapter 25: The Afghan Rule In Kashmir 1752-1819

103. G.M.D. Sufi, *Kashir: Being a History of Kashmir*, Vols I & II (Capital Publishing House, New Delhi, 1996).
104. A thirteenth century tyrant who invaded Kashmir a number of times and devastated it. Many historians say that Zulchoo was a Mongol and he continuously plundered Kashmir at the behest of Halakoo Khan.
      ikashmir.net/baharistan/chapter2.html
      https://shahishaharyar.wordpress.com/tag/kashmirs-5000-years-recorded-history-hindu-buddhist-period-muslim-period-to-follow/
105. Tej K. Tiku, *Kashmir: Its Aborigines and Their Exodus* (Lancer Publishers

and Distributors, New Delhi, 2013).

106. Jia Lal Kilam, *A History of Kashmiri Pandits* (Utpal Publications, New Delhi, 2003).

107. George Forster, *A Journey from Bengal to England* (R. Faulder, London, 1798).

108. It was Azad Khan whom Ferguson describes as Asad Khan.

Chapter 26: The Sikh Rule In Kashmir 1819-46

109. Dewan Chand Sharma, *Kashmir Under the Sikhs* (Seema Publications, 1983).

110. Cis Indus District of Hazara, and the trans-Indus territories of Dir, Swat and Chitral.
    sentence.yourdictionary.com › Sentence Examples › CIS

111. G.M.D. Sufi, *Kashir: Being a History of Kashmir* (Capital Publishing House, New Delhi, 1996).

112. William Moorcroft, George Trebeck, *Travels in the Himalyan Provinces of Hindustan* (New York Public Library, 1841).

113. Victor Jacquemont, *The British Dominions of India, Tibet, Lahore and Kashmir, Letters from India* (Gulshan Books, Srinagar, 2013).

114. George Trebeck (1800–25) was born in Middlesex, England. He was trained as a solicitor and recruited by William Moorcroft at the age of nineteen as his geographer and draftsman and second-in-charge of an exploratory expedition which was to take him through the Himalayan provinces of Hindustan, the Punjab, Ladakh, Kashmir, Peshawar, Kabul, Kunduz, Bokhara and eventually led to his death.
    https://en.wikipedia.org/wiki/George_Trebeck

Chapter 27: Sheikh Ghulam Mohiuddin: Kashmir's Great Friend

115. Mohammad-ud-Din Fouq, *A Complete History of Kashmir: The Ancient Hindu Kings, The Muslim Kings, The Khalsa Kings* (Gulshan Books, Srinagar, 2009).

116. Shodhganga is a portal hosted by the Information and Library Network, an autonomous body promoted by the University Grants Commission (UGC). More than 100 universities have already joined the project, a national repository of electronic theses and dissertations.
    shodhganga.inflibnet.ac.in/handle/10603/1203

117. Dina Nath Raina, *Kashmir: Distortions and Reality* (Reliance Publishing House, New Delhi, 1994).

Chapter 29: J&K Constituent Assembly

118. Alastair Lamb, *Kashmir: A Disputed Legacy* (Oxford University Press, Karachi, 1992).
119. Ajit Bhattacharjea, *Kashmir: The Wounded Valley* (UBS Publishers & Distributors, New Delhi, 1994).
120. H.V. Hodson, *The Great Divide: Britain-India-Partition* (Hutchinson and Co., London, 1969).
121. Sheikh Mohammad Abdullah, *Aatish-e-Chinar* (Ali Mohammad and Sons, Srinagar, 1986).
122. Arvind Lavakare, *The Truth About the Article 370* (Rambhau Mhalgi Prabodhini, Mumbai, 2005).

Chapter 30: The Delhi Agreement Of 1952

123. Syed Mir Qasim, *Dastan-e-Hayat* (Idarah Adbiyat, New Delhi, 2009).
124. Prem Nath Bazaz, *The History of Struggle for Freedom in Kashmir: Cultural and Political, from the Earliest Times to the Present Day* (Gulshan Books, Srinagar, 2009).
125. Krishen Dev Sethi, *Yad-e-Rafta* (Modern Publications, New Delhi, 1986).
126. Y.D. Gundevia, *The Testament of Sheikh Mohammad Abdullah* (Palit & Palit Publishers, New Delhi, 1974).

Chapter 31: The Armed Militancy And Its Aftermath

127. Shabnam Qayoom, *History of Kashmir Movement* (Ali Mohammad & Sons, Srinagar, 2014).
128. Shoukeen Kashmiri, *Khatoon-e-Kashmir* (Kaus-e-Qazah Publications, Srinagar).

Chapter 32: The Pandit Exodus

129. Sanaullah Bhat, *Ahad Nama-e-Kashmir* (Ali Mohammad and Sons, Srinagar).
130. Dina Nath Raina, *Kashmir Distortions and Reality* (Reliance Publishing House, New Delhi, 1994).

Chapter 33: Kashmir-The Way Forward

131. See *Greater Kashmir* dated 12 October 2016.
http://epaper.greaterkashmir.com/Details.aspx?id=1835&boxid=124917866

132. P.N. Dhar, *Indira Gandhi; the Emergency and Indian Democracy* (Oxford University Press, New Delhi, 2000).

133. Sofi Mohiuddin, *Kashmir* (Snober Publications, Srinagar).

134. Sirdar Shaukat Hayat Khan, *The Nation That Lost Its Soul* (Jang Publishers, Lahore, 1995).

135. Atish Fishan Publications, Lahore. (The reference to this interview is carried in the book *Ilhaq: Haqeeqat Key Aayine Mein* by M. Ghulam Rasool Gadda, Shamaswari, Kalashpora, Srinagar).

136. C. Bilquees Taseer, *Kashmir of Sheikh Mohammad Abdullah* (Ferozsons, Lahore, 1986).

137. Mian Amiruddin, *Yade-e-Ayam* (Anjuman-e-Himayatul Islam, Railway Road, Lahore, 1983).

138. Kuldip Nayar, *Beyond the Lines: An Autobiography* (Roli Books, New Delhi, 2012).

139. Chaudhri Muhammad Ali, *The Emergence of Pakistan* (Research Society of Pakistan, University of Punjab, Lahore, 1973).

140. A.G. Noorani, 'A Tale of Two States' (*Frontline*, June 10–23, 2000).

141. B.N. Mullik, *My Years with Nehru* (Allied Publishers, 1971).

142. Ram Jethmalani, *Maverick Unchanged, Unrepentant* (Rupa Publications, 2014).

143. D.S. Hooda, 'In Valley, No Magic Bullet' (*The Indian Express*, 19 July 2017).

144. Khurshid Mahmud Kasuri, *Neither A Hawk Nor A Dove* (Penguin Books, 2015).

145. Durga Das Basu, *Shorter Constitution of India, Eleventh Edition* (Prentice Hall of India, New Delhi, 1994).

146. Eric Arthur Blair (25 June 1903–21 January 1950), better known by his pen name George Orwell, was an English novelist, essayist, journalist and critic. https://en.wikipedia.org/wiki/George_Orwell

BIBLIOGRAPHY

Ahmad, Khalid Bashir, *Kashmir: Exposing the Myth Behind the Narrative* (Sage Publications, 2017).

Aijaz, Ghulam Hassan, *Tahreekh-e-Kashmir from 1905 to 1947* (Sheikh Mohammad Usman & Sons, Srinagar, 2012).

Abdullah, Sheikh Mohammad, *The Blazing Chinar: An Autobiography* (Gulshan Books, Srinagar, 2013).

Baba, Yasir Muhammad, *My Land, My People: Kashmir in Perspective* (Gulshan Books, Srinagar, 2007).

Banday, Aijaz Ahmad, *Prehistoric Kashmir* (Dilpreet Publishing House, New Delhi, 2009).

Basu, Durga Das, *Shorter Constitution of India*, Eleventh Edition (Prentice Hall, New Delhi, 1994).

Bazaz, Prem Nath, *Azad Kashmir: A Democratic Socialist Conceptions* (Gulshan Books, Srinagar, 2005).

———. *The Untold Story of Kashmir Politics: Democracy Through Intimidation and Terror* (Gulshan Books, Srinagar, 2007).

———. *A Last Chance For India in Kashmir* (Pamposh Publication, New Delhi, 1964).

———. *The History of Struggle for Freedom in Kashmir: Cultural and Political, from the Earliest Times to the Present Day* (Gulshan Books, Srinagar, 2009).

Bates, Charles Ellison, *A Gazetteer of Kashmir and Adjacent Districts of Kishtwar, Badrawah, Jammu, Naoshera, Poonch, and the Valley of the Kishen Ganga* (Gulshan Books, Srinagar, 2005).

Bamzai P.N.K., *Socio-Economic History of Kashmir 1846–1925* (Gulshan Books, Srinagar, 2007).

———. *Kashmir and Central Asia* (Light and Life Publishers, New Delhi, 1980).

———. *A History of Kashmir* (Gulshan Books, Srinagar, 2016).

Bakshi S.R., *History of Economic Development in Kashmir* (Gulshan Books, Srinagar, 2002).

Beal, Samuel, *Buddhist Kashmiri Record of the Western World* translated from the Chinese by Hiuen Tsiang (Price Publishers, New Delhi).

Bernier, Francis, *Travels in the Mughal Empire AD 1656–1688* (Gulshan Books, Srinagar, 2012).

Bhattacharjea, Ajit, *Kashmir: The Wounded Valley* (UBS Publishers & Distributers, New Delhi, 1994).

———. *Sheikh Mohammad Abdullah: Tragic Hero of Kashmir* (Roli Books, 2008).

Birdwood, Lord, *Two Nations and Kashmir* (Gulshan Books, Srinagar, 2005).

Bhat, Khawaja Sonaullah, *Ahad Nama-e-Kashmir* (Ali Mohammad & Sons, Srinagar, 1995).

Bhat R.L., *Lal And Her Vaakh: An Encyclopedic Collection* (Gulshan Books, Srinagar, 2015).

Butt Abdul Gani, *Beyond Me* (Gulshan Books, Srinagar, 2016).

Cunningham, Bingley, *Introduction to the History and Culture of Dogras* (Ajaya Prakashan, Jammu Tawi, 2008).

Chaudhary, Mohammad Ali, *The Emergence of Pakistan, Research Society of Pakistan* (University of Punjab, Lahore, 1973).

Chittick, William C., *The Sufi Path of Love: The Spiritual Teachings of Rumi* (Gulshan Books, Srinagar, 2009).

Dabla, A. Bashir, *Pandit Migration in Jammu and Kashmir* (Jay Kay Books, Srinagar, 2015).

Dar, Saifur Rahman, *Taxila and the Western World* (Al-Waqar Publishers, Lahore, 1984).

Dhar P.N., *Indira Gandhi, the Emergency and India Democracy* (Oxford University Press, New Delhi, 2000).

Duguid J., *Letters from India & Kashmir: 1873* (British Library, Historical Print Editions, 1795).

Fazal, Hussain Malik, *Kashmir and Dogra Raj* (Maliha Publishers, New Delhi, 1989).

Fazili, Manzoor, *Kashmir Government and Politics* (Gulshan Books, Srinagar, 1982).

———. *Cultural Glimpses of Kashmir* (Gulshan Books, Srinagar, 2002).

Ferguson J.P., *Kashmir: An Historical Introduction* (London Centaur Press, 1961).

Fouk, Mohammad-ud-din, *A Complete History of Kashmir, The Ancient Kings, The Muslim Kings, The Khalsa Kings* (Gulshan Books, Srinagar, 2009).

———. *Tareekh-e-Budshahi* (Sheikh Mohammad Usman & Sons, Srinagar, 2015).

Francke A.H., *A History of Ladakh* (Gulshan Books, Srinagar, 2008).

Gadda, Ghulam Rasool, *Ilhaq: Hakikat Ke Aayine Main* (Ali Printers, Srinagar, 1984).

——— . *Kashmir Ki Infiradiyat* (Shagufa Publications, Srinagar, 1984).

Ganai, Abdul Jabbar, *Kashmir and National Conference and Politics 1975–1980,* (Gulshan Books, Srinagar, 1984).

——— . *Personality Behind Oration: Sheikh Mohammad Abdullah: Agreements, Speeches and Statements* (Gulshan Books, Srinagar, 2009).

Ghulam, Ahmad, *My Years with Sheikh Abdullah: Kashmir from 1971–1987* (Gulshan Books, Srinagar, 2008).

Gompert M.L.A., *Magic Ladakh: An Intimate Picture of a Land of Topsy-Turvy Customs and Great Natural Beauty* (Gulshan Books, Srinagar, 2009).

Grierson, A. George and Barnett D. Lionel, *Lalla Vakyani: The Wise Sayings of Lal Ded: Mystic Poetess of Ancient Kashmir* (Gulshan Books, Srinagar, 2013).

Gupta, Mahander M., *Troubled Kashmir: Exasperated Essays in its Contemporary Politics* (Gulshan Books, Srinagar, 2008).

Haider, Malik Chadurah, *History of Kashmir* (Bhavna Prakashan, New Delhi, 1991).

Hassnain, Fida Mohammad, *British Policy Towards Kashmir 1846–1946* (Gulshan Books, Srinagar, 2009).

——— . *Sri Amarnath Ji Tirtha Kashmir* (Gulshan Books, Srinagar, 2009).

——— . *Kashmir the History of Himalayan Valley* (Gulshan Books, Srinagar, 2002).

——— . *Heritage of Kashmir* (Gulshan Books, Srinagar, 2007).

——— . *Historic Kashmir* (Gulshan Books, Srinagar, 2002).

——— . *Advent of Islam in Kashmir* (Gulshan Books, Srinagar, 2013).

——— . *Kashmir: The Focus of Asiatic Civilization* (Gulshan Books, Srinagar, 2007).

Hassan, Askari Kazim, *The Makers of Medieval Muslim Geography*: Alberuni (Renaissance Publications, Covington, USA, 1995, original from the University of Michigan).

Hugel, Charles, *Travels in Kashmir and Punjab* (Gulshan Books, Srinagar, 2008).

——— . *Kashmir Under Maharaja Ranjit Singh* (Atlantic Publishers & Distributors, New Delhi, 1984).

Hugel, Charles, *Travels in Kashmir & the Punjab* (Asian Educational Services, New Delhi, 1995).

Jacquemont, Victor, *Letter from India* (E. Churton, London 1835).

Jain, Ajit Prasad, *Kashmir: What Really Happened* (Jaico Publishing House, Bombay, 1972).

John, Collett, *A Guide for Visitors to Kashmir—1884* (W. Newman & Co., Calcutta, 1898).

Jethmalani, Ram, *Maverick Unchanged, Unrepentant* (Rupa Publications, New Delhi, 2014).

Khan, Hayat Sirdar Shoukat, *The Nation That Lost Its Soul* (Jang Publishers, Lahore, 1995).

Kilam, Jai Lal, *A History of Kashmiri Pandits* (Gandhi Memorial College Publication, 2003).

Khan, Muhammad Ishaq, *Crisis of a Kashmiri: Spiritual and Intellectual* (Gulshan Books, Srinagar, 2008).

——. *Kashmir's Transition to Islam: The Role of Muslim Rishis* (Gulshan Books, Srinagar, 2005).

Khan, Maulana Wahiduddin, *Hind–Pak Diary* (Goodword Books, New Delhi, 2006).

Khan, Major General Akbar, *Raiders in Kashmir* (National Book Foundation, Islamabad, 1975).

Kirpa Ram, *Gulabnama: A History of Maharaja Gulab Singh of Jammu and Kashmir* (Gulshan Books, Srinagar, 2005).

Knight, (Captain) William Henry, *Diary of the Pedestrian in Kashmir and Tibet* (Asian Educational Service, 1998/2007).

Knight F.F., *Where Three Empires Meet: A Narrative of Recent Travels in Kashmir, Western Tibet, Gilgit and the Adjoining Countries* (London Longmans, 1893).

Knowles, J. Hinton, *Folklore of Kashmir* (Gulshan Books, Srinagar, 2009).

Kasuri, Khurshid Mahmud, *Neither A Hawk Nor A Dove* (Penguin Books, 2015).

Lamb, Alastair, *Kashmir: A Disputed Legacy 1846–1990* (Oxford University Press, 1991).

Lawrence, Sir Walter, *The Valley of Kashmir* (Gulshan Books, Srinagar, 2005).

Majumdar R.C., *Age of Imperial Unity* (Bharatiya Vidya Bhavan, Bombay, 1963).

——. *British Paramountcy and Indian Renaissance* (Bharatiya Vidya Bhavan, Bombay, 1963).

Mattoo, Neerja, *The Stranger Beside Me: Short Stories of Kashmir* (Gulshan Books, Srinagar, 2007).

Mattu, Abdul Majid, *The Prolonged Agony: Kashmir Saga* (Gulshan Books, Srinagar, 2004).

Manzoor, Fazili, *The Constitutional System of Jammu and Kashmir* (Gulshan Books, Srinagar, 2008).

Morison, Margaret Cotter, *A Lonely Summer in Kashmir* (Gulshan Books, Srinagar, 2007).

Mohammad, Zahid G., *Kashmir in War and Diplomacy* (Gulshan Books, Srinagar, 2007).

Mohammad, Ashraf, *Kashmir First: The Kashmir Story* (Gulshan Books, Srinagar, 2008).

Mullik B.N., *Kashmir: My Years with Nehru* (Allied Publishers, 1971).

Mohi-ud-din, Akthar, *A Fresh Approach to the History of Kashmir* (Books Bank Publishers, Srinagar, 1998).

Moorcroft William and Trebeck George, *Travels in the Himalayan Provinces of Hindustan and the Punjab in Ladakh and Kashmir: In Peshawar, Kabul,*

Kunduz and Bokhara from 1819–1825 (edited by H.W. Wilson, Gulshan Books, Srinagar, 2012).

Najar G.R., *Kashmir Accord (1975): A Political Analysis* (Gulshan Books, Srinagar, 1988).

Narain A.K., *The Indo-Greeks* (Oxford Clarendon Press, London, 1957).

Neve, Arthur, *Thirty Years in Kashmir* (Edward Arnold Publications, London, 1913).

Neve, Ernest .F., *Things Seen in Kashmir* (Gulshan Books, Srinagar, 2012).

———· *A Crusader in Kashmir* (Gulshan Books, Srinagar, 2007).

———· *Beyond the Pir Panjal: Life Among the Mountains and Valley of Kashmir* (Gulshan Books, Srinagar, 2003).

Notovitch, Nicholas, *Journey Into Kashmir and Tibet: With The Life of Jesus* (Ramakrishna Vedanta Math Publication Department, New Delhi, 1987).

Pandit, Mohammad Amin, *Ladakh: Land of Possessive Powers and Charms* (Gulshan Books, Srinagar, 2016).

Percy, Brown, *Chinar Leaves, Poems of Kashmir* (Gulshan Books, Srinagar, 2013).

Puri, Balraj, *Jammu and Kashmir: Triumph and Tragedy of Indian Federalism* (Asia Book Corporation, New Delhi, 1993).

———· *Kashmir Towards Insurgency: Tracts for the Times* (Orient Longman, New Delhi, 1993).

———· *5000 Years of Kashmir* (Ajanta Publications, New Delhi, 1997).

Pandit R.S., *Rajatarangini: The Saga of the Kings of Kashmir* (Sahitya Akademi, New Delhi, 1935).

Qadri, Shafi Ahmad, *Kashmiri Sufism* (Gulshan Books, Srinagar, 2002).

Qayoom, Shabnam, *Mufasil Tareekh-wa-Tehreek-e-Kashmir* (Ali Mohammad & Sons, Srinagar, 2014).

Qureshi A.S., *Srinagar: Heritage Treasure* (Gulshan Books, Srinagar, 2007).

Qasim, Syed Mir, *Dastan-e-Hayaat* (Jaid Offset Press, New Delhi, 1985).

Rabbani G.M., *Kashmir: Social and Cultural History* (Gulshan Books, Srinagar, 2007).

Rafiqi A.Q., *Letters to Mir Saiyid Ali Hamdani (Maktubat-e-Mir Saiyid Ali Hamdani): An annotated edition with English translation and historical analysis* (Gulshan Books, Srinagar, 2007).

Rafiqi, Abdul Qayoom, *History of Kashmir* (Gulshan Books, Srinagar, 2011).

Raina, Dina Nath, *Kashmir Distortions and Reality* (Reliance Publishing House, New Delhi, 1994).

Saki, Moti Lal, *Agur Naib* (published with financial assistance from the Ministry of HRD, Government of India, 1998).

Saraf, Muhammad Yousuf, *Kashmiris Fight for Freedom 1819–1946* (Ferozsons, Lahore, 1977).

Sethi, Krishan Dev, *Yad-e-Rafta* (Modern Publications, New Delhi, 1986).

Sen, Lt. Gen. L.P, *Slender was the Thread: Kashmir Confrontation 1947–48* (Orient Longman, New Delhi, 1969).

Shali S.L., *Settlement Pattern in Relation to Climate Changes in Kashmir* (O.M. Publications, New Delhi, 2001).

Shauq, Shafi, *Europeans on Kashmir* (Summit Publishers, Srinagar, 1997).

Sheeraza, *Jammu, Kashmir & Ladakh* (J&K Academy of Art, Culture & Languages).

Singh N.K., *Buddhism in Kashmir* (Gulshan Books, Srinagar, 2000).

Sofi, Mohiuddin, *Kashmir From 1931 to 1977* (Shaheen Book Stall and Stationers, Srinagar, 1996).

Soz, Saifuddin, *Kashmir Crisis: Agenda for an Effective Dialogue* (Kashmir Centre for Asian Studies, New Delhi, 1993).

———. *Why Autonomy to Kashmir?* (India Centre of Asian Studies, New Delhi, 1995).

Sodhi, S. Anoop Singh, *Kashmir and the Sikh: An Insight* (Gulshan Books, Srinagar, 2007).

Stein M.A., *Kalhana's Rajatarangini: A Chronicle of the Kings of Kashmir translated with an introduction, commentary and appendices, Vol. I & II* (Gulshan Books, Srinagar, 2013).

———. *Ancient Geography of Kashmir* (Gulshan Books, Srinagar, 2005).

Sufi G.M.D, *Islamic Culture in Kashmir* (Gulshan Books, Srinagar, 2007).

———. *Kashir: Being a History of Kashmir From the Earliest Times to Our Own* (Capital Publishing House, New Delhi, 1996).

Swinburne T.R., *Kashmir: Holiday in the Happy Valley* (Gulshan Books, Srinagar, 2008).

Syed, Tassadque Hussain, *Kashmir Engima: Entangled Strands: A Kashmir View Point* (Gulshan Books, Srinagar, 2009).

Taseer, C. Bilquues, *The Kashmir of Sheikh Abdullah* (Gulshan Books, Srinagar, 2005).

Taseer, Rashid, *Tahreek-e-Hurriyat-e-Kashmir 1936 to 1953* (Muhafiz Publications, Srinagar, 1983).

Temple, Richard, *Journals kept in Hyderabad, Kashmir, Sikkim and Nepal* (W.H. Allen, Oxford University Press, London, 1887).

Thorp, Robert, *Kashmir: Misgovernment* (Longmans & Co. New Delhi, 1870).

Tyndale-Biscoe, Cecil Earle, *Tyndale Biscoe of Kashmir: An Autobiography* (Gulshan Books, Srinagar, 2003).

Van Douzel and Ch. Pellat, *The Encyclopaedia of Islam* (edited by E. Brill, Infobase Publishing, New York, 2009).

Vigne G.T., *Travel in Kashmir, Ladak and Iskardo* (H. Colburn, London, 1842).

Villiers, Stuart C.M., *Gardens of the Great Mughals* (Gulshan Books, Srinagar, 2009).

Wakefield W., *The Happy Valley: Sketches of Kashmir and the Kashmiris* (Gulshan Books, Srinagar, 2011).

Wakhlu S.N., *Habba Khatoon: Nightingale of Kashmir* (Gulshan Books, Srinagar, 2007).

Wilson H.H., *The Hindu History of Kashmir* (Sushil Gupta Publications, Calcutta, 1960).

Younghusband, Sir Francis, *Kashmir* (A&C Black Publisher, London, 1866).

Zutshi, N.K., *Sultan Zain-ul-Abidin of Kashmir: An Age of Enlightenment* (Gulshan Books, Srinagar, 2012).

www.ingramcontent.com/pod-product-compliance
Lightning Source LLC
Chambersburg PA
CBHW070945150426
42812CB00067B/3316/J